Fine Art of Bondage

Beauty of Rope

Rod Meier
Photographer
www.Fine-Art-of-Bondage.com

Warning:
Be careful with bondage! It can cause serious injury to the tied person. Begin with easy knots, learn about where, what and how to tie or work with someone experienced or take a course about bondage. You should know the medical aspects and you only should do this with people you trust. This book is a photo art book and not a bondage guide!

Legal notice
This is an art photo book. The author assumes no responsibility when you try this at home. There is no medical advice, the laws in your country or any information how to tie in this book. You also should take care with who you work (or play)!

All models in this book are at least 18 years old. Written model releases for commercial use of the images are available.

(c) 2016 by Rod Meier Media - all rights reserved

Photos, concept, rigging and most of the retouching by Rod Meier
www.Fine-Art-of-Bondage.com
Mail: Info@Fine-Art-of-Bondage.com
Photography Homepage - www.Model-Space.de

published by Rod Meier Media, Brueckenstr. 1, 89231 Ulm/Germany
http://Rod-Meier-Media.com

ISBN: 978-3-946768-00-5
First Edition

Fine Art of Bondage
- Beauty of Rope -

Rod Meier

Preamble

I want to thank all the models in this book.

They all gave their best to get great artistic and creative photos with lots of rope around their beautiful bodies.

We had a lot of fun doing all the images, but sometimes it was a real torture for the models to be tied in helpless and painful poses. Nevertheless all of them enjoyed the ropes, bindings and even a little pain.

About bondage
For a lot of people it´s hard to understand why someone likes to be tied, helpless or dominated. But I think it´s a private pleasure and everybody should try this at least one time in his life. Be open minded and enjoy the new experience. After a first try it will be much easier to understand the pleasure of bondage.

About the book
This is a photographic art book about bondage, shibari and kinbaku. Amazing girls, creative and inspirational ties and poses. All images very colorful with high-end retouching. I just wanted to produce stunning bondage art, so I mixed elements of shibari, kinbaku, hojojutsu and western bondage.

The Story behind
I am a pro photographer and love to do creative photography projects. At the end of 2014 I stumbled about some really great bondage art photos. Totally blown away and with no knowledge about rope, bondage or bdsm, I did some more research and an idea was born:

I wanted to produce stunning images for a wide audience. Espcially for people with no affinity to bondage/bdsm, but also for experienced people. So the result should be high-end, focused on art, beautiful models, cool ties, poses and light. On top of this with several types of high end retouching - ideal for a photo book, art prints, calendars or posters.

With no idea about knots, ropes and such things, I watched some youtube videos, read some articles about it and bought 3 books - you´ll find them on amazon:

- „Decorative Fusion Knots: A Step-by-Step Illustrated Guide to New and Unusual Ornamental Knots" , ISBN-10: 1931160783
- „Two Knotty Boys Showing You The Ropes: A Step-by-Step, Illustrated Guide for Tying Sensual and Decorative Rope Bondage" , ASIN: B009CRMORO
- „Two Knotty Boys Back on the Ropes" , ISBN-10: 1931160694

These books and some inspiration from my artwork is all you need...

Table of Contents

Chair Bondage — 8
Girls tied to a chair

Wedding — 12
Brides in a wedding dress - sensual ties

Portraits — 16
A look into the face of tied beauties.

Bamboo — 26
Girls tied to bamboo poles

Rope Harness — 37
hard rope, bound close to beautiful bodies.

Housemaids, Schoolgirls, Nuns,… — 55
Girls, tied in costumes

Fine Art of Bondage - Beauty of Rope
Rod Meier
Fine-Art-of-Bondage.com

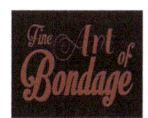

Hard tied   62

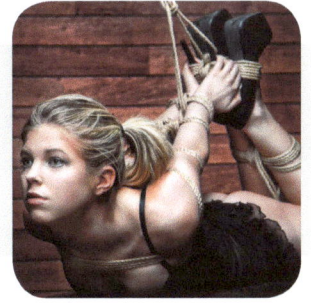

Hogtied, helpless and painful - great tied women

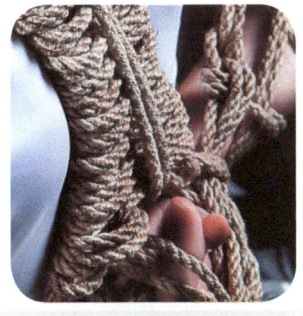

Close up   74

focused on rope...

Ropemarks   84

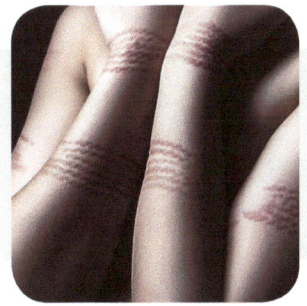

symbols after the pleasure of rope bondage...

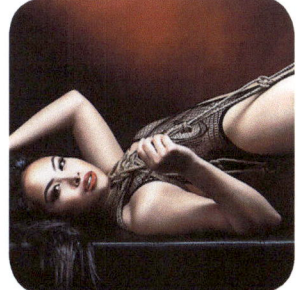

Thank you   88

for watching and all the response...

more books to come   89

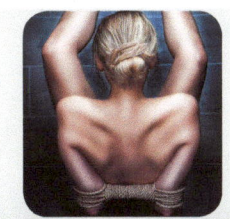

More (planned) Fine Art of Bondage books...

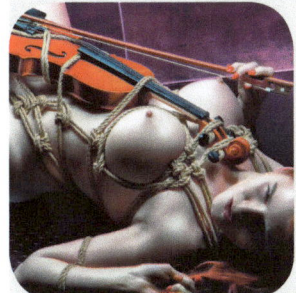

Nudes and Rope

"just skin and rope"
the second book..

91

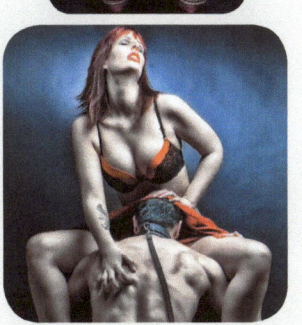

Couples and Rope

"couples and rope, playing"
the third book..

97

The Models

I did some test shoots with models I already knew from my work. Some of those images have been published on the new homepage www.Fine-Art-of-Bondage.com and on my social media accounts.

The response was really outstanding: I gained a lot of fans, received messages from photographers, magazines, people from the bondage/shibari/kinbaku scene and especially from a lot of stunning models....

For publishing this book, I had about 50 photoshoots with newcomer models, experienced freelance models and some „famous" girls. They came from the United Kingdom, Switzerland, Austria, Brazil, Italy, Poland, Ireland, Ukraine, Bulgaria, Russia and on top some really stunning asian girls living in germany.

So this book is really international. Some girls have been on the cover of penthouse/USA, playboy germany or acted in TV series. Others are well known, professional models in the fashion or commercial business.

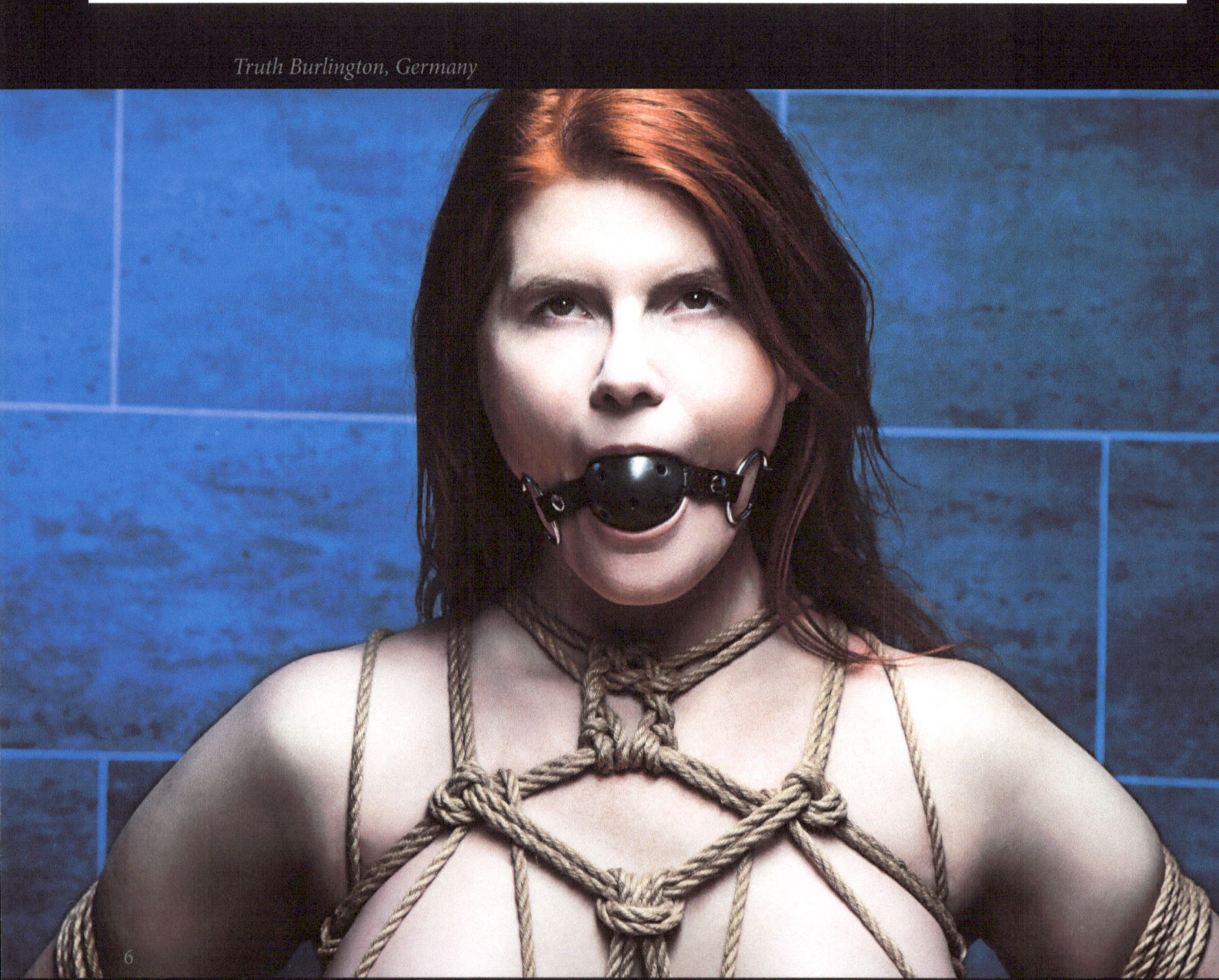

Truth Burlington, Germany

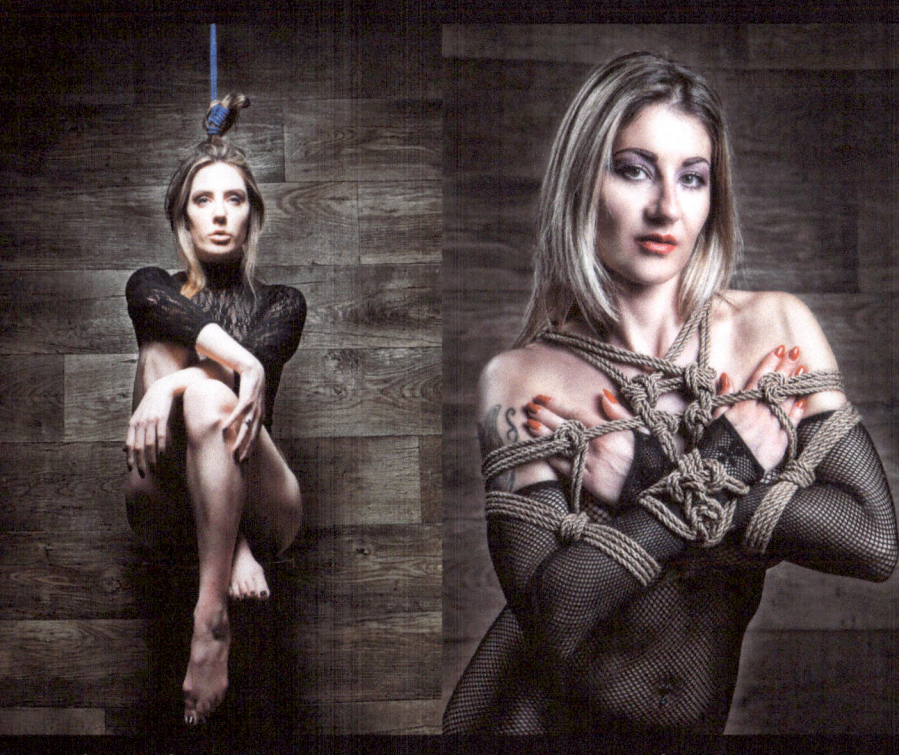

Samantha Bentley, UK   *Eva Kisimova, Italy*   *Leonora Burkhardt, Brazil*

Some of the VIP´s Girls

Samantha Bentley, UK
Multi AVN award winning pornstar, Penthouse Pet USA August/2015, Game of Thrones actress. Changing her life actually to a great DJ career!

Eva Kisimova
Professional nude model from italy. Working almost all over europe. Published in a lot of magazines and well know in italy.

Truth Burlington
Professional model and actress e.g. „Alarm fuer Cobra 11"/german TV series translated in a lot of countries all over the world. Published model in a lot of magazines.

Jessica K.
„Wiesn Playmate 2015" / the yearly, elected playboy playmate for the oktoberfest munich

Leonora Burkhardt
Actress, model and dancer from brazil, living in germany. Well known from several TV shows in germany.

Model Contacts
Most of the models are listet here with homepage/social media accounts:
http://fine-art-of-bondage.com/models/
(some models wanted to stay anonymous - please respect this)

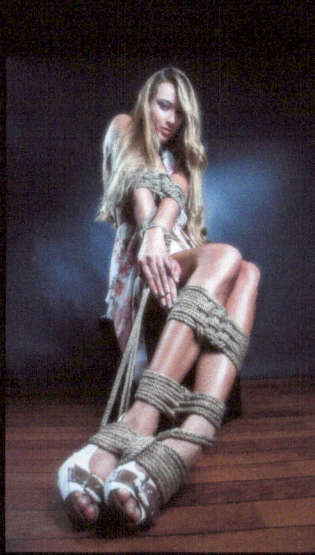

Jessica K., Wiesn Playmate 2015

Chairs

Chair bondage - girls tied to a chair.

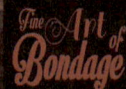

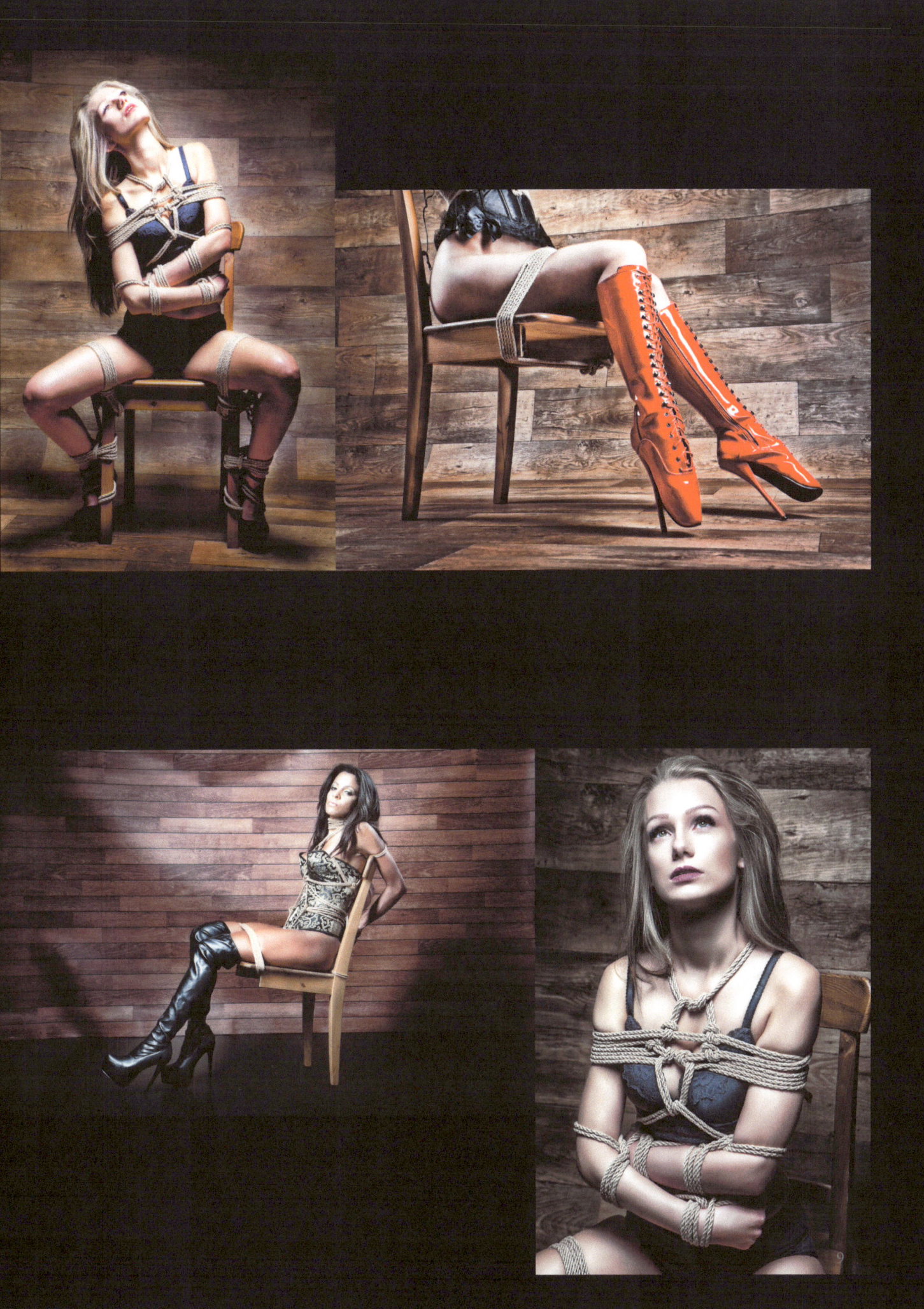

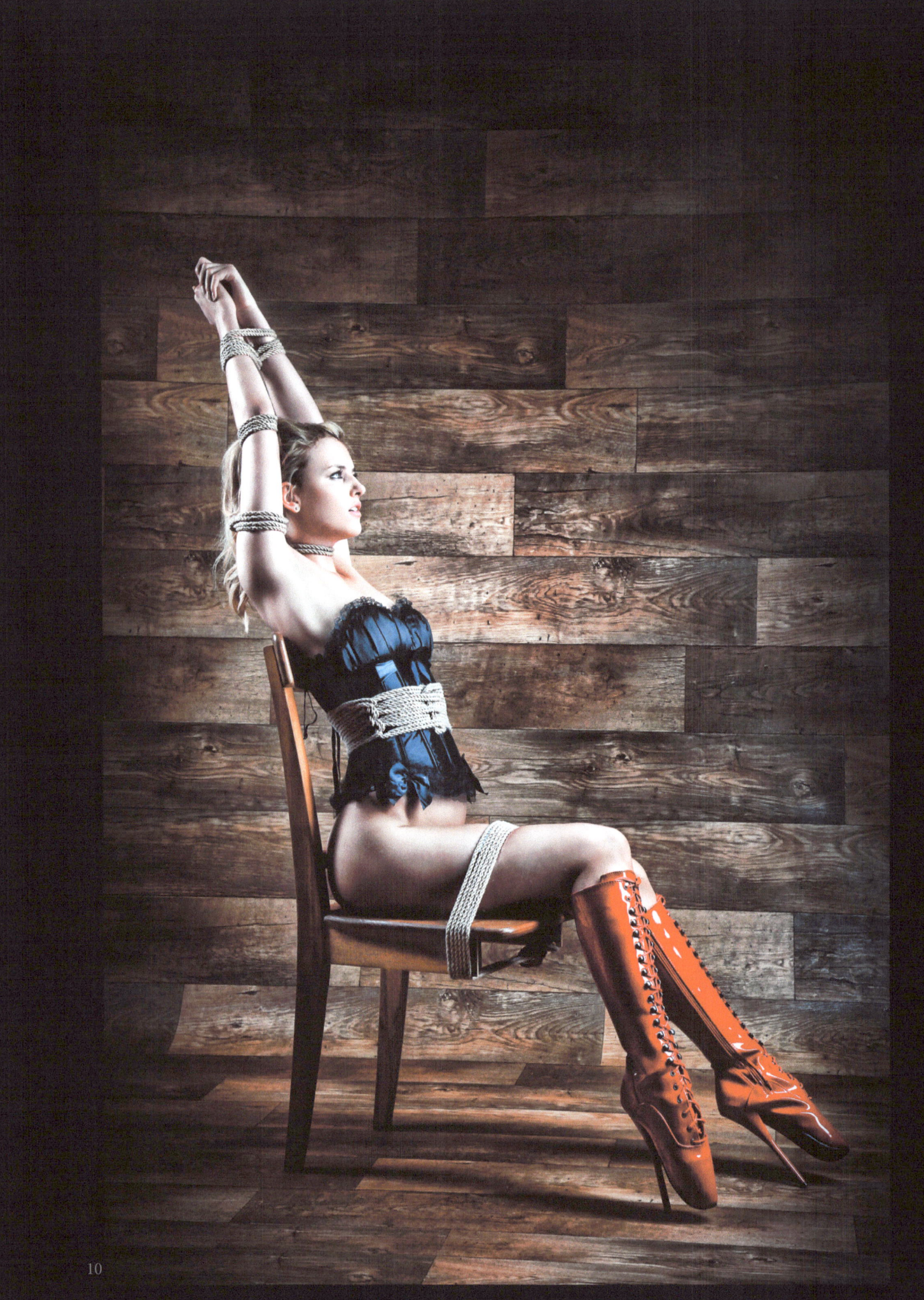

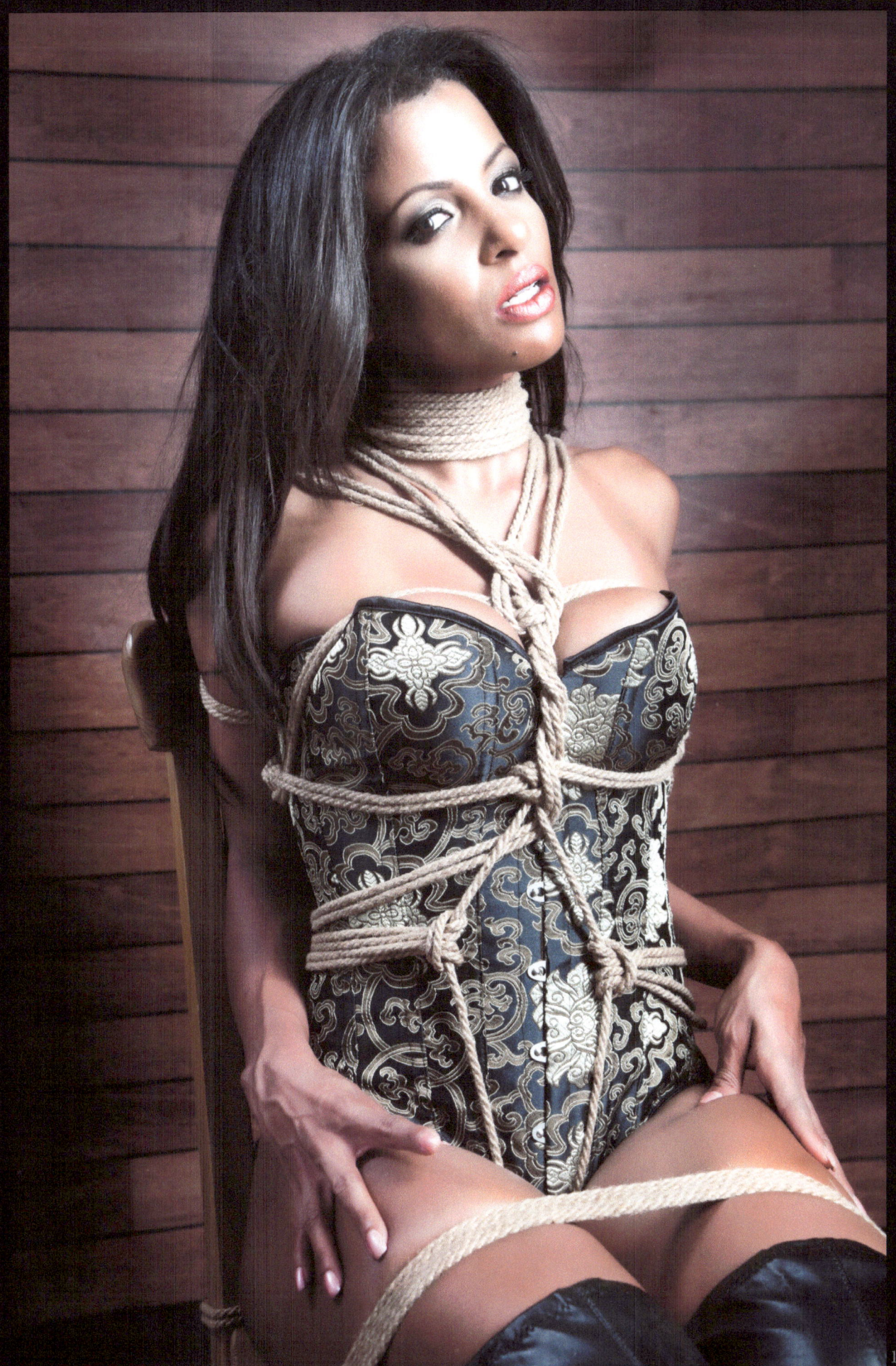

Wedding

Tied in a wedding dress

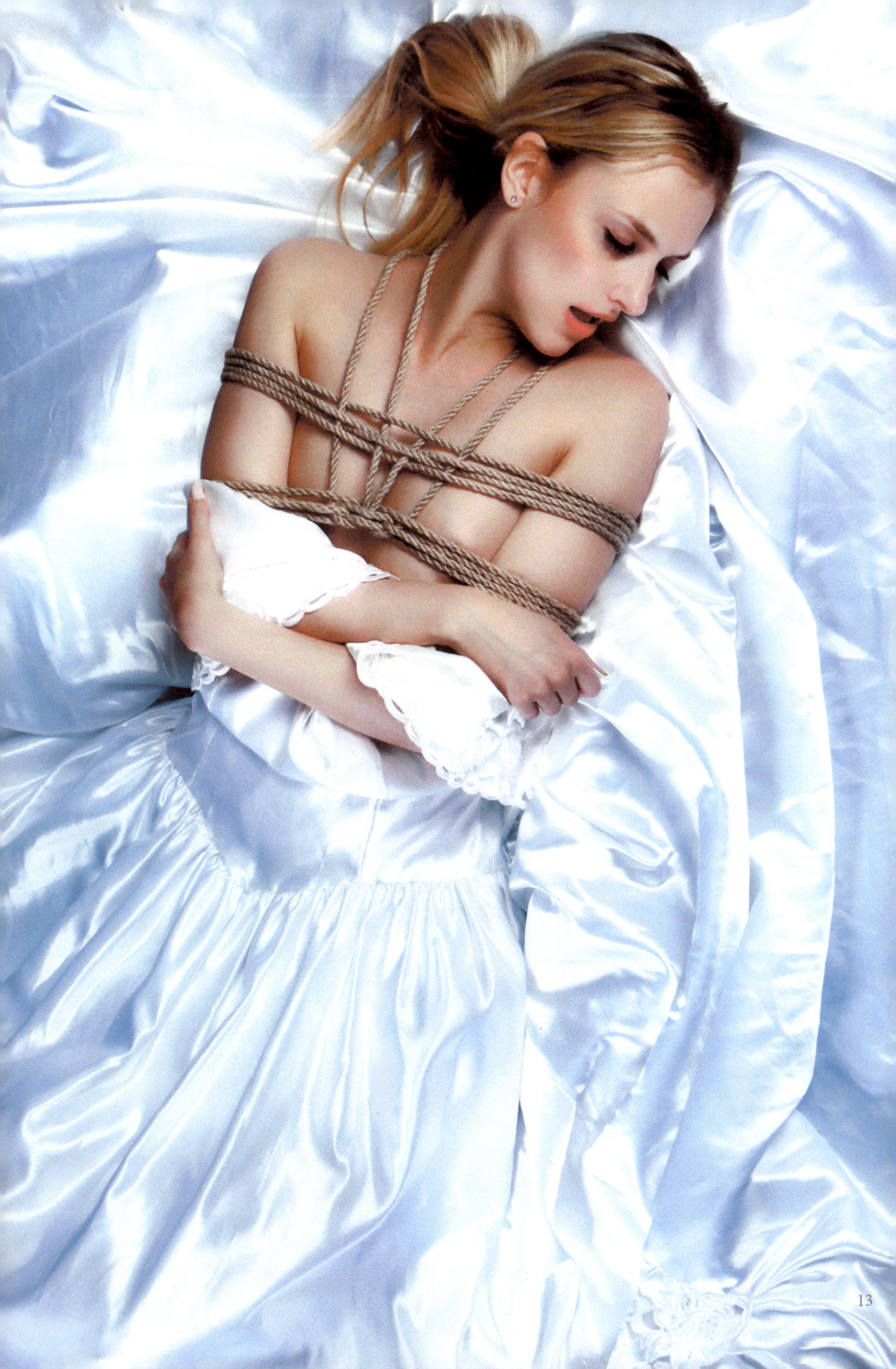

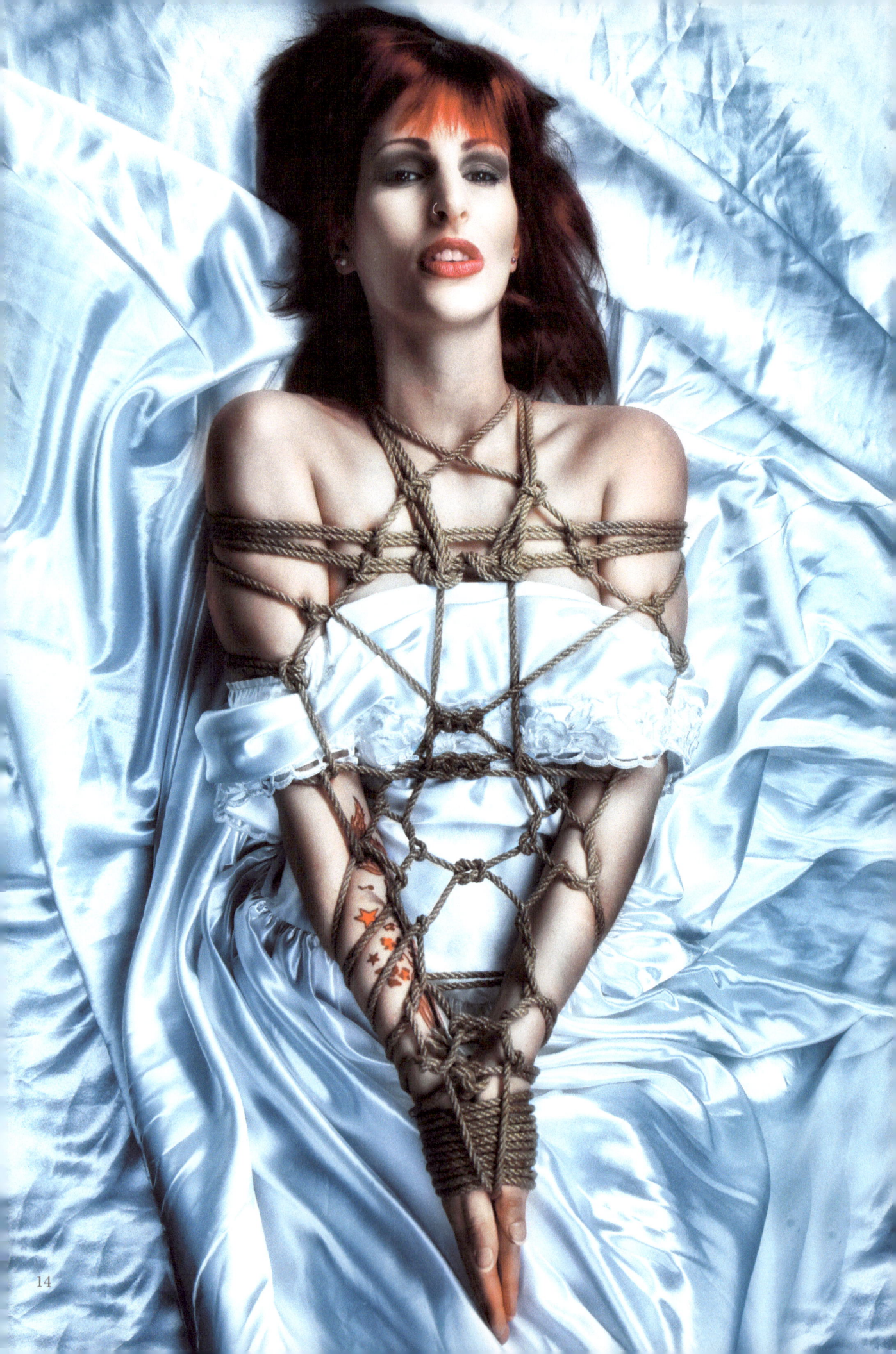

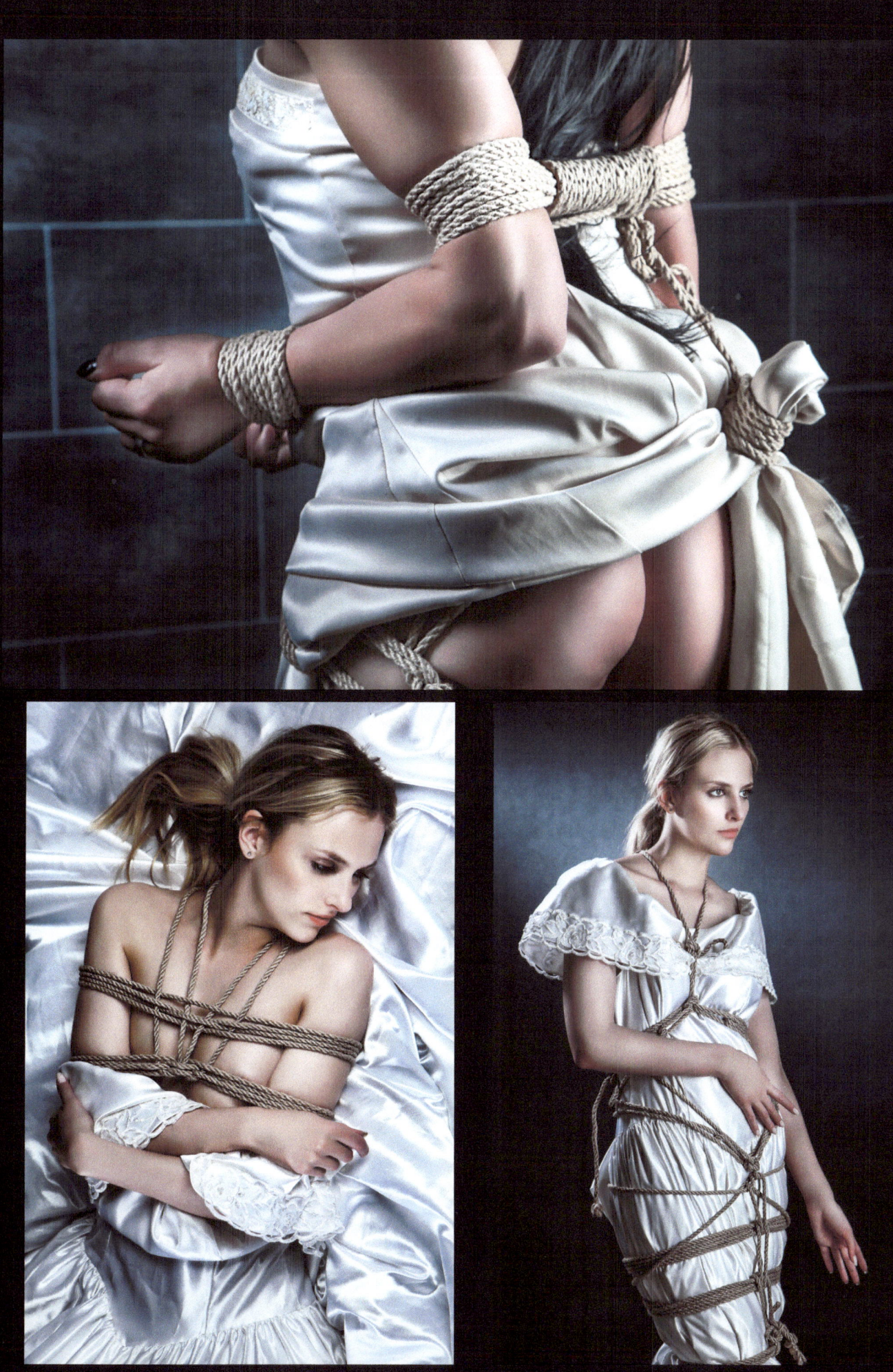

Portraits

A look into the face of tied beauties..

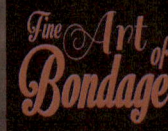

Samantha Bentley, UK

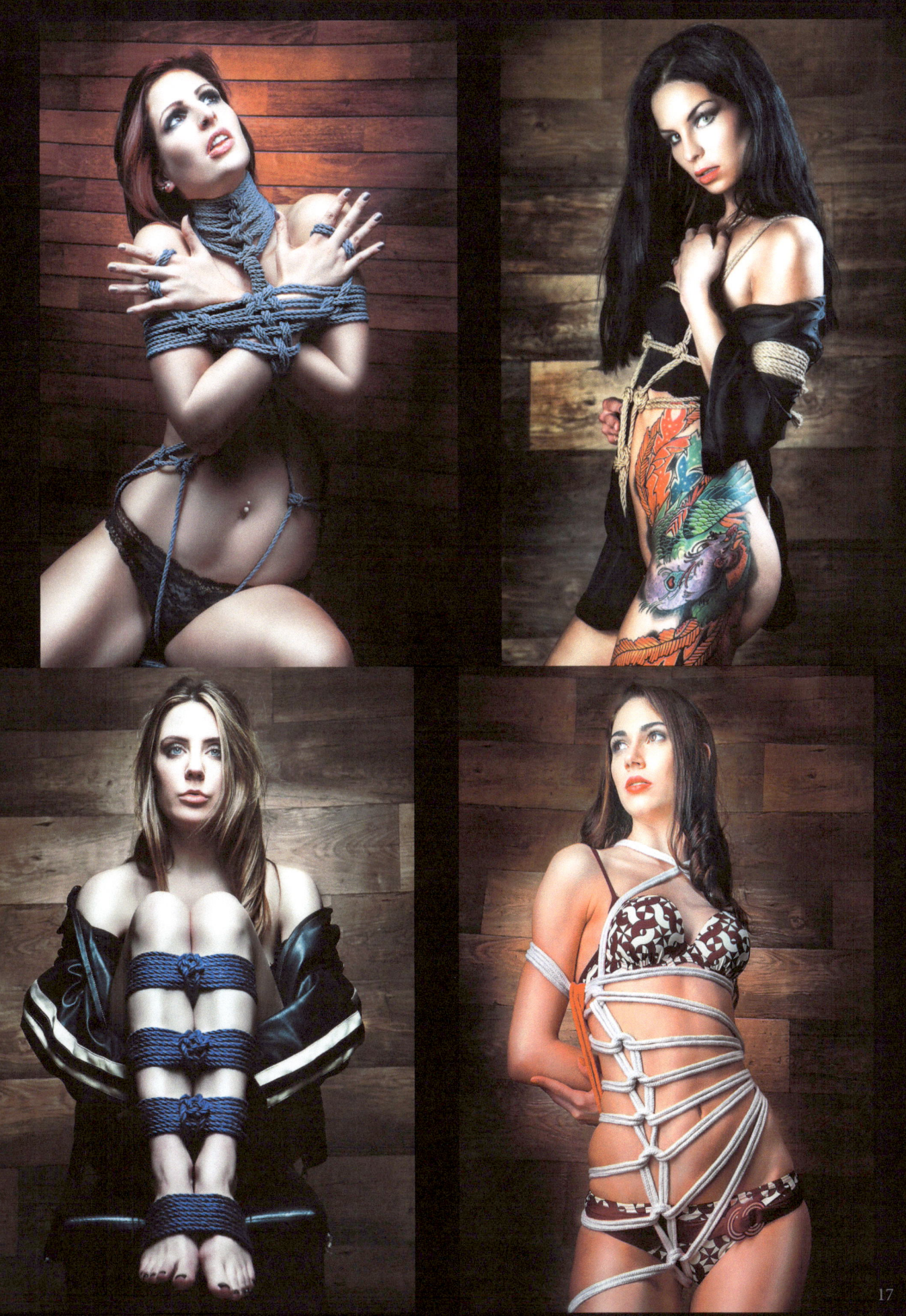

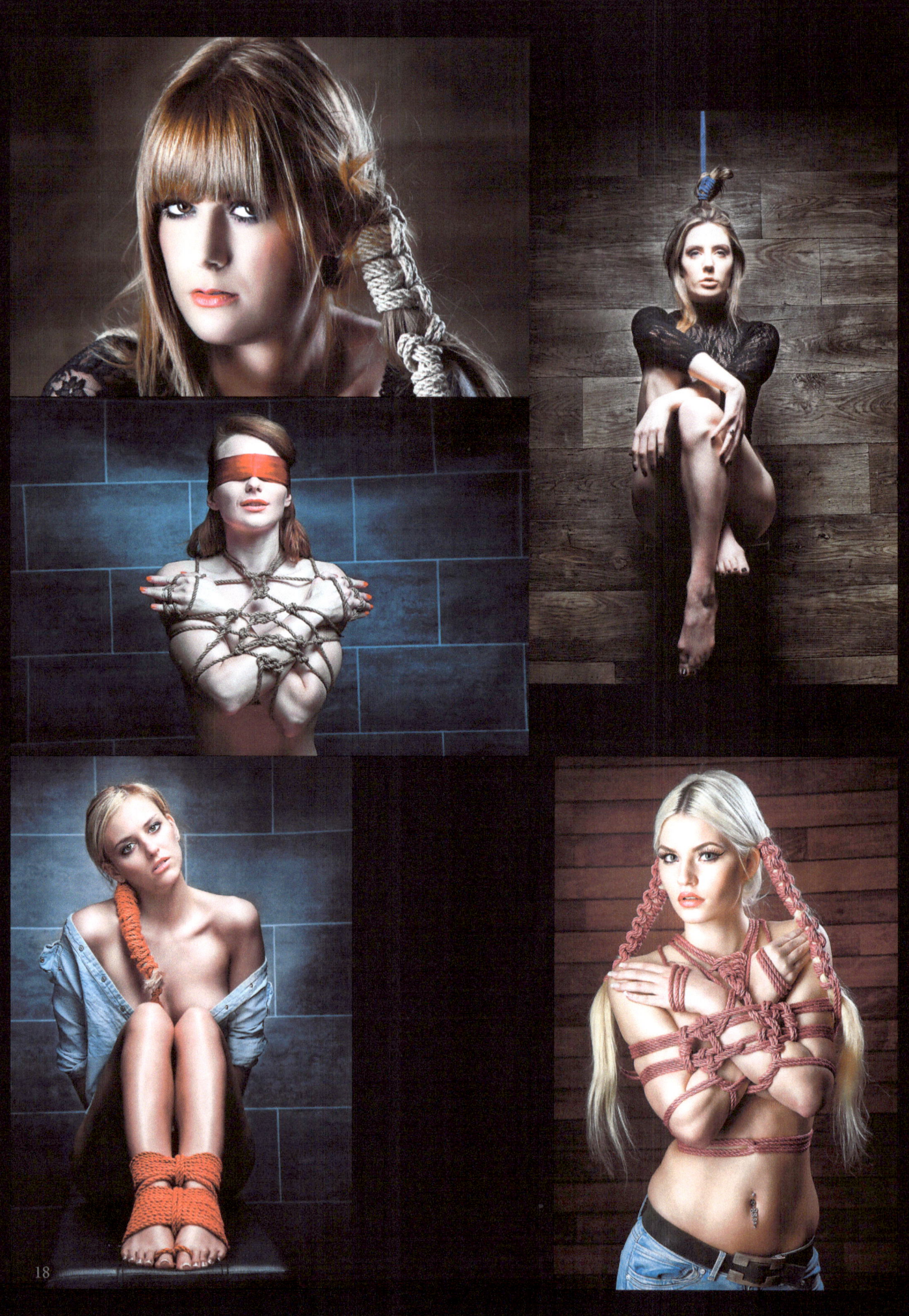

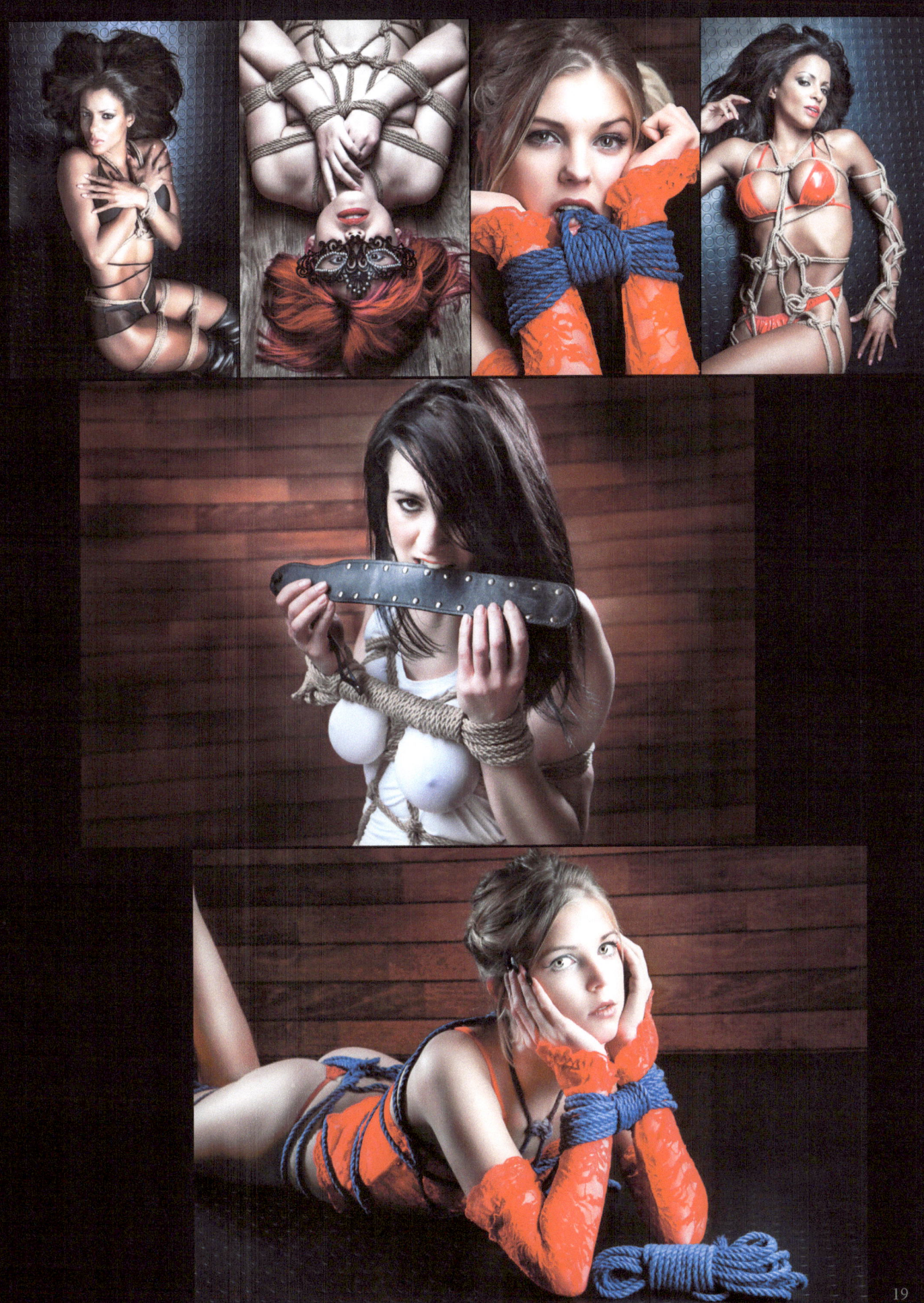

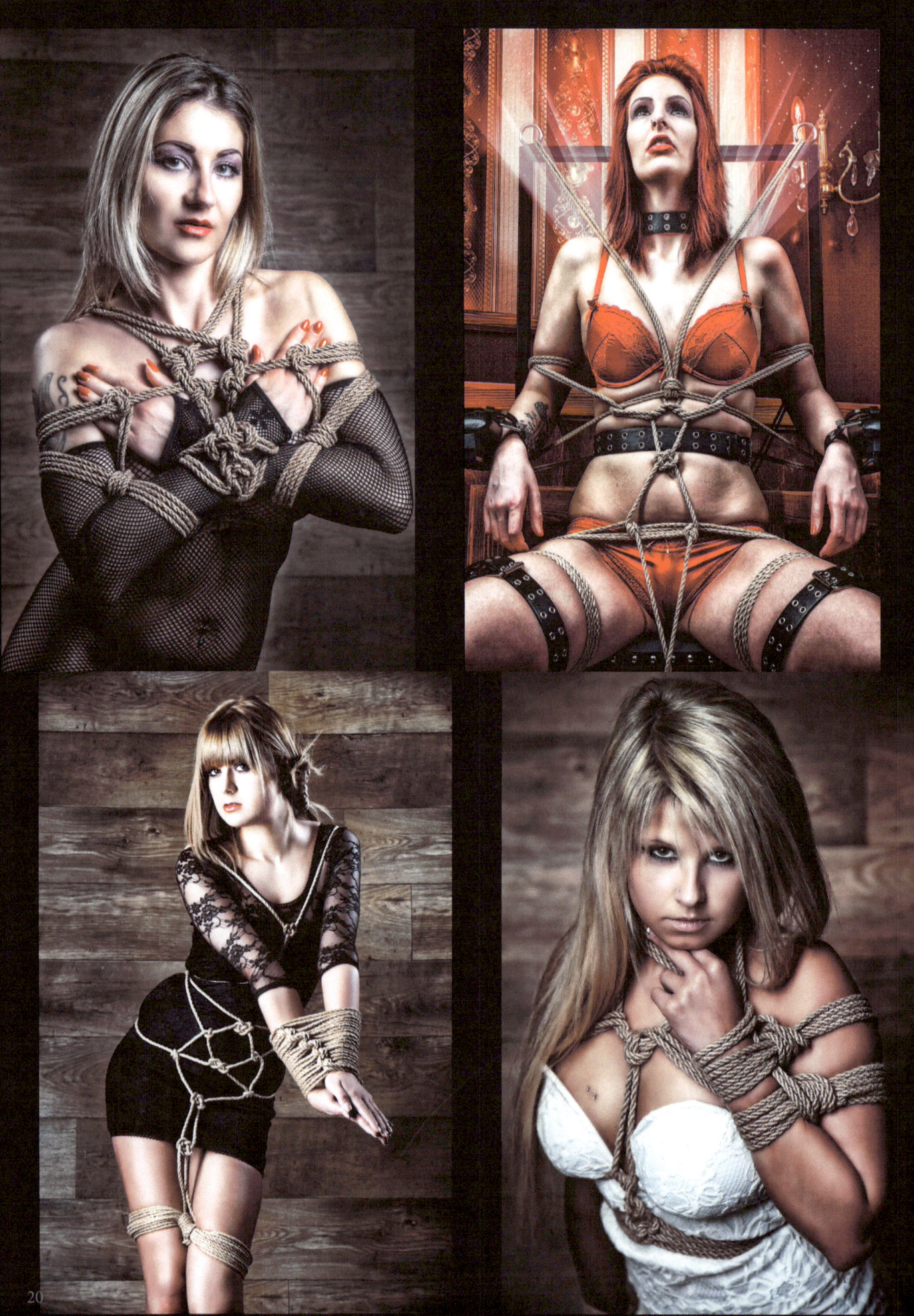

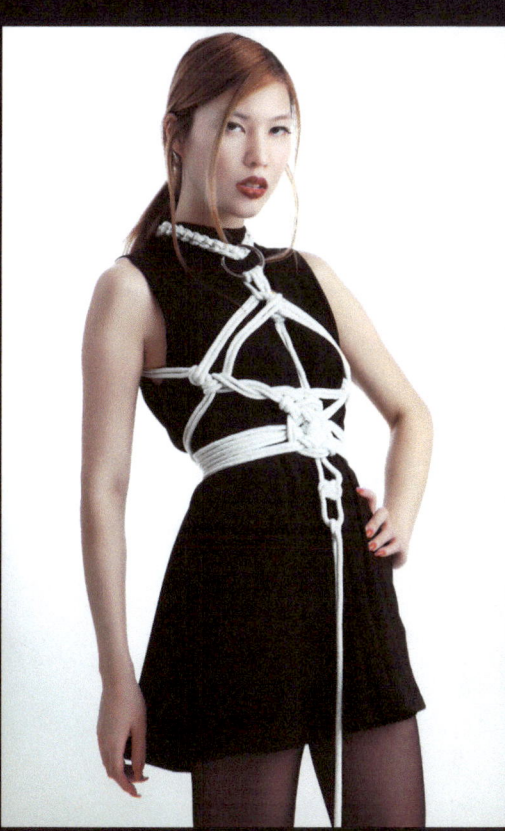
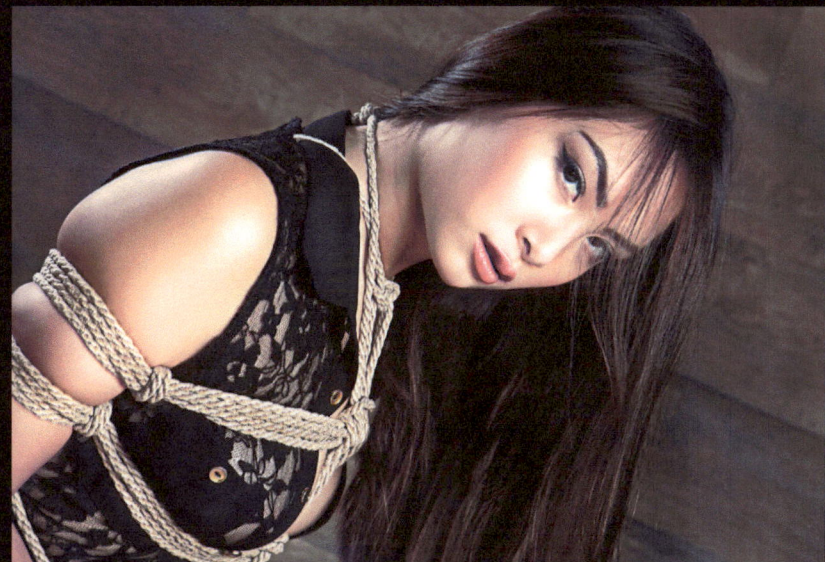

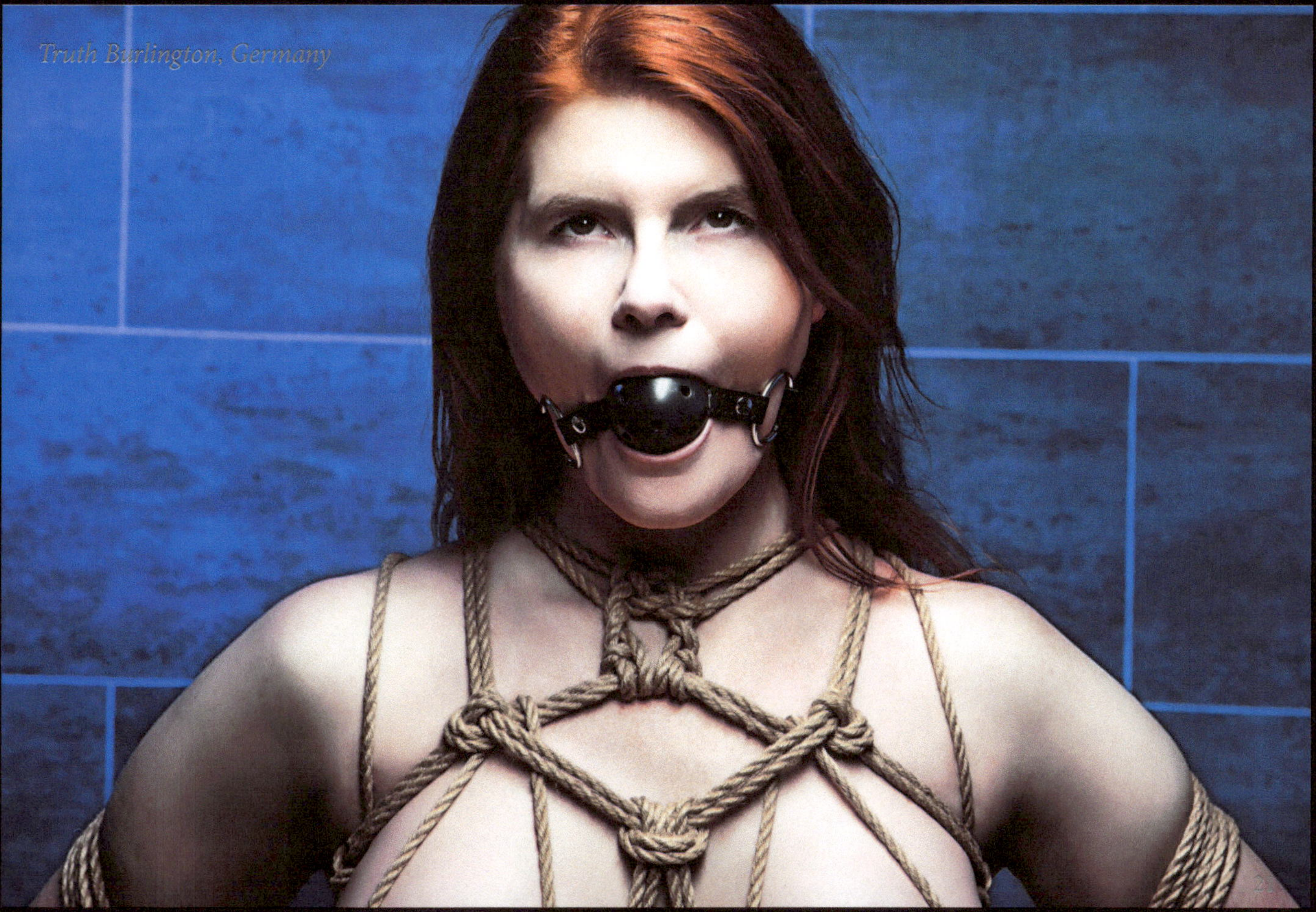

Truth Burlington, Germany

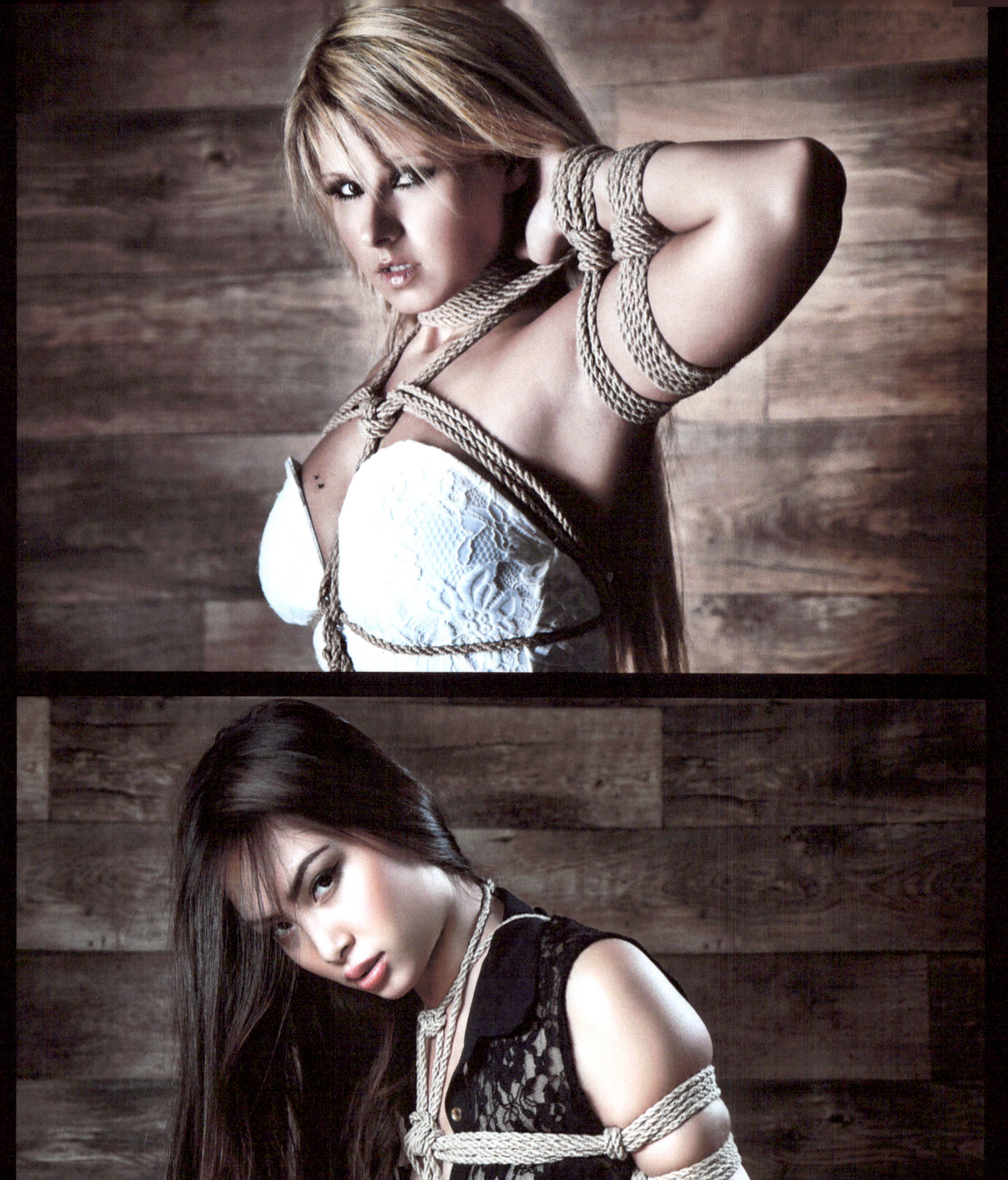

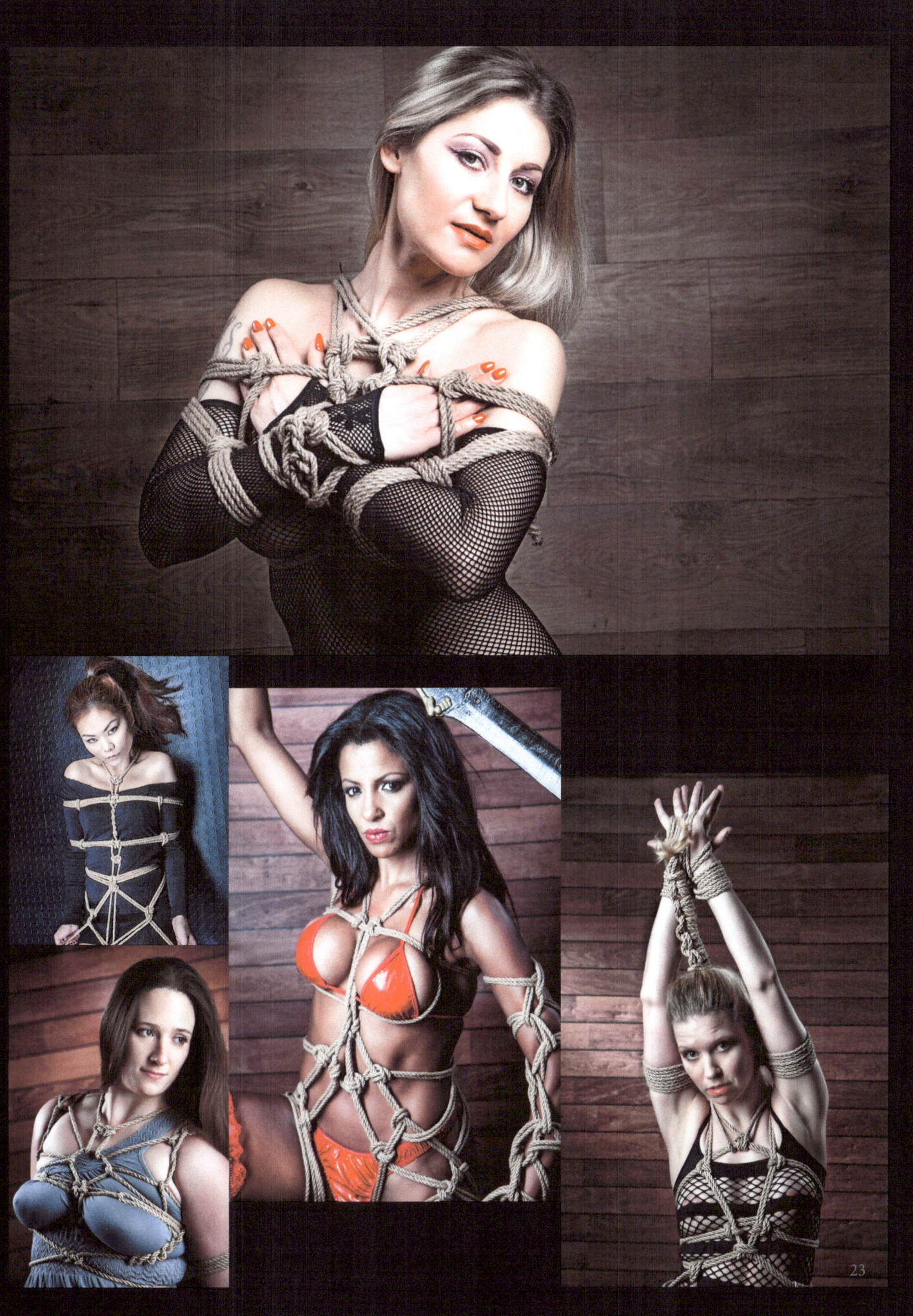

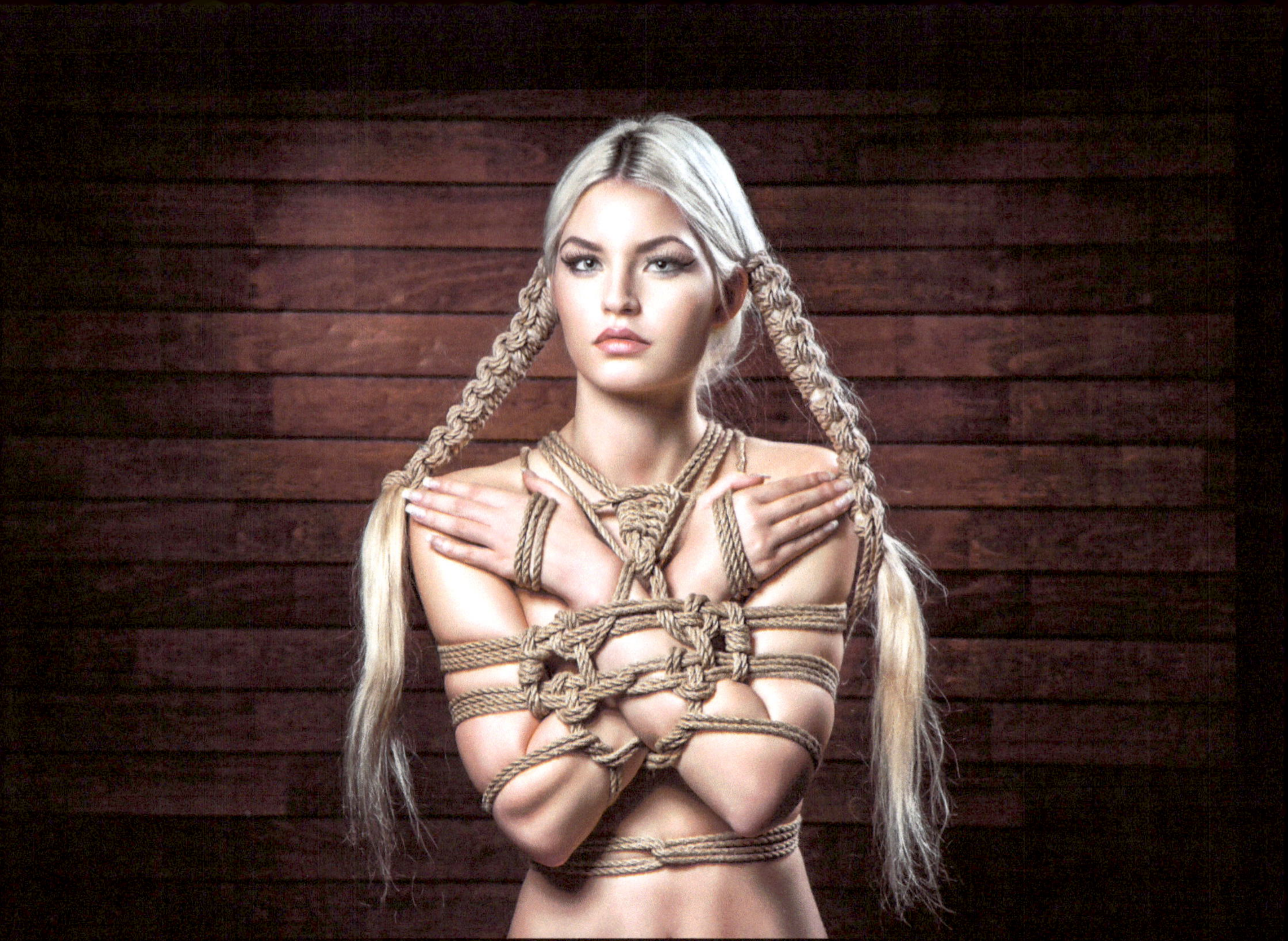

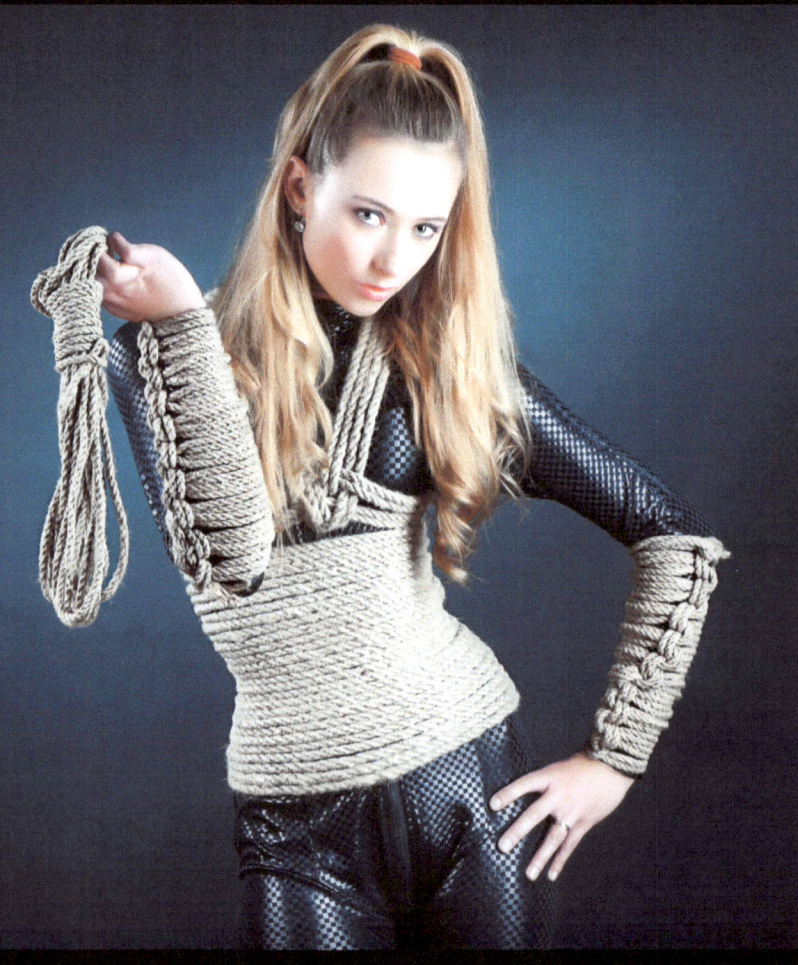

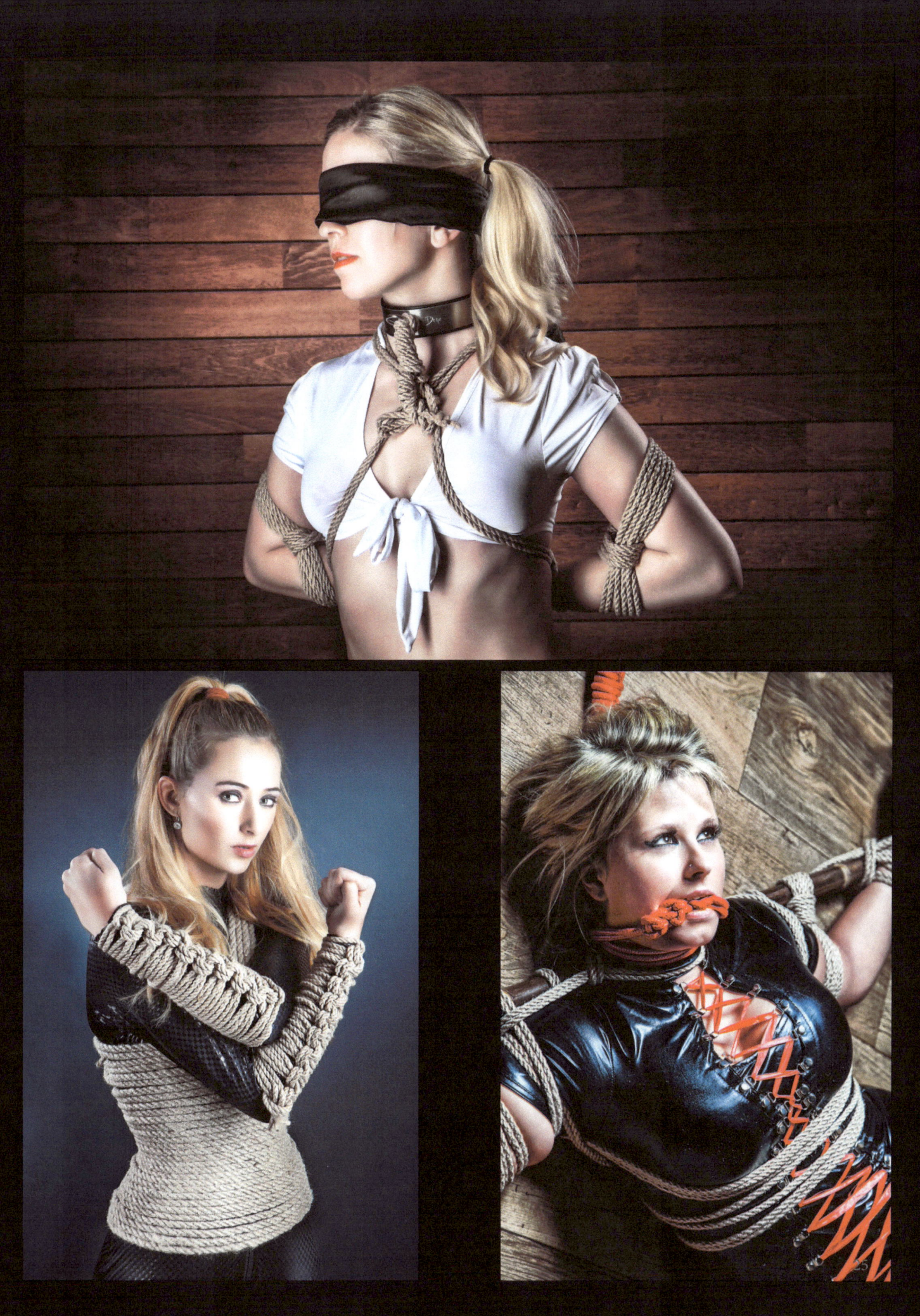

Bamboo

girls tied to bamboo poles

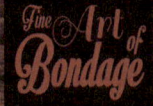

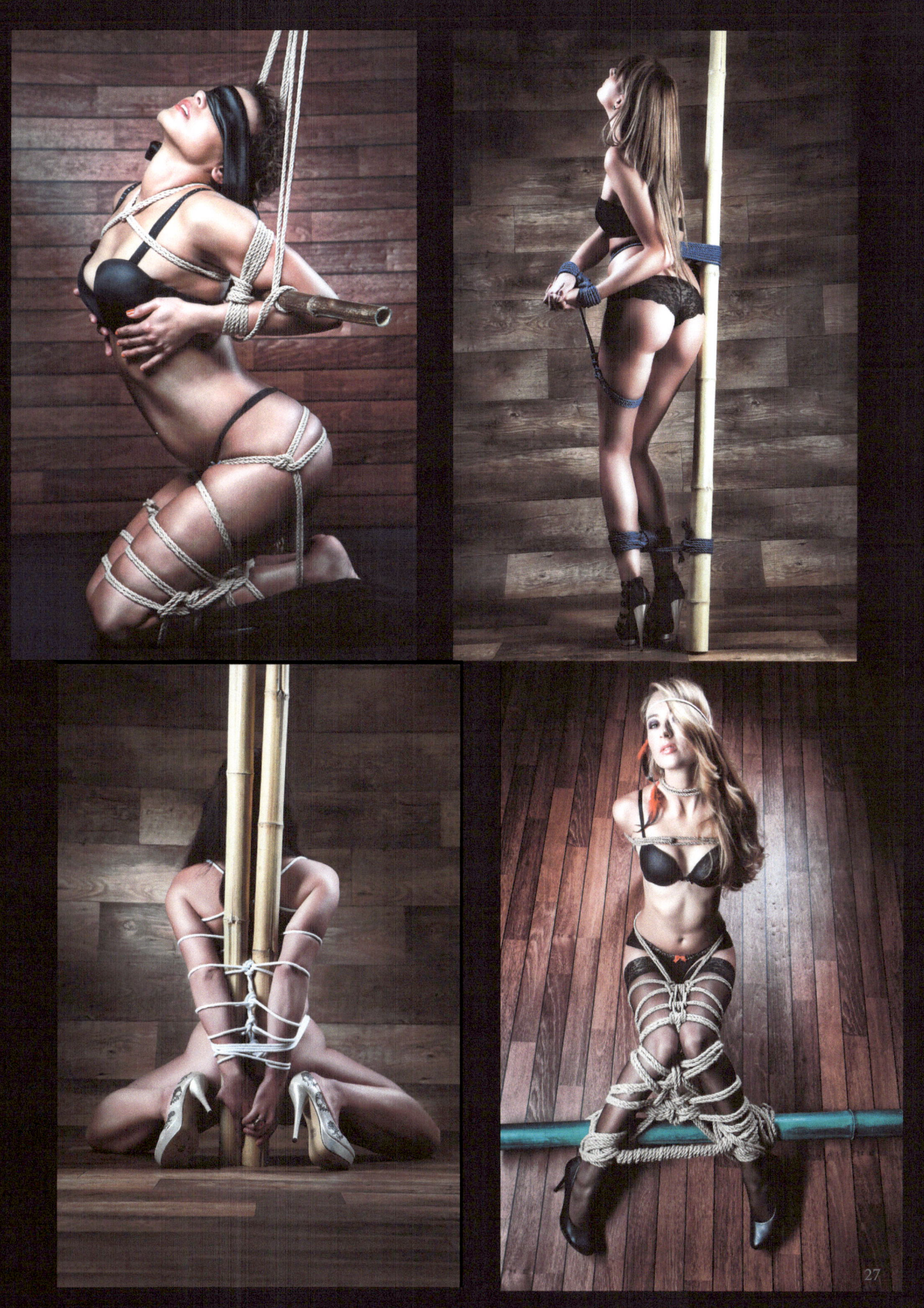

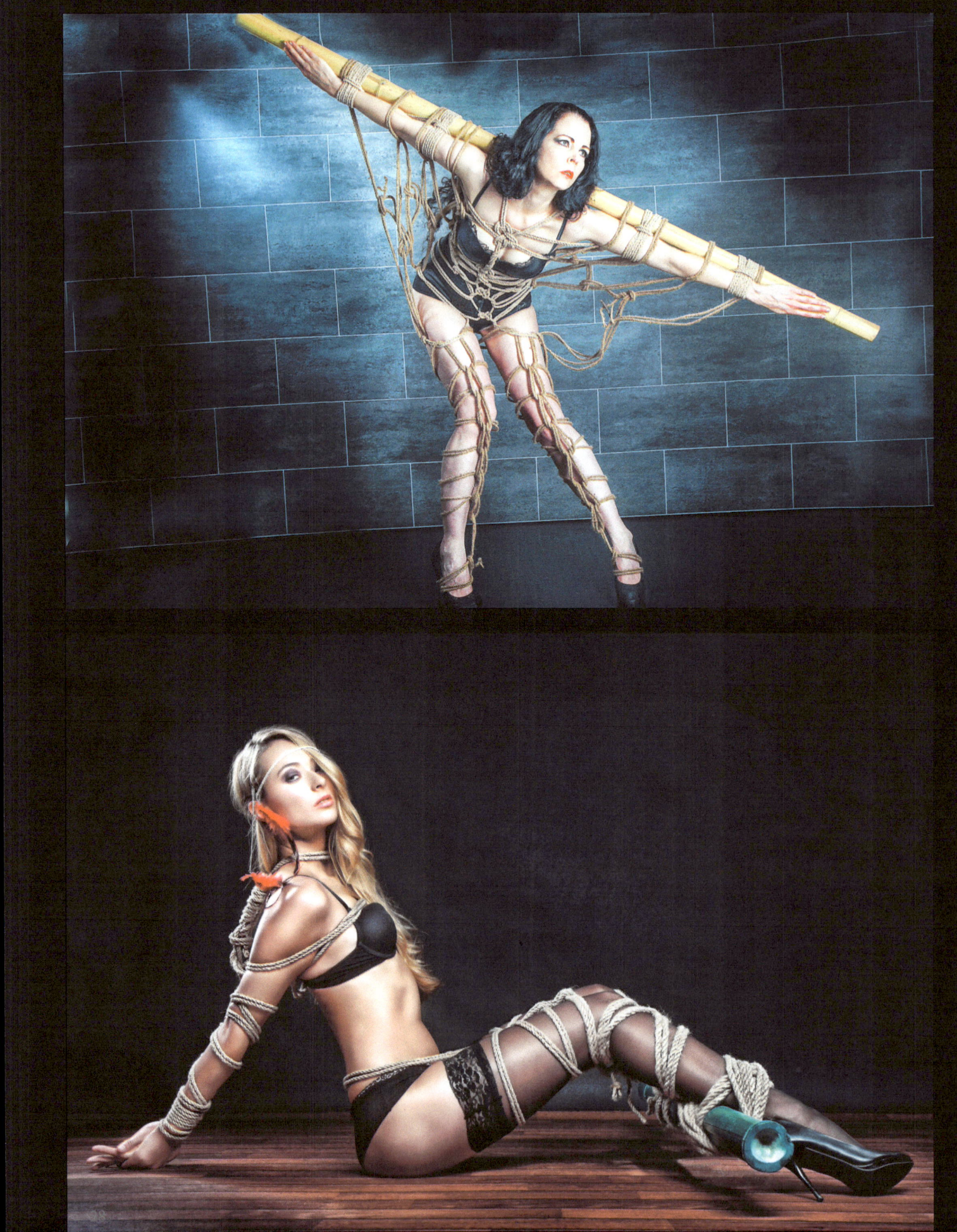

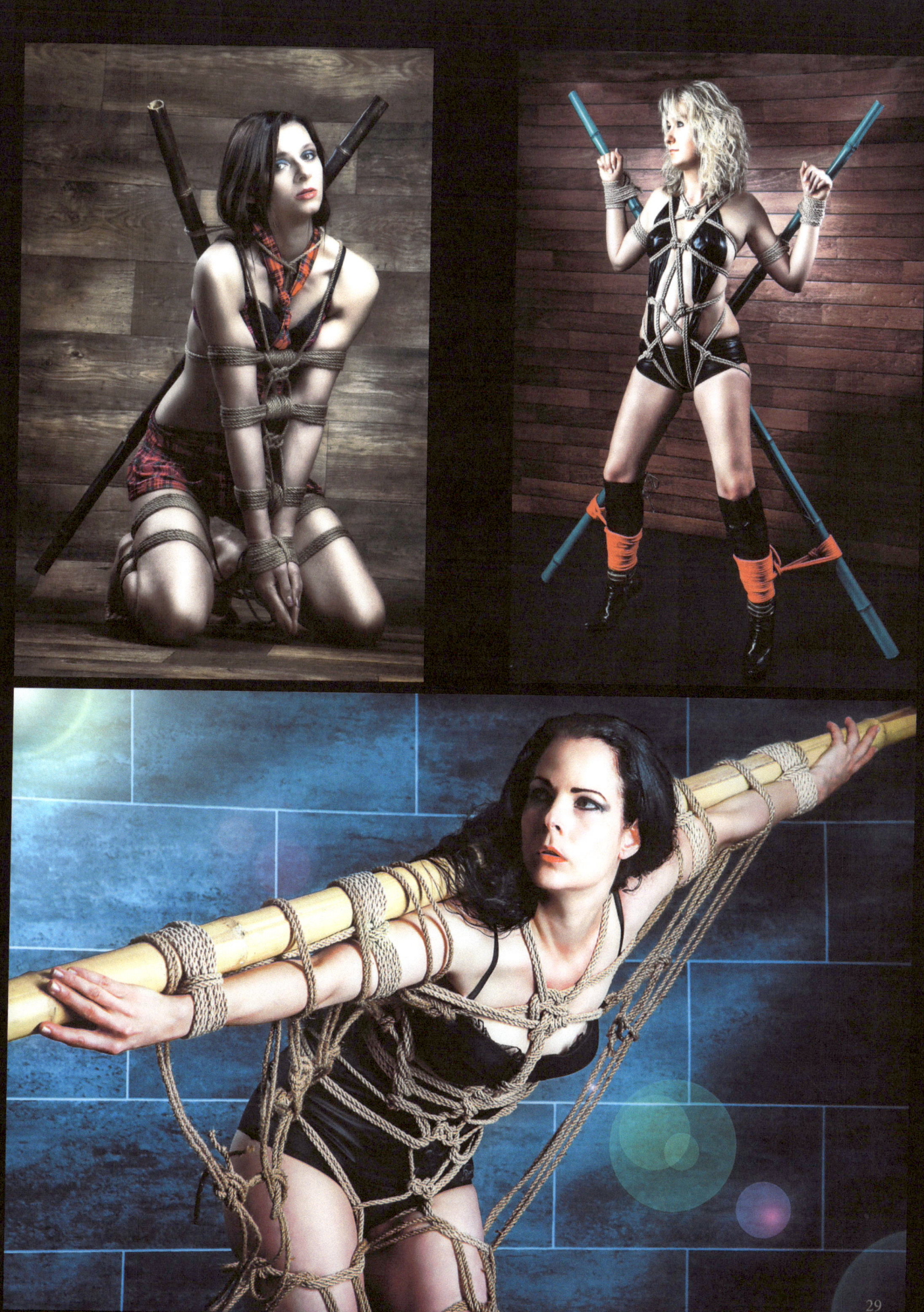

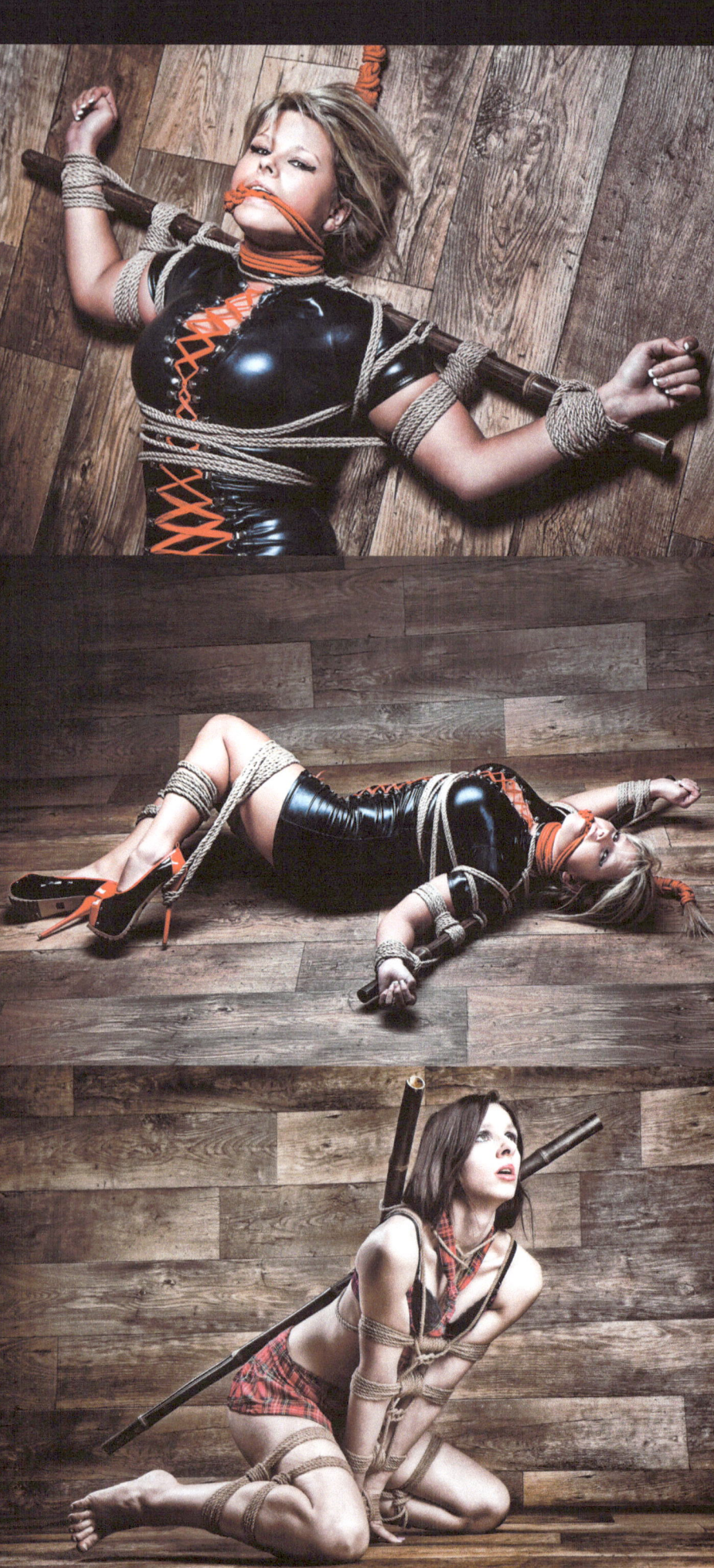

Bamboo

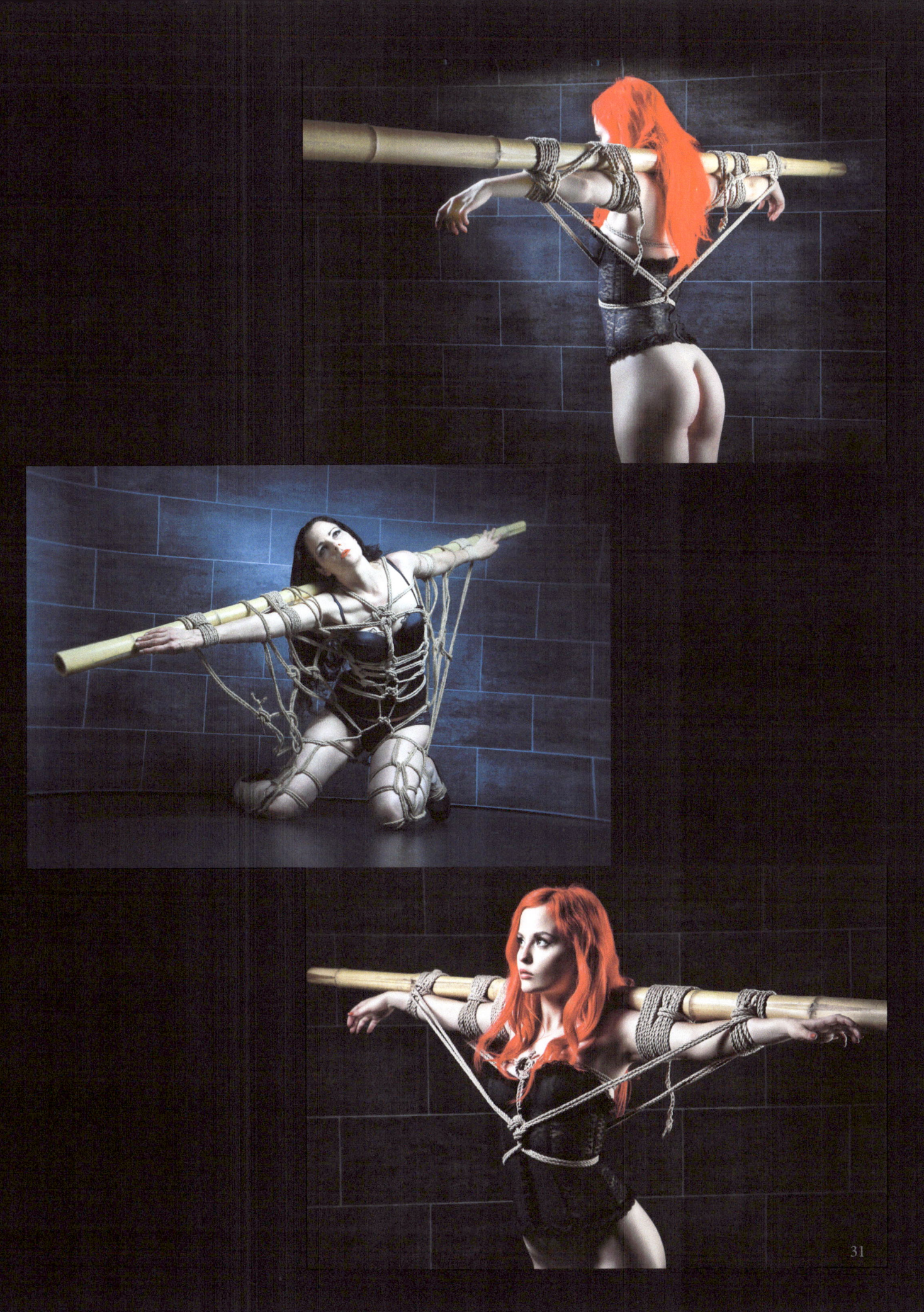

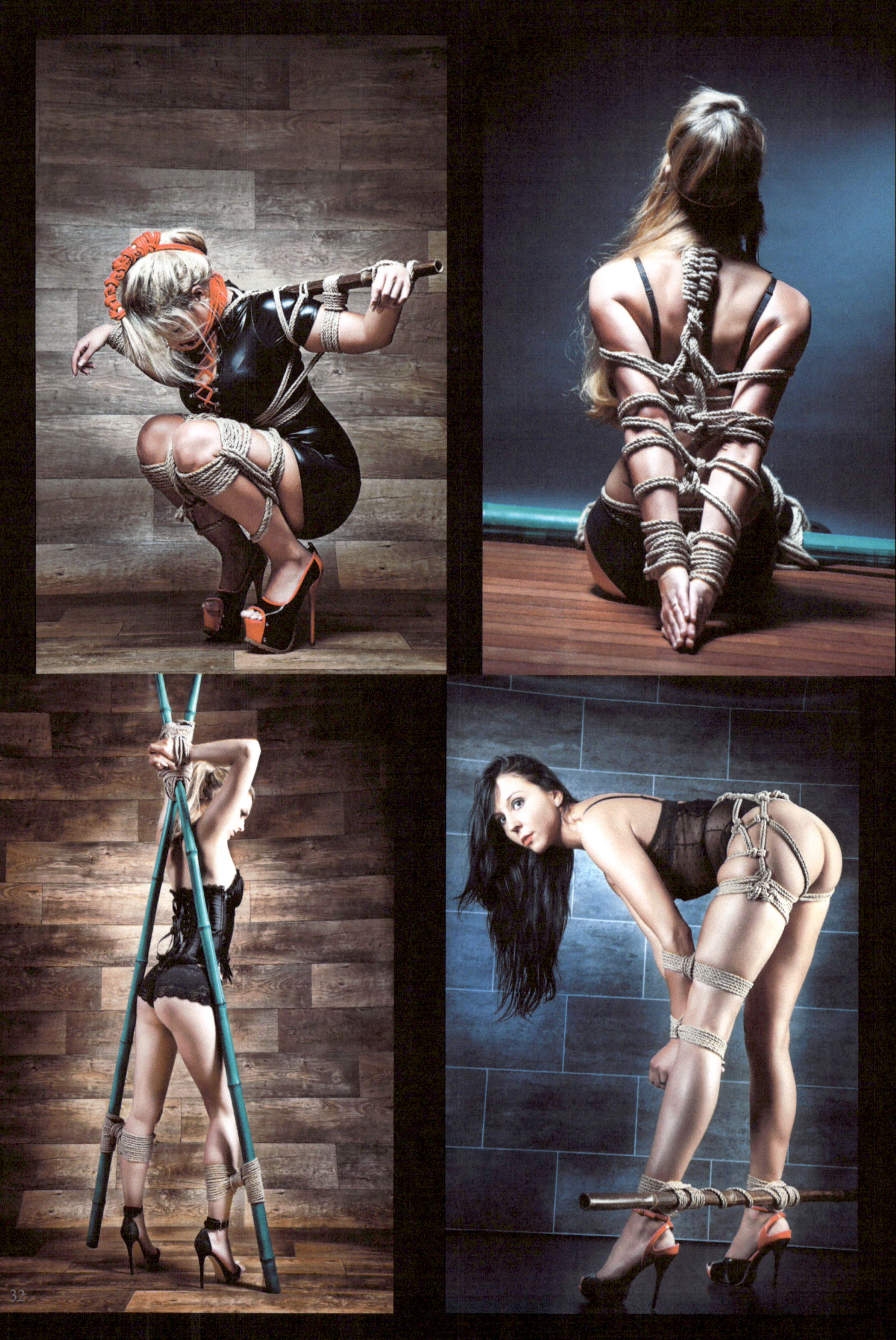

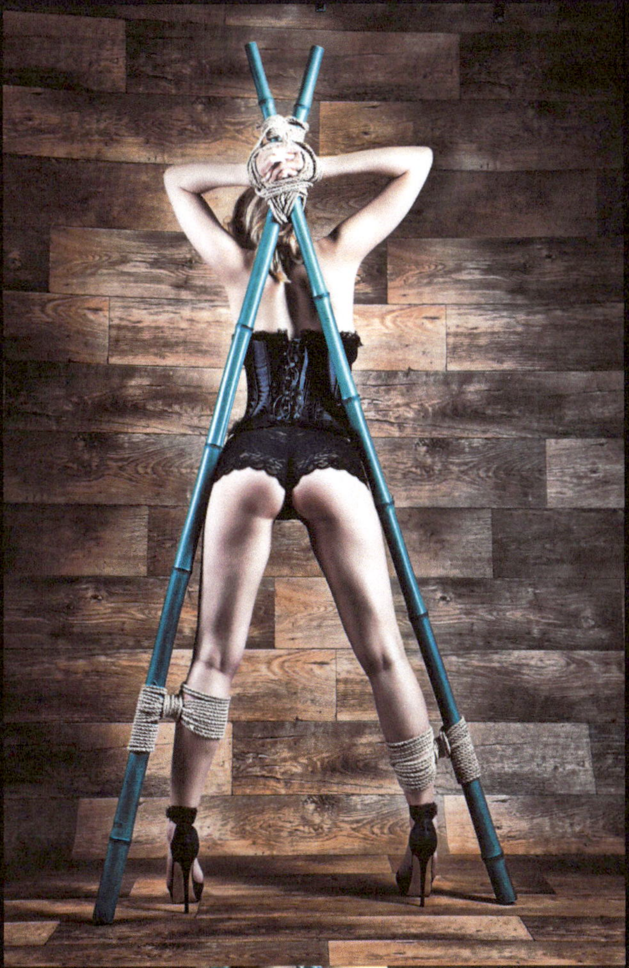

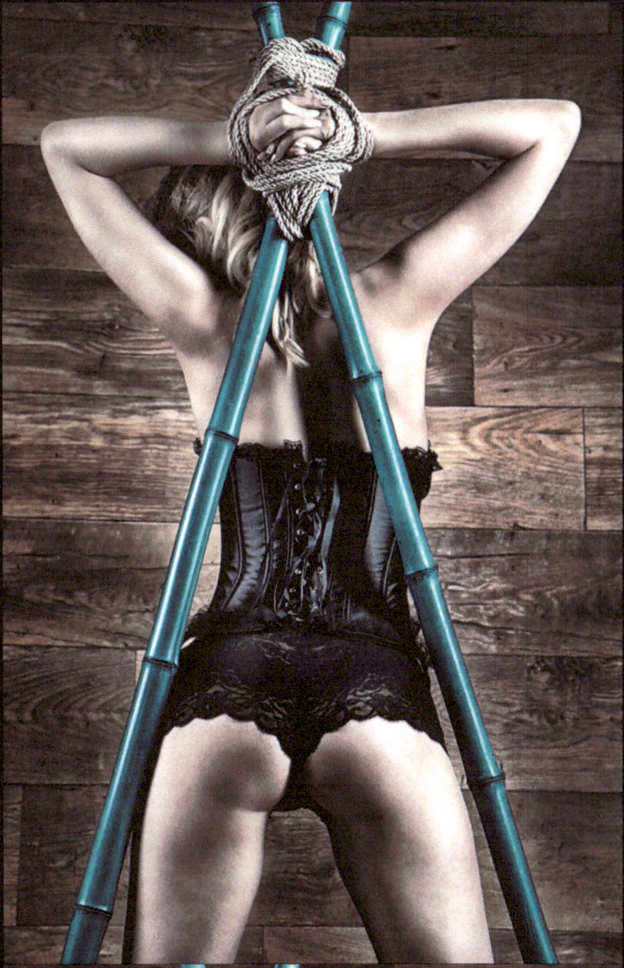

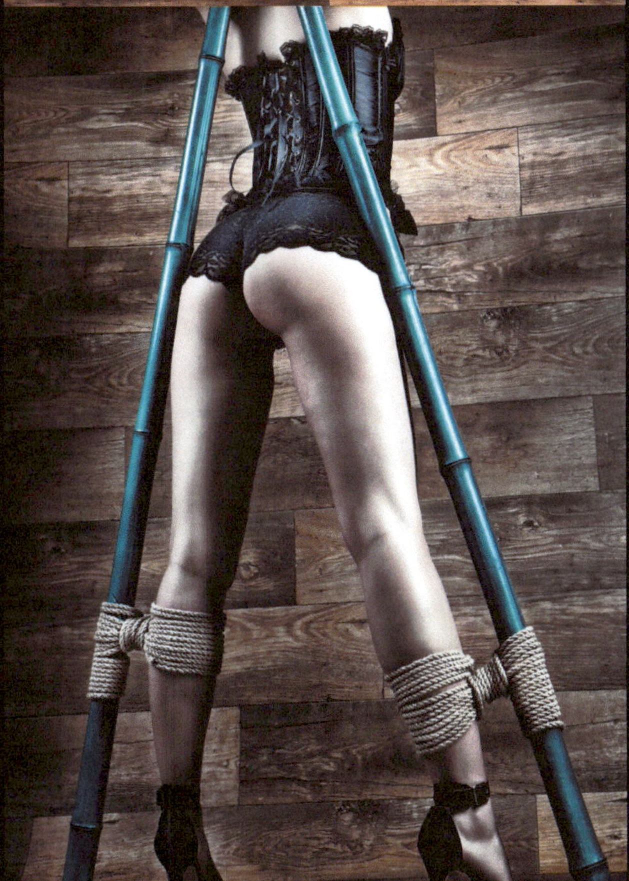

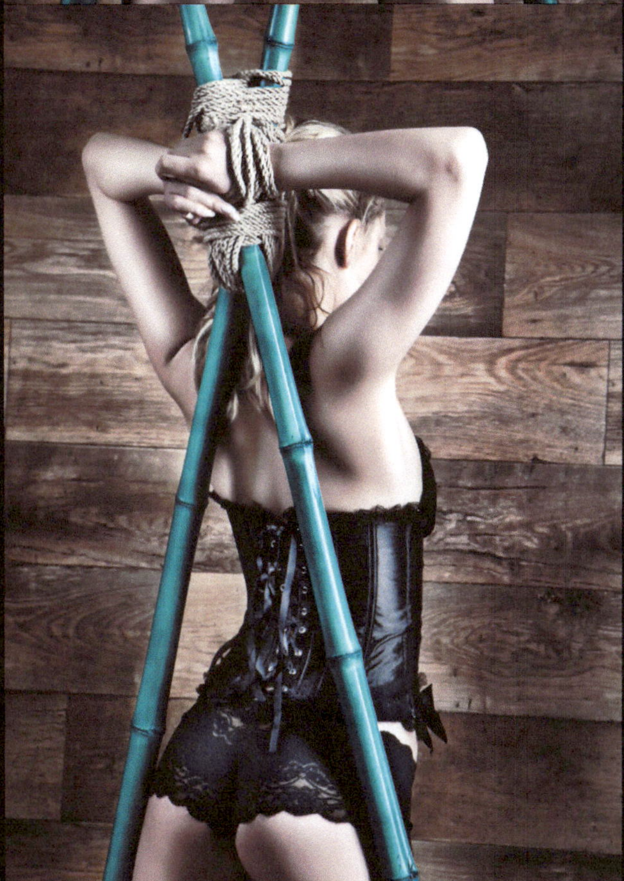

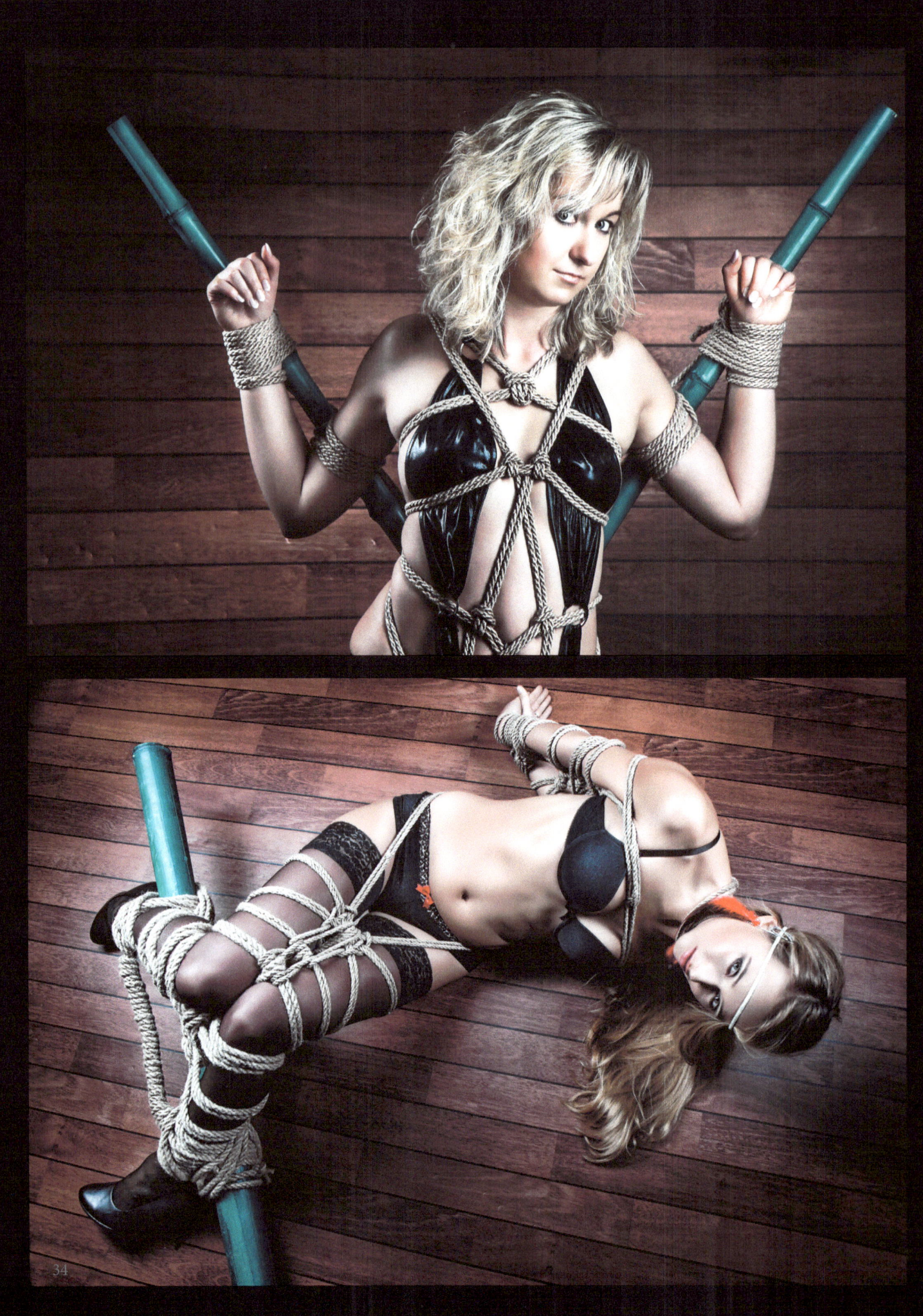

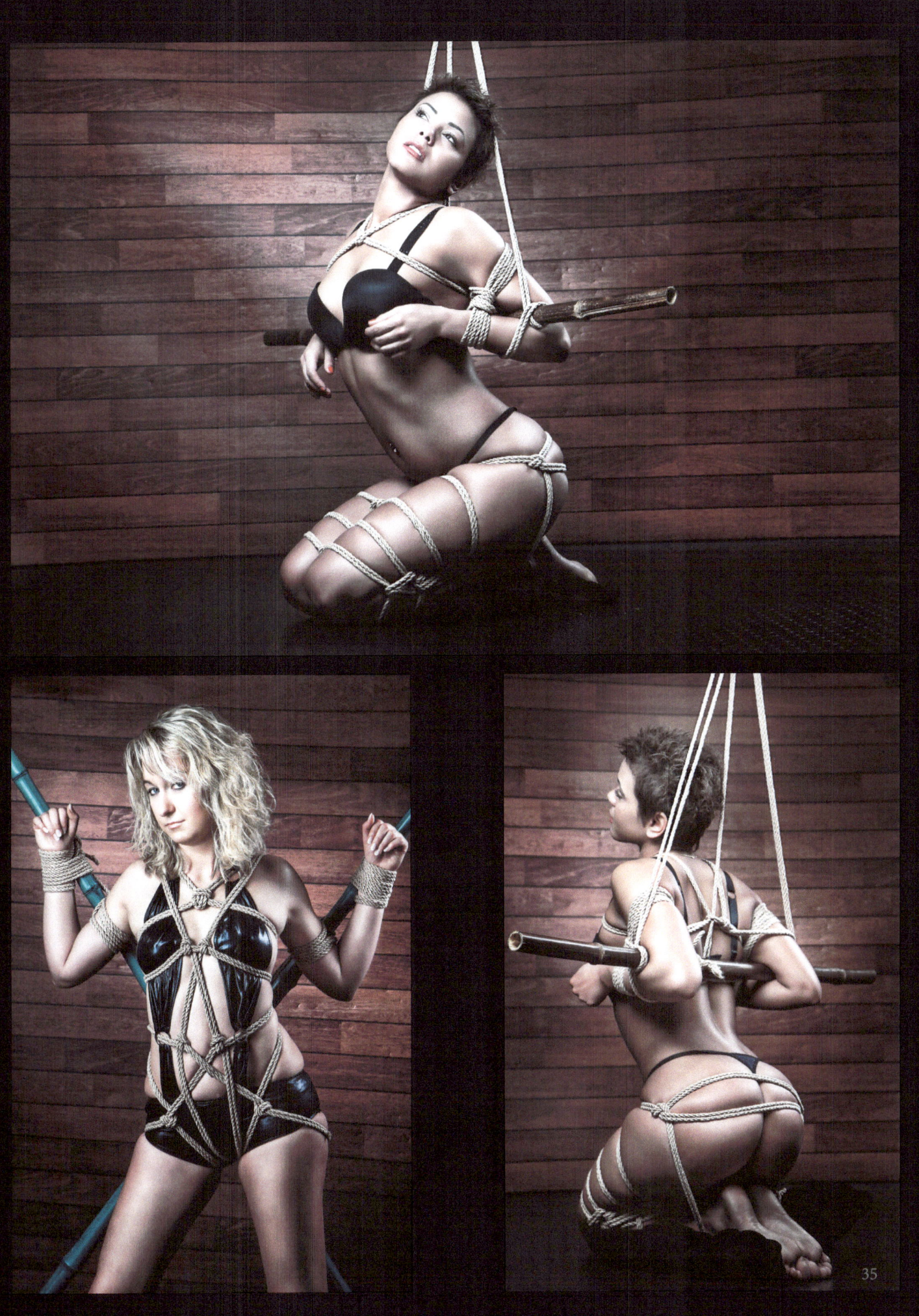

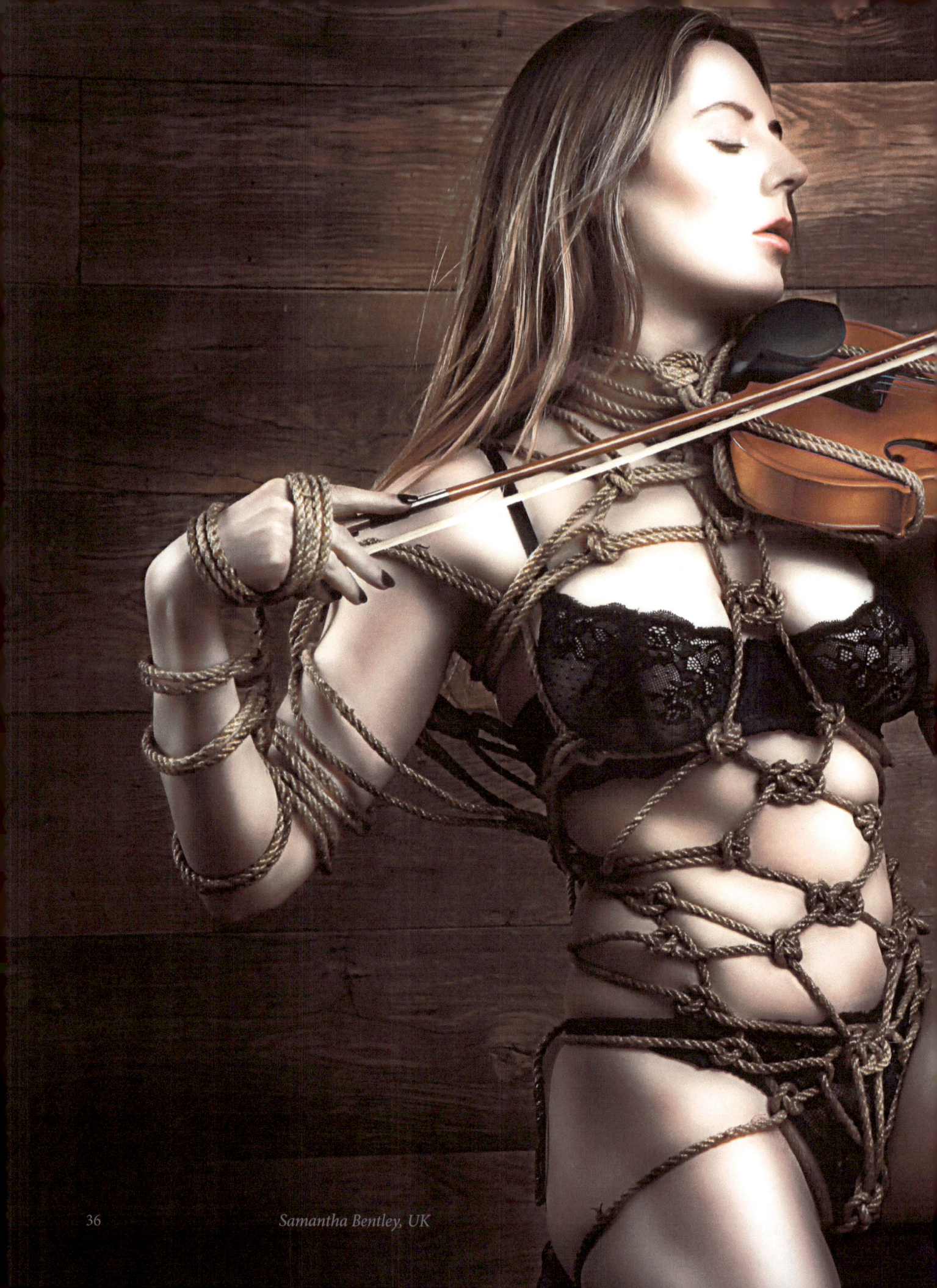
Samantha Bentley, UK

Rope Harness

hard rope, bound close to beautiful bodies

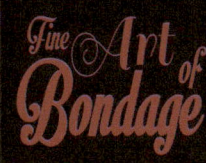

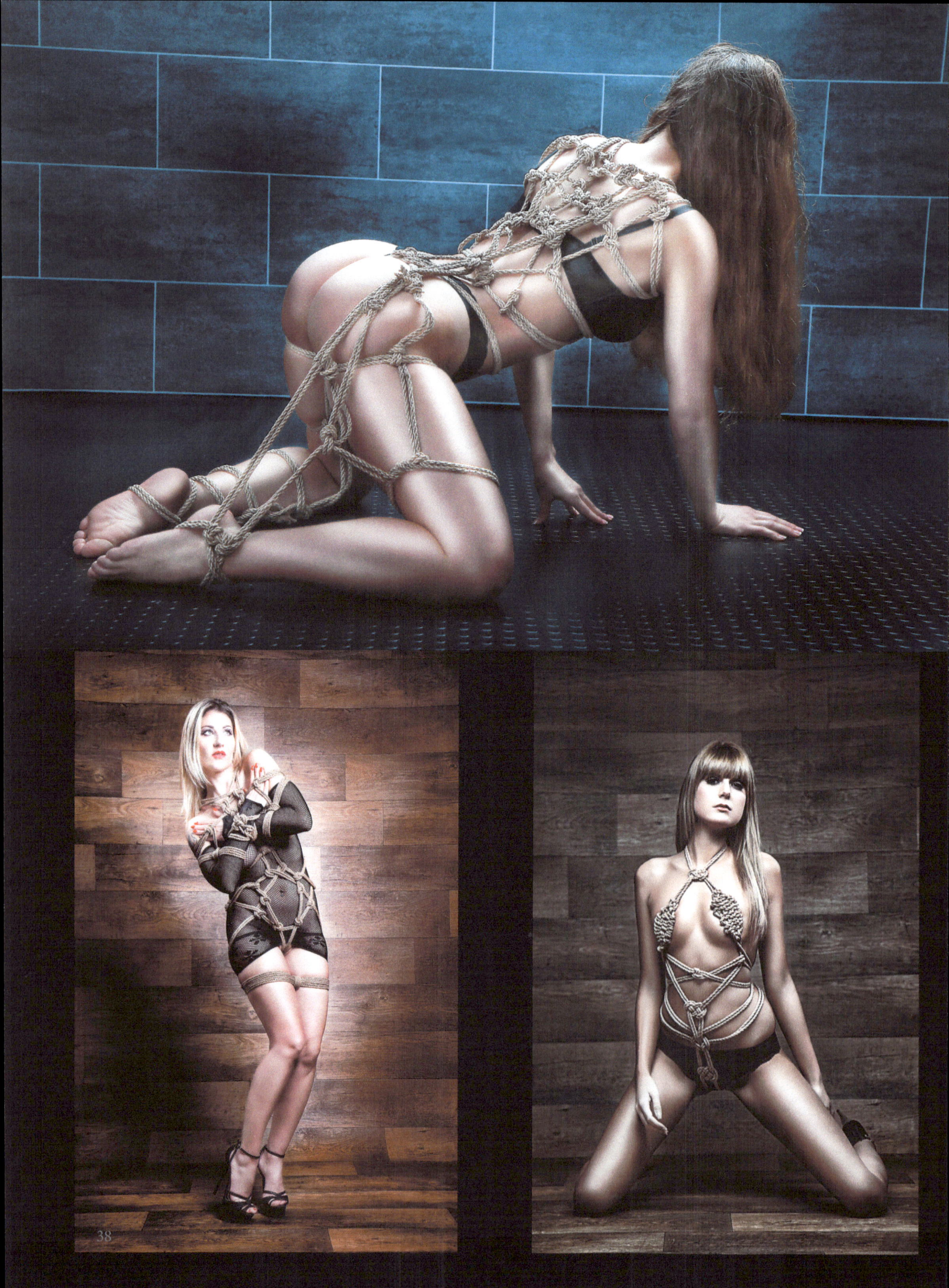

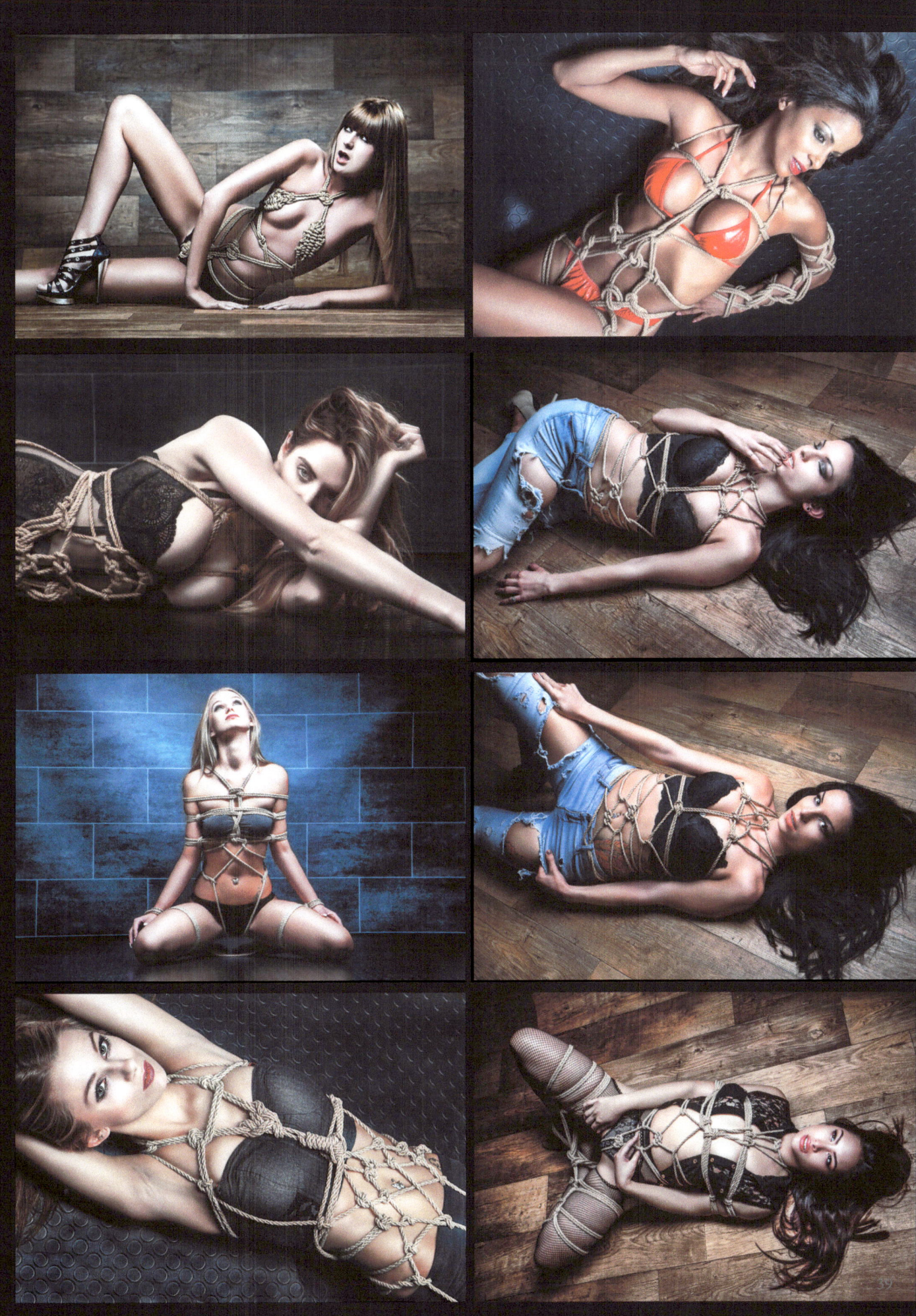

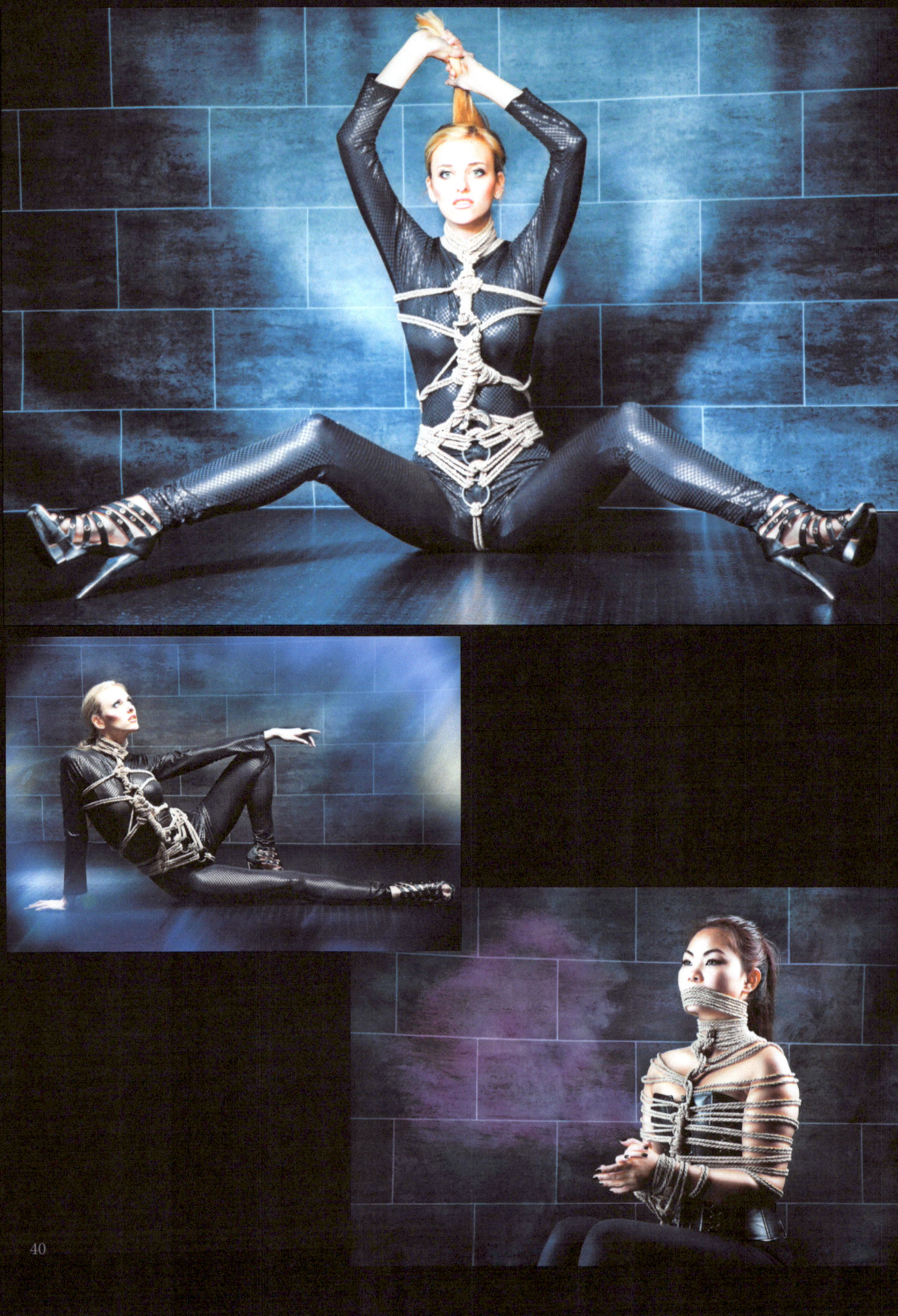

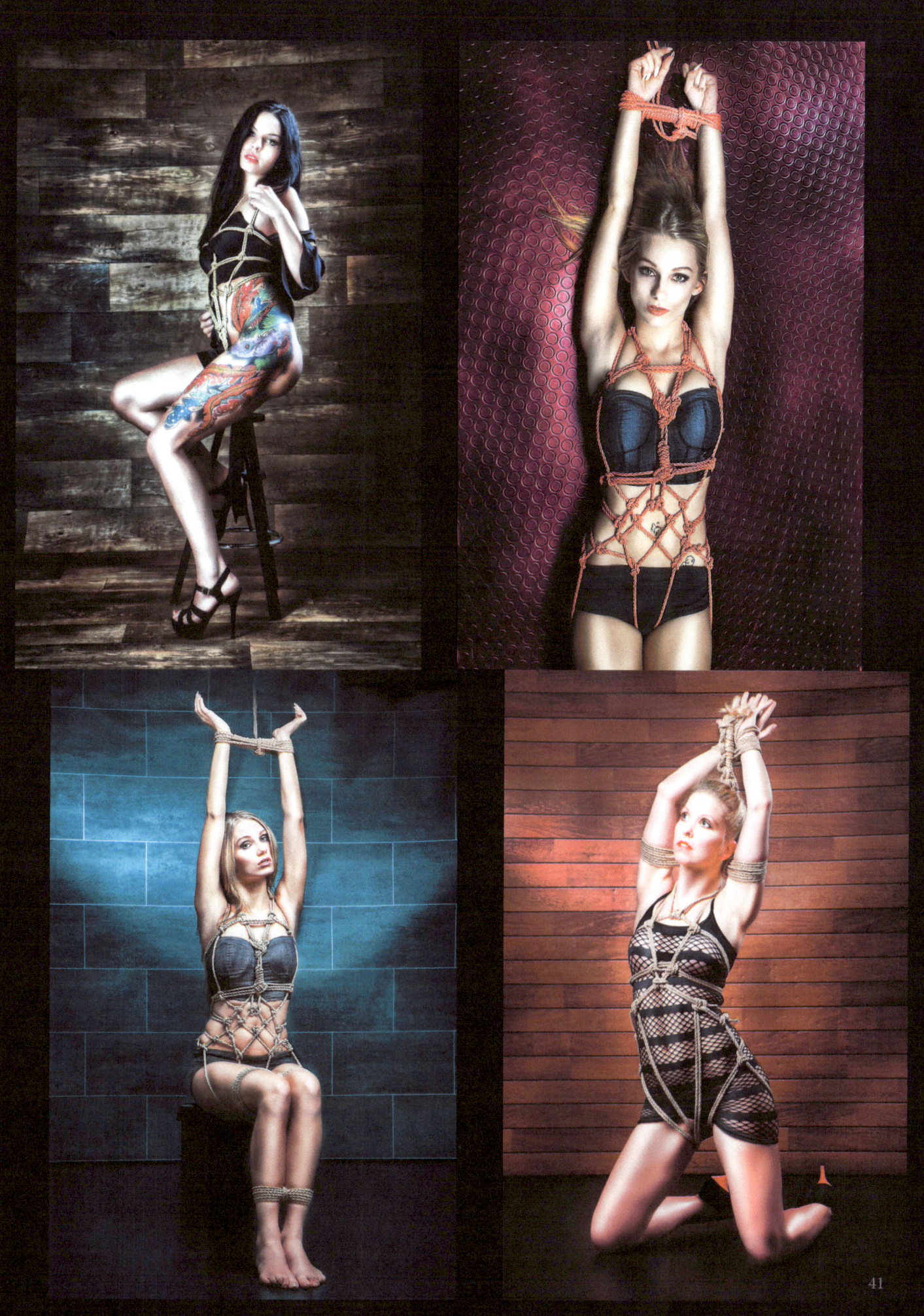

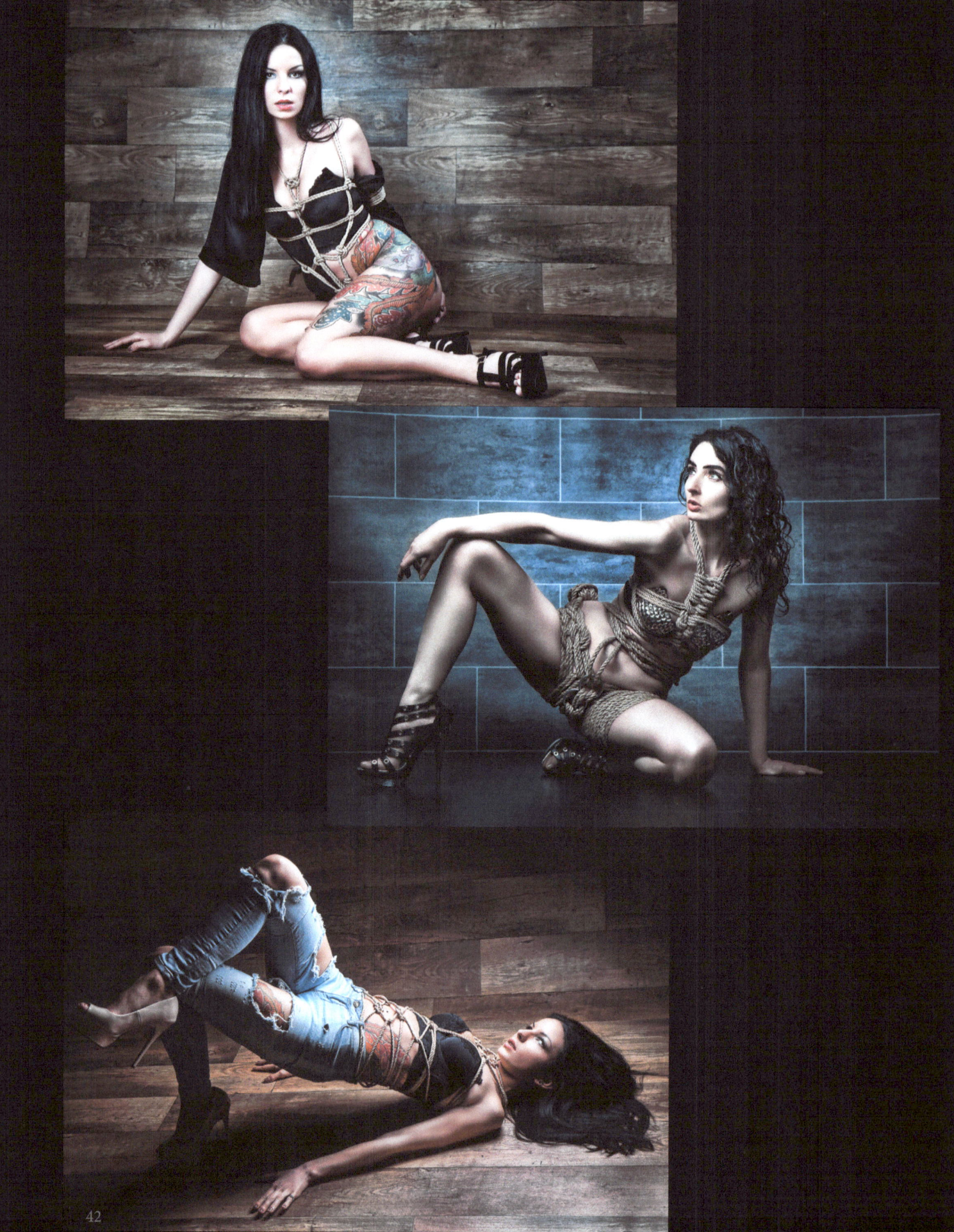

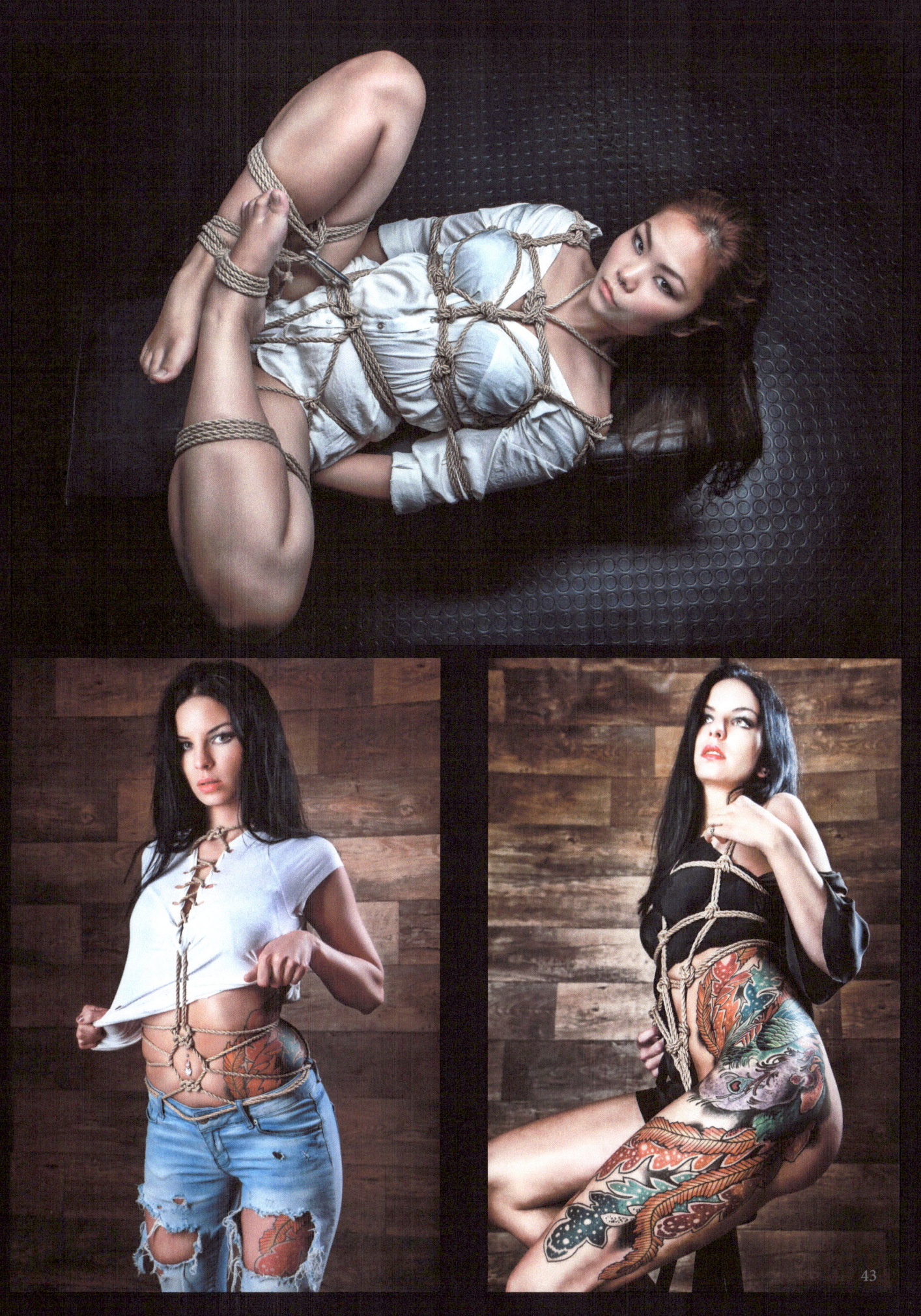

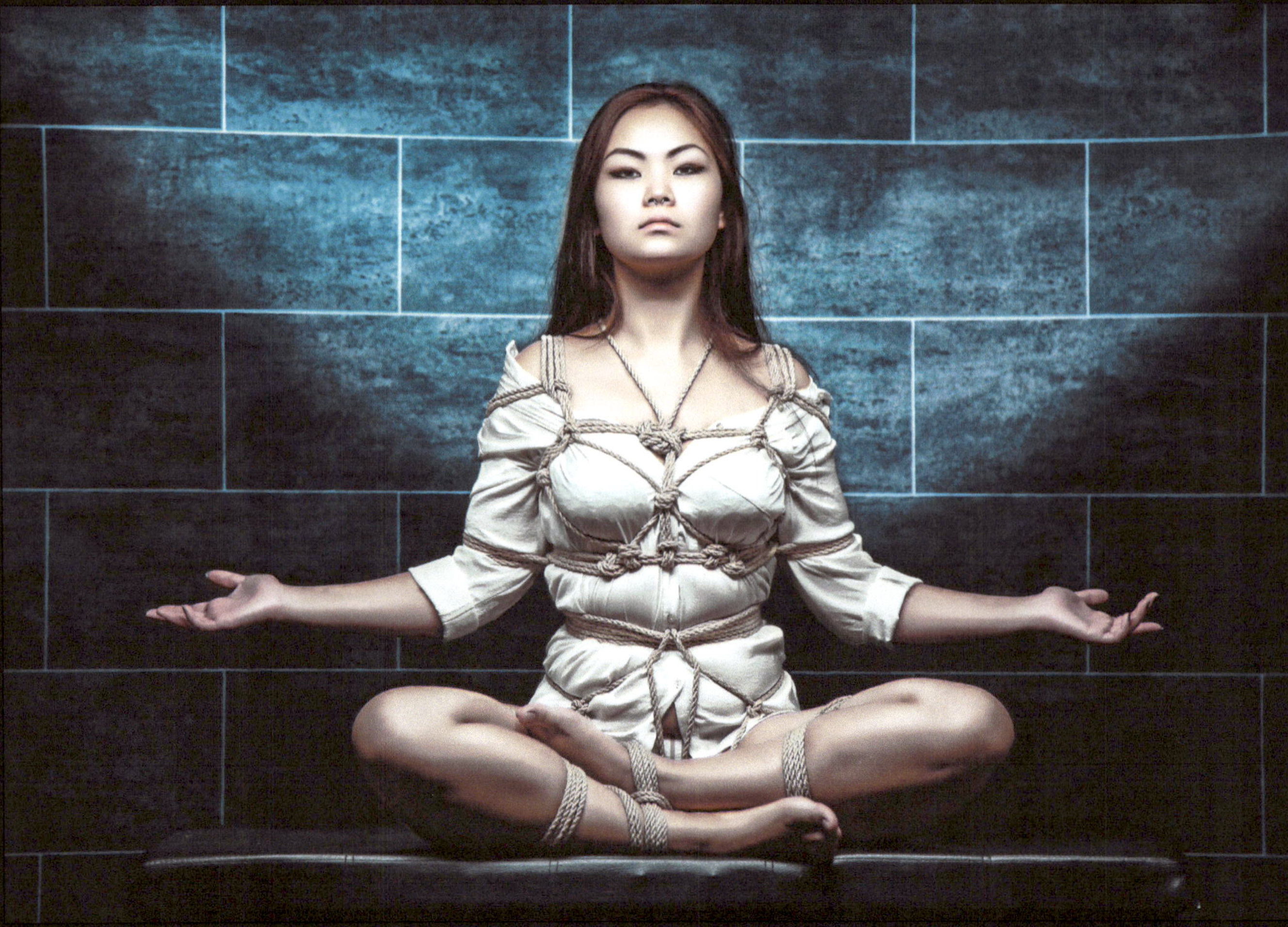

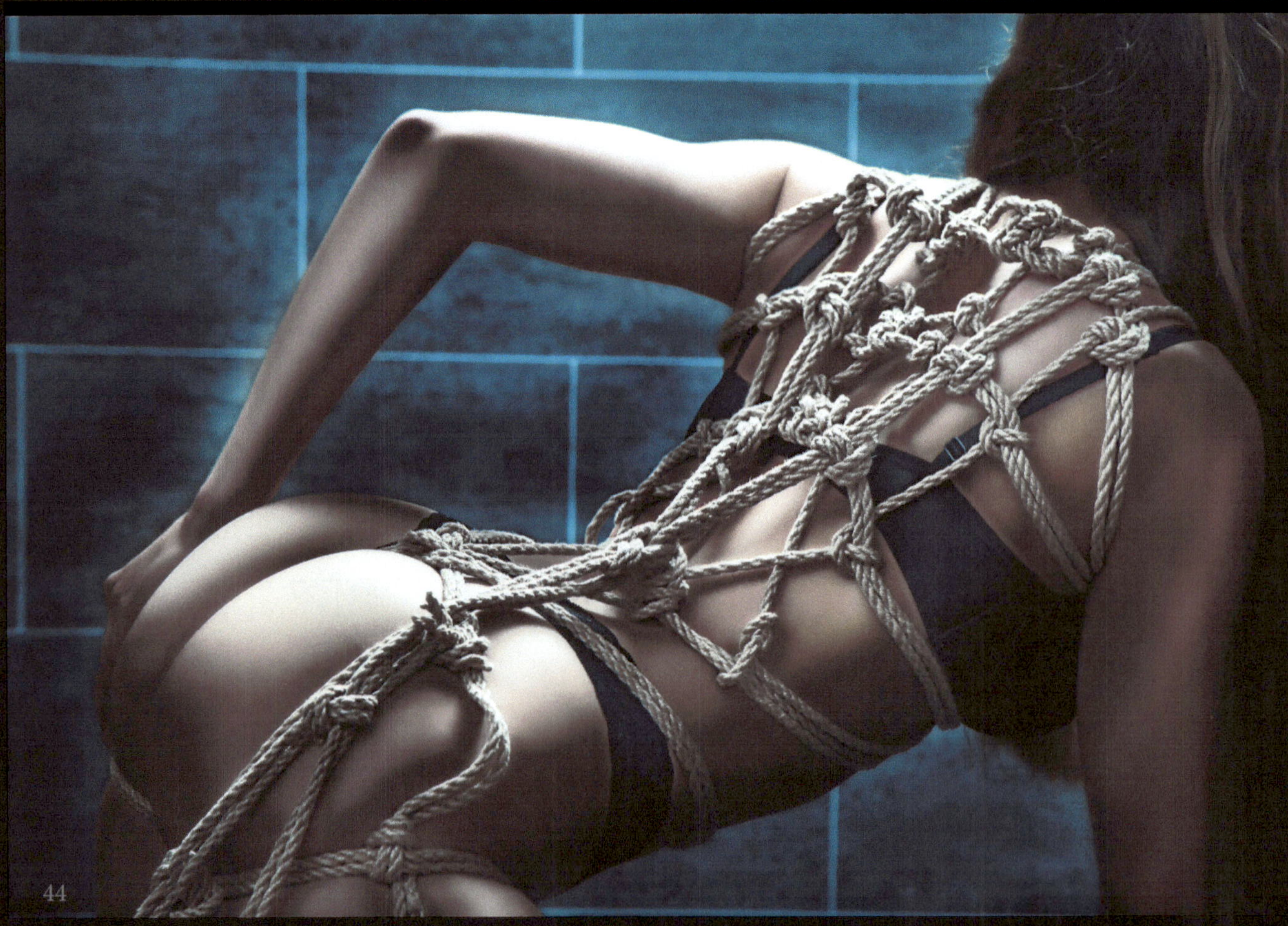

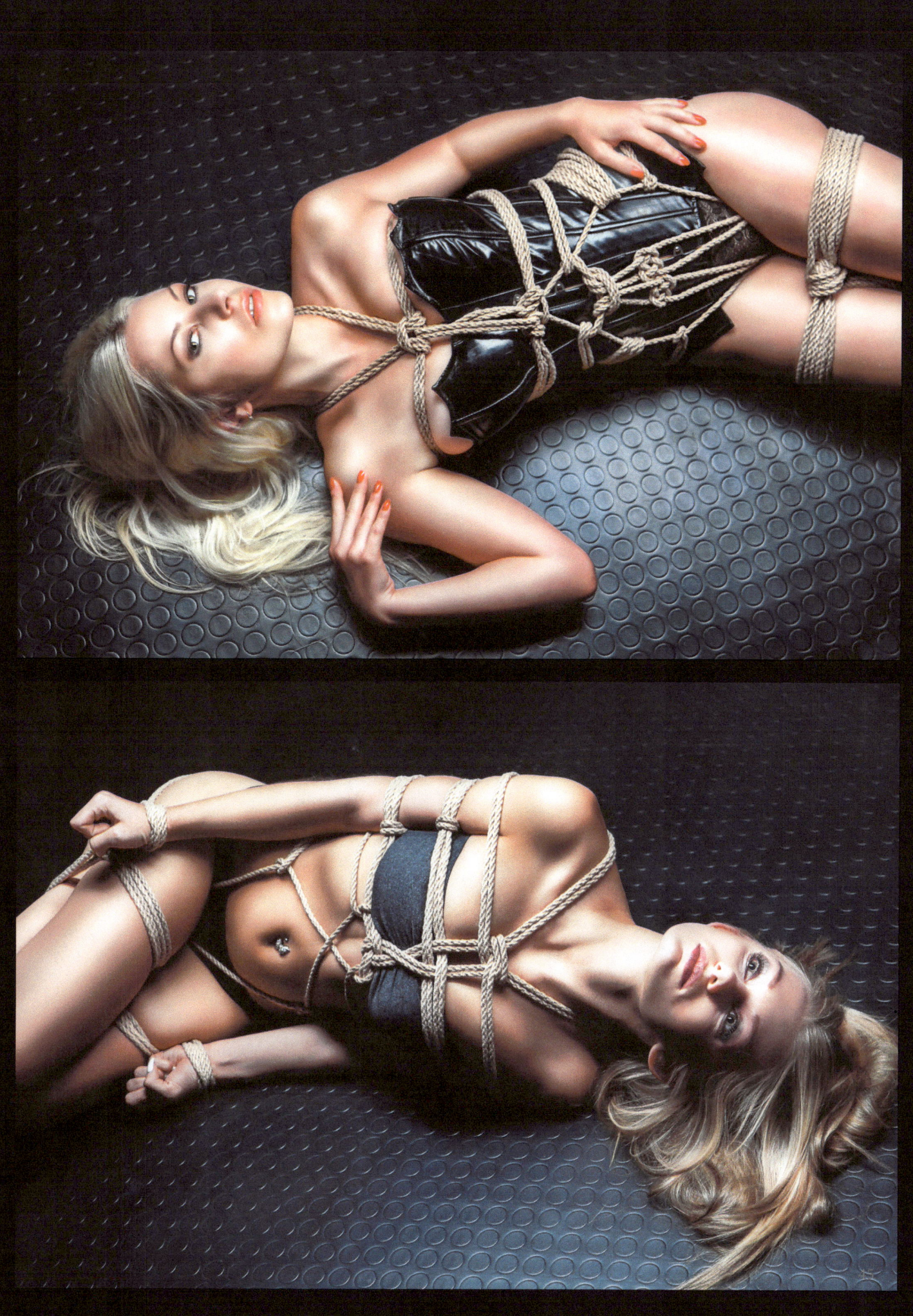

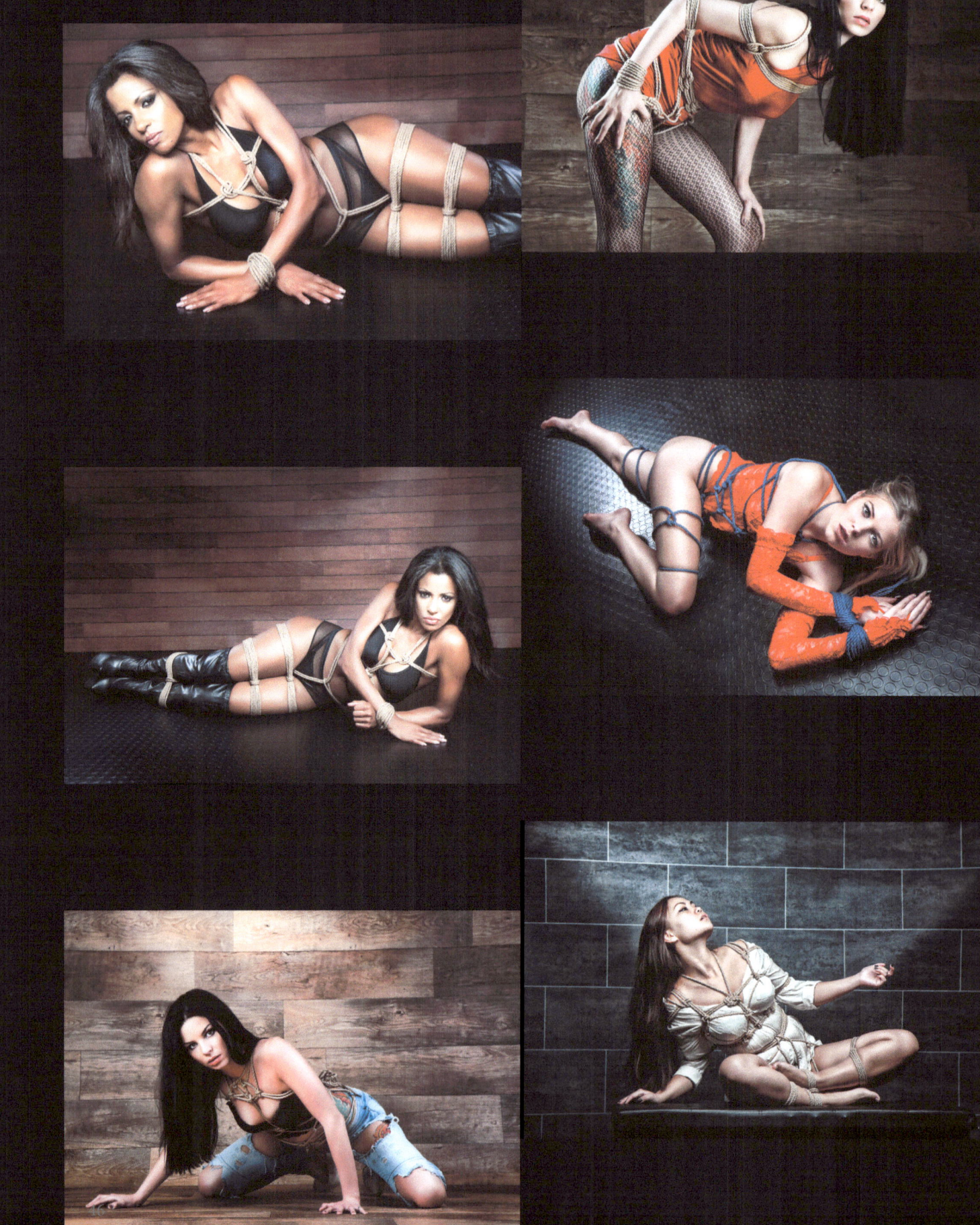

Wall Calendars

Several bondage art calendars are available too. Small and large sized for a monthly changing inspiration of bondage art at your wall. Starting with calendars for the year 2017 you´ll find all links to the shops on the homepage.

...so perhaps you´ll take a try to order one of those fantastic calendars.

It´s also nice as a gift to someone interested in ropes and art...

All available calendars are listed at the projects homepage:
http://Fine-Art-of-Bondage.com

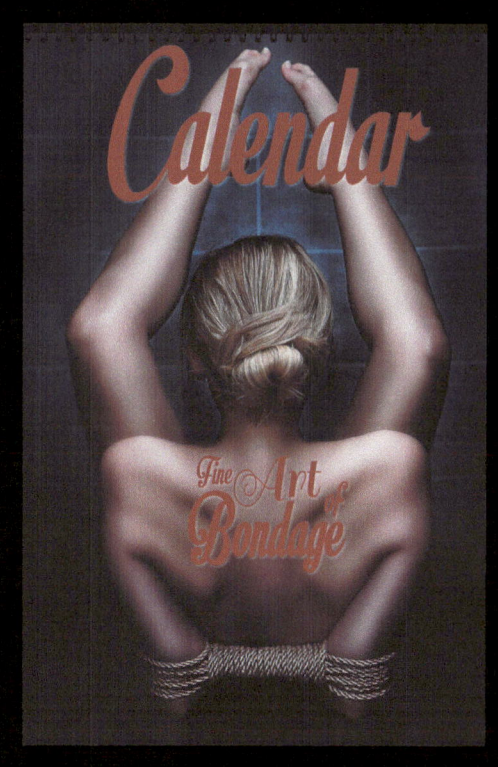

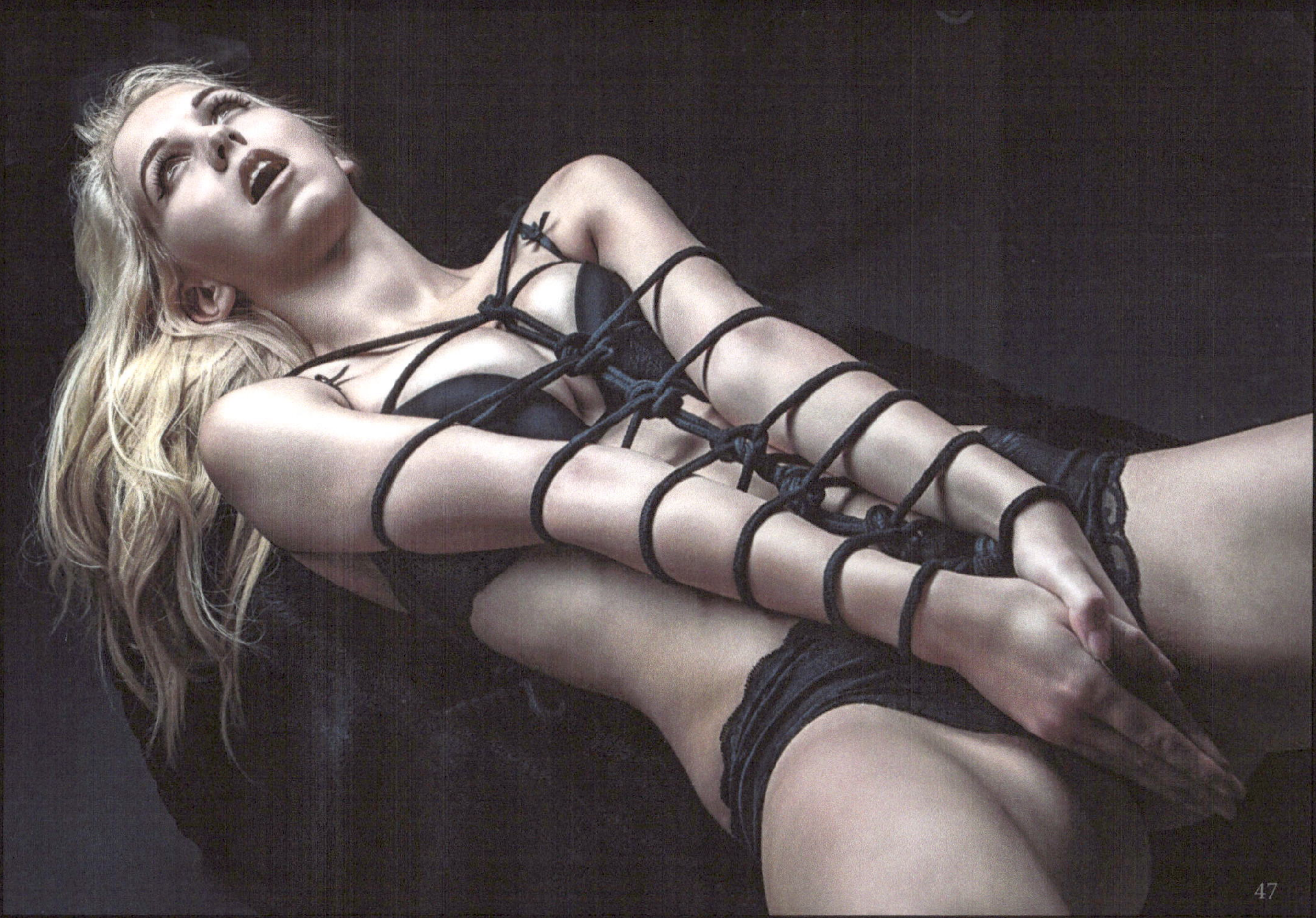

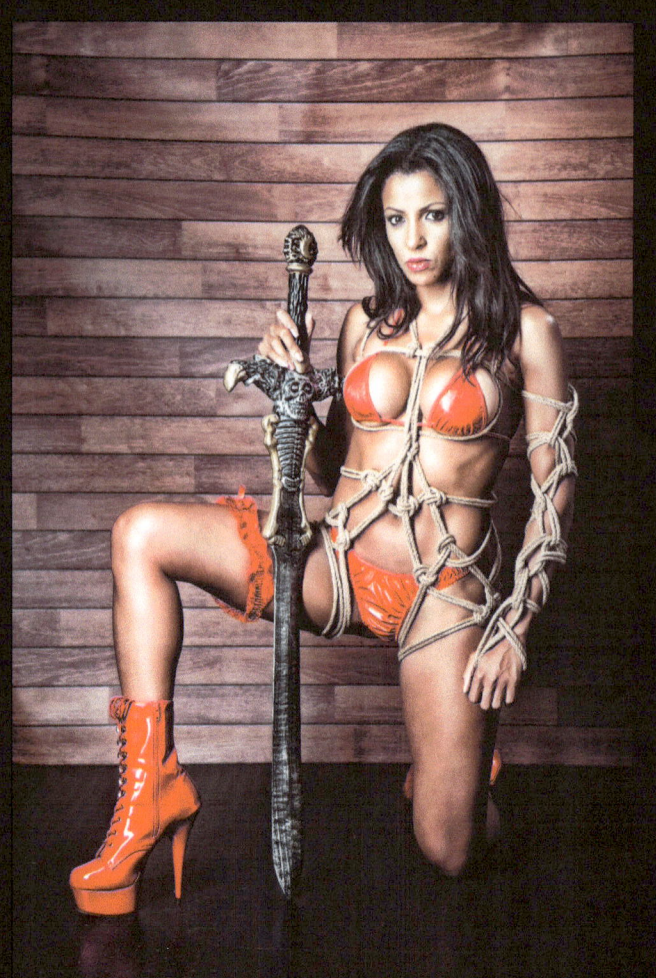
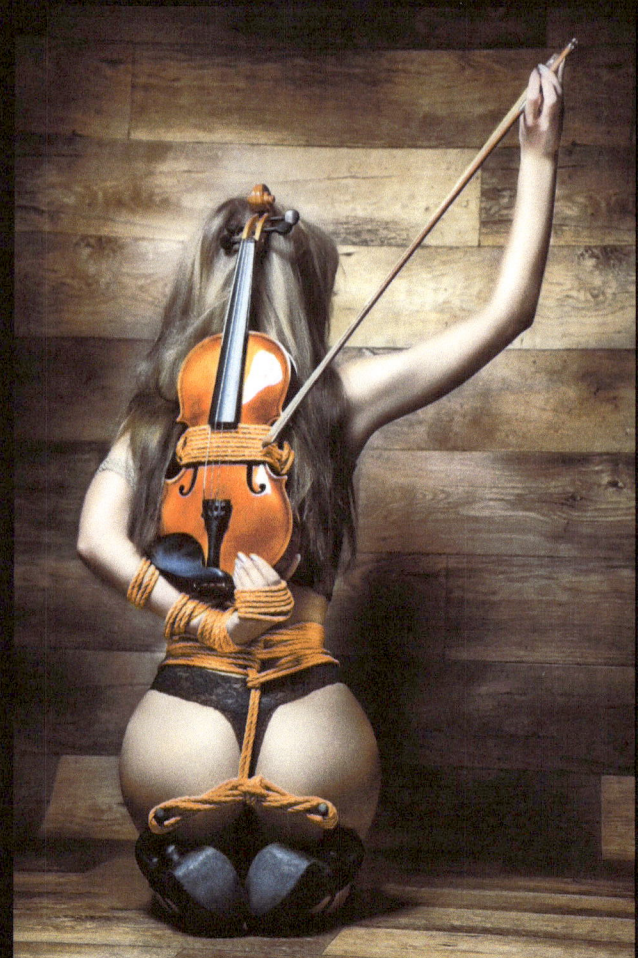
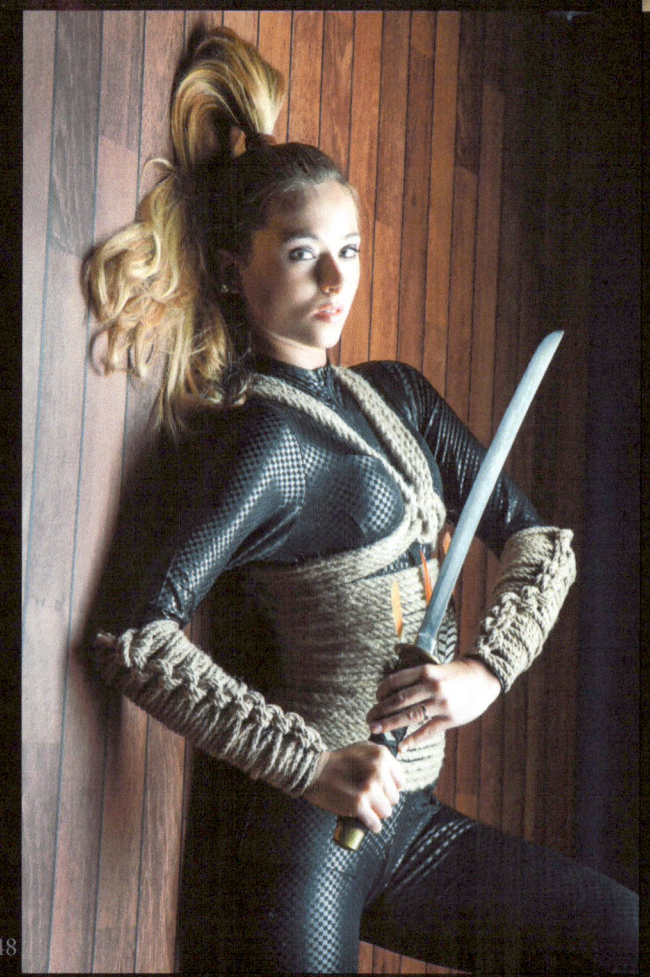
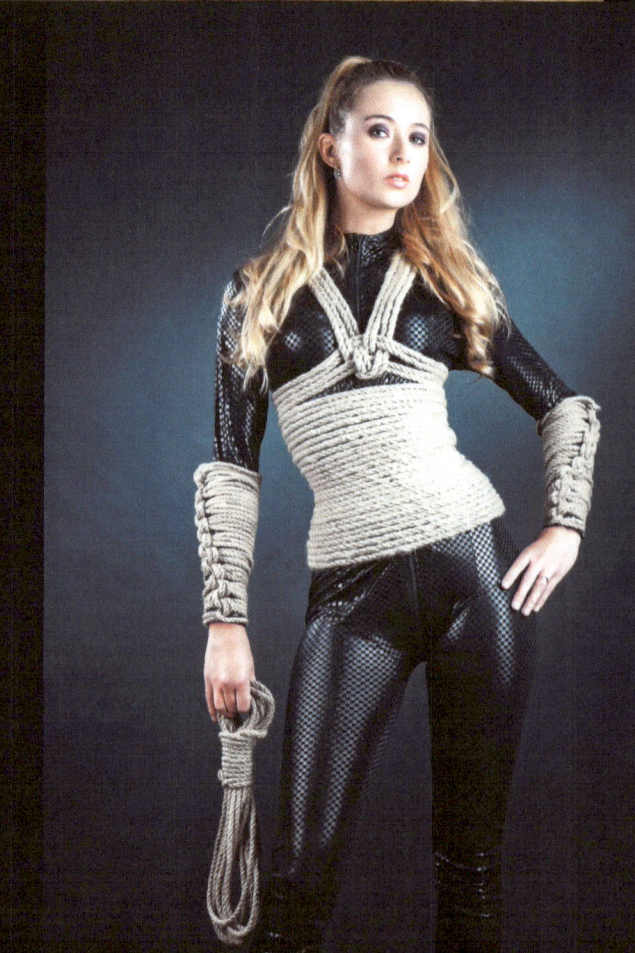

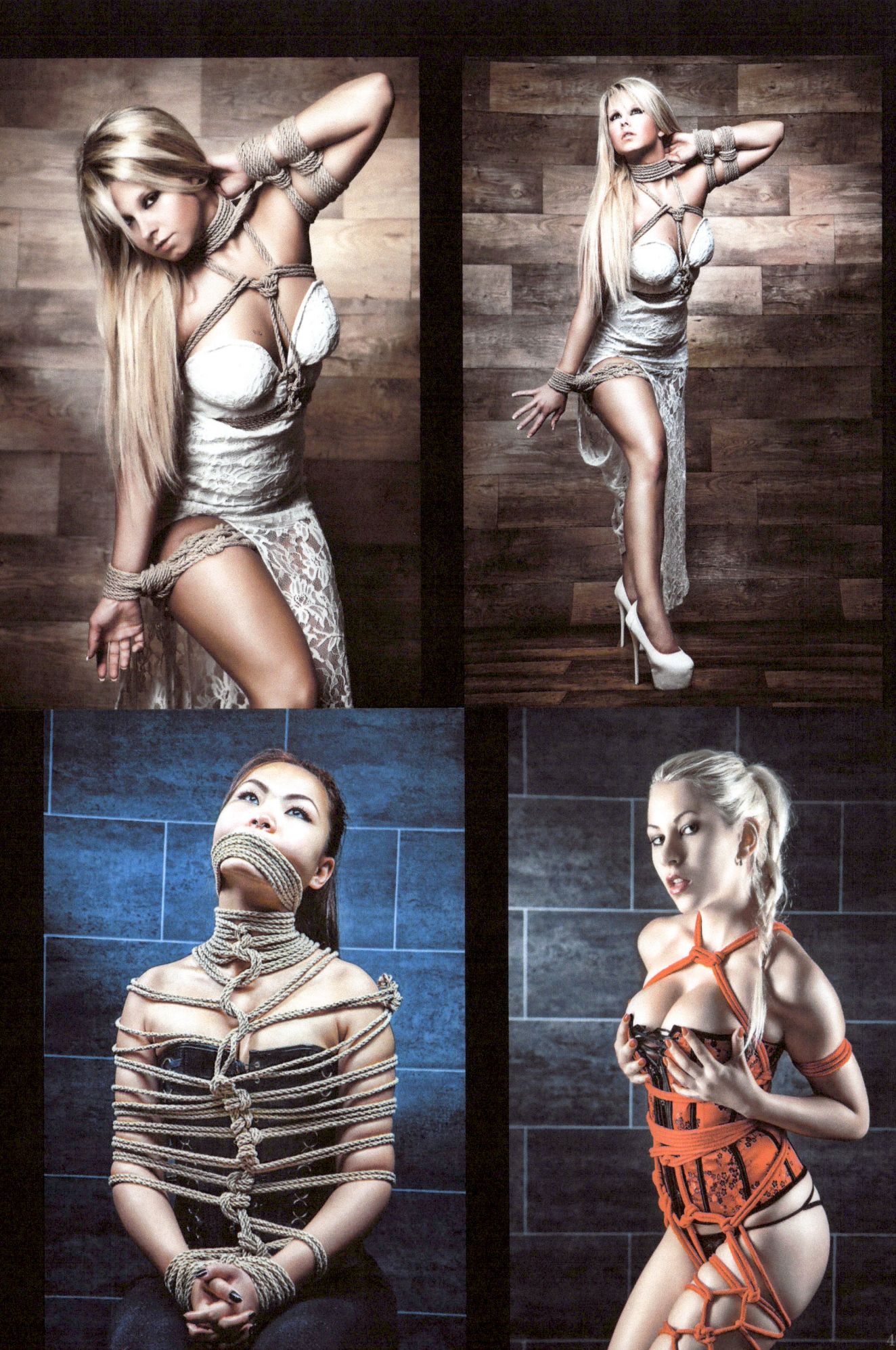

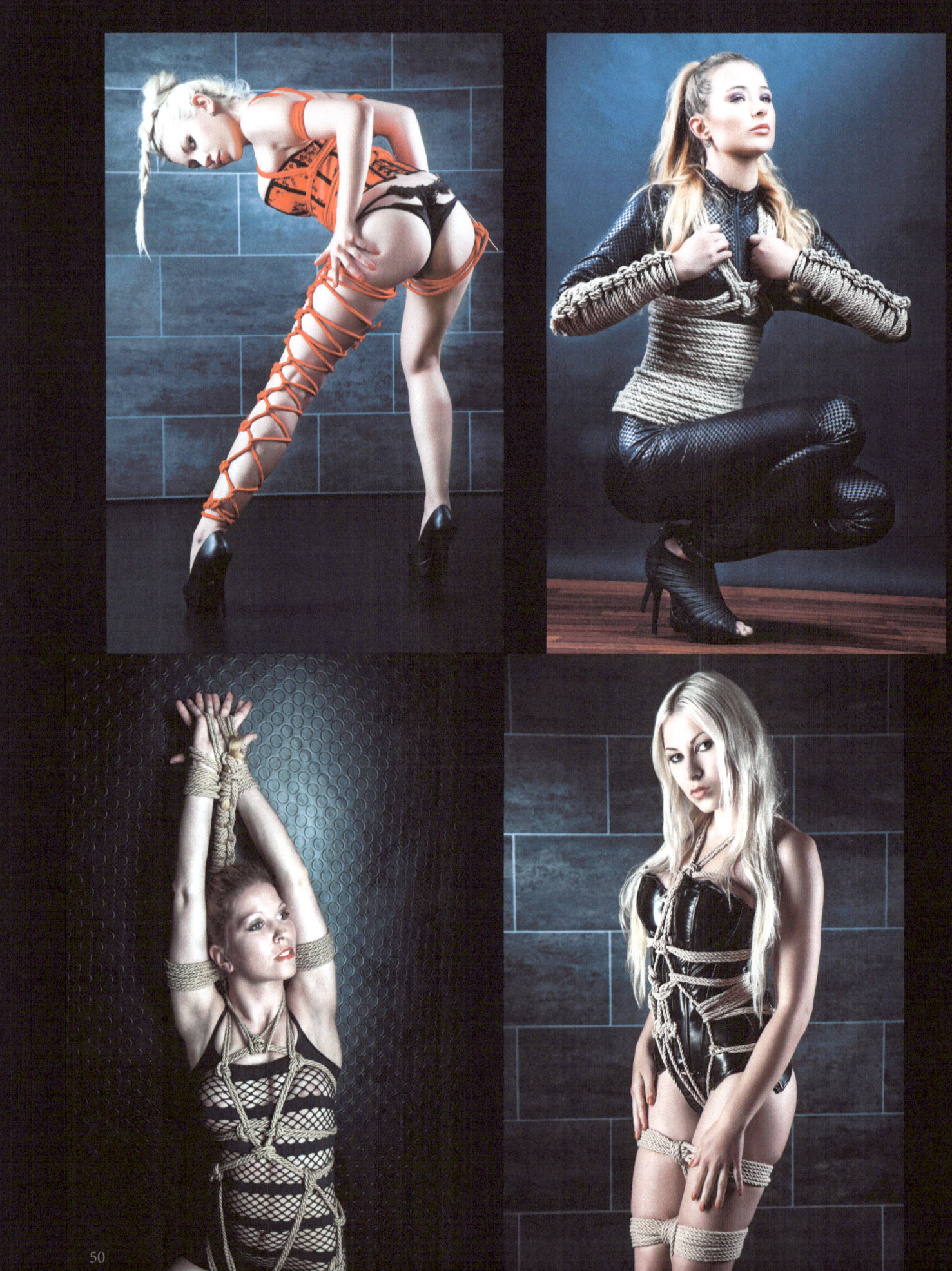

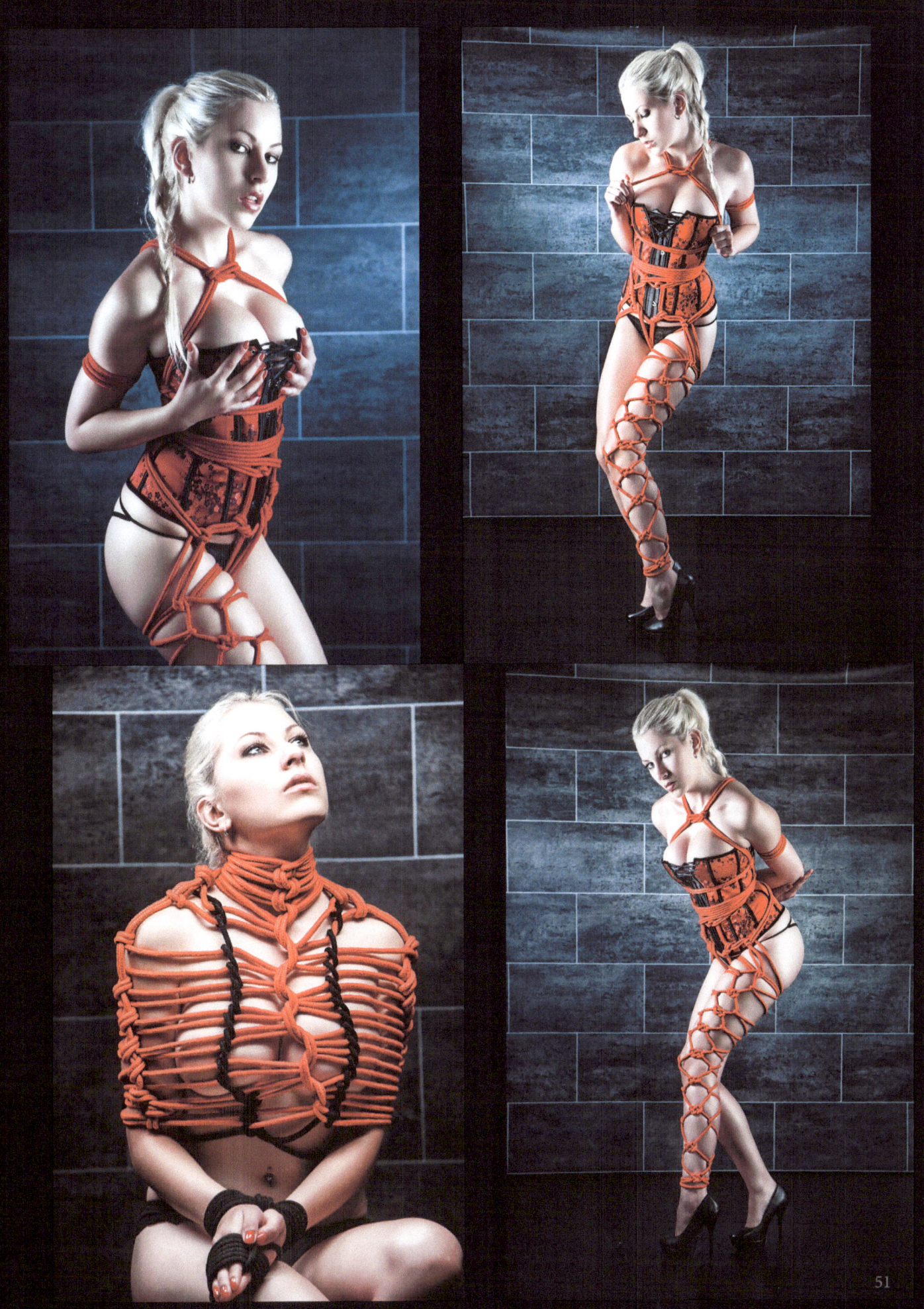

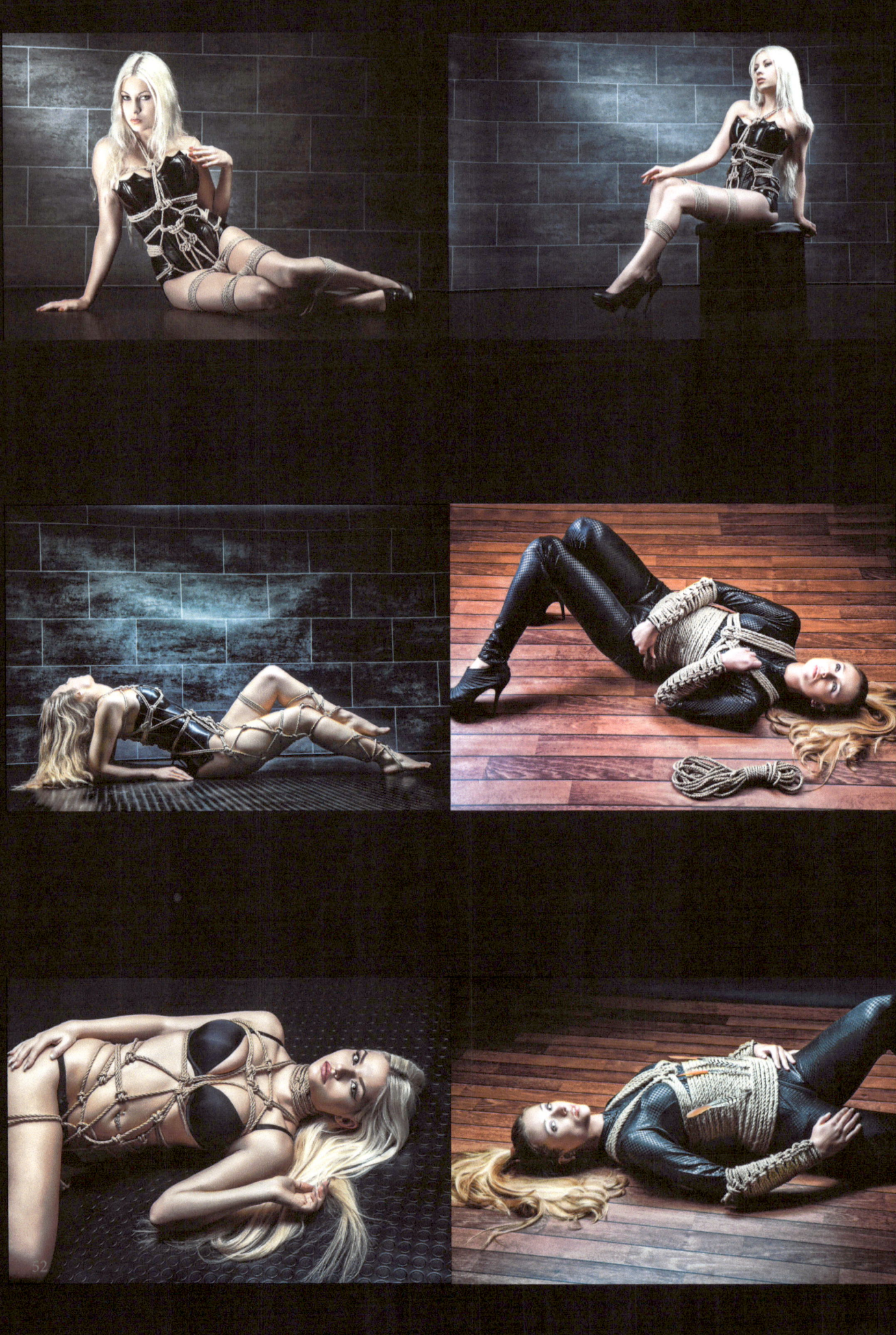

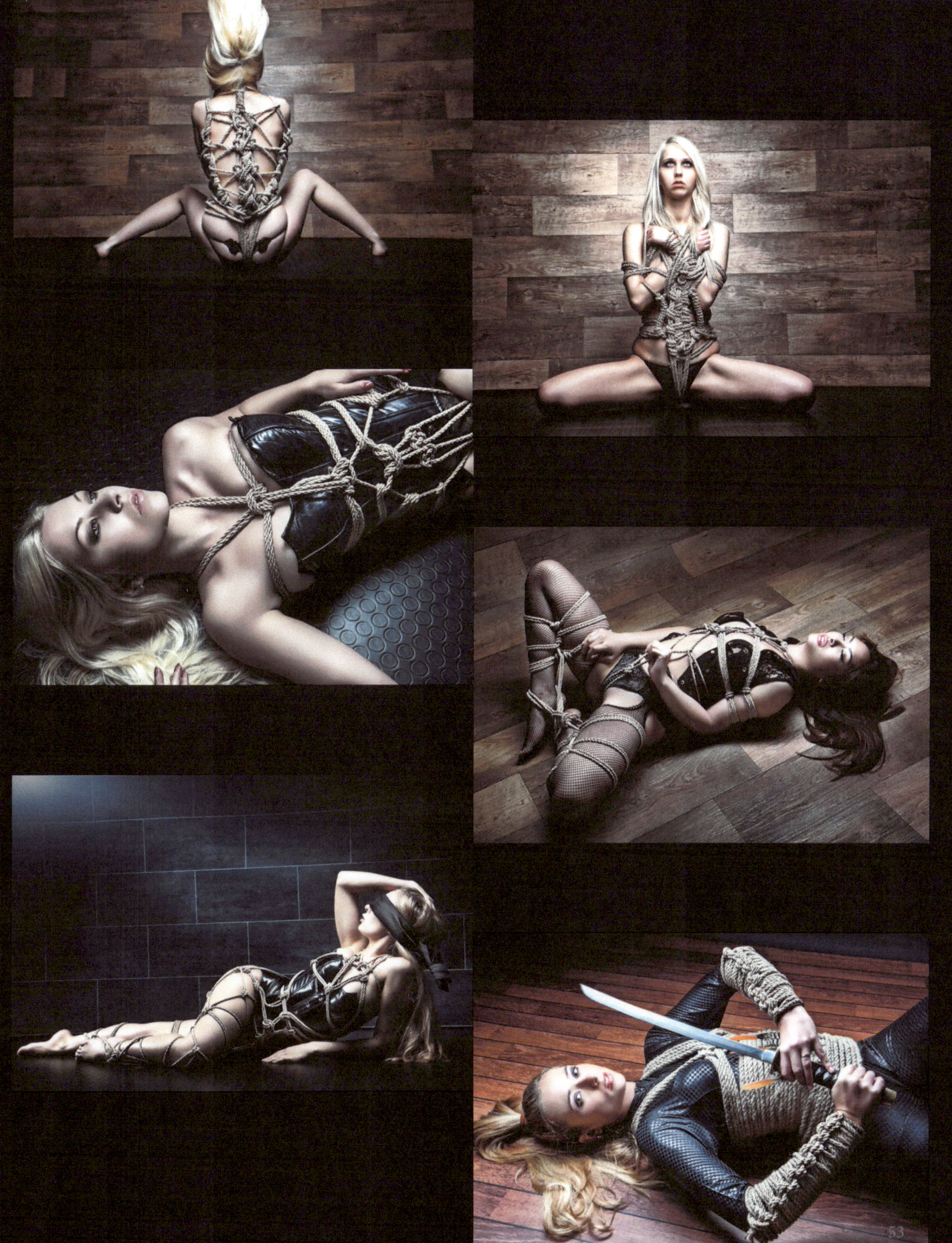

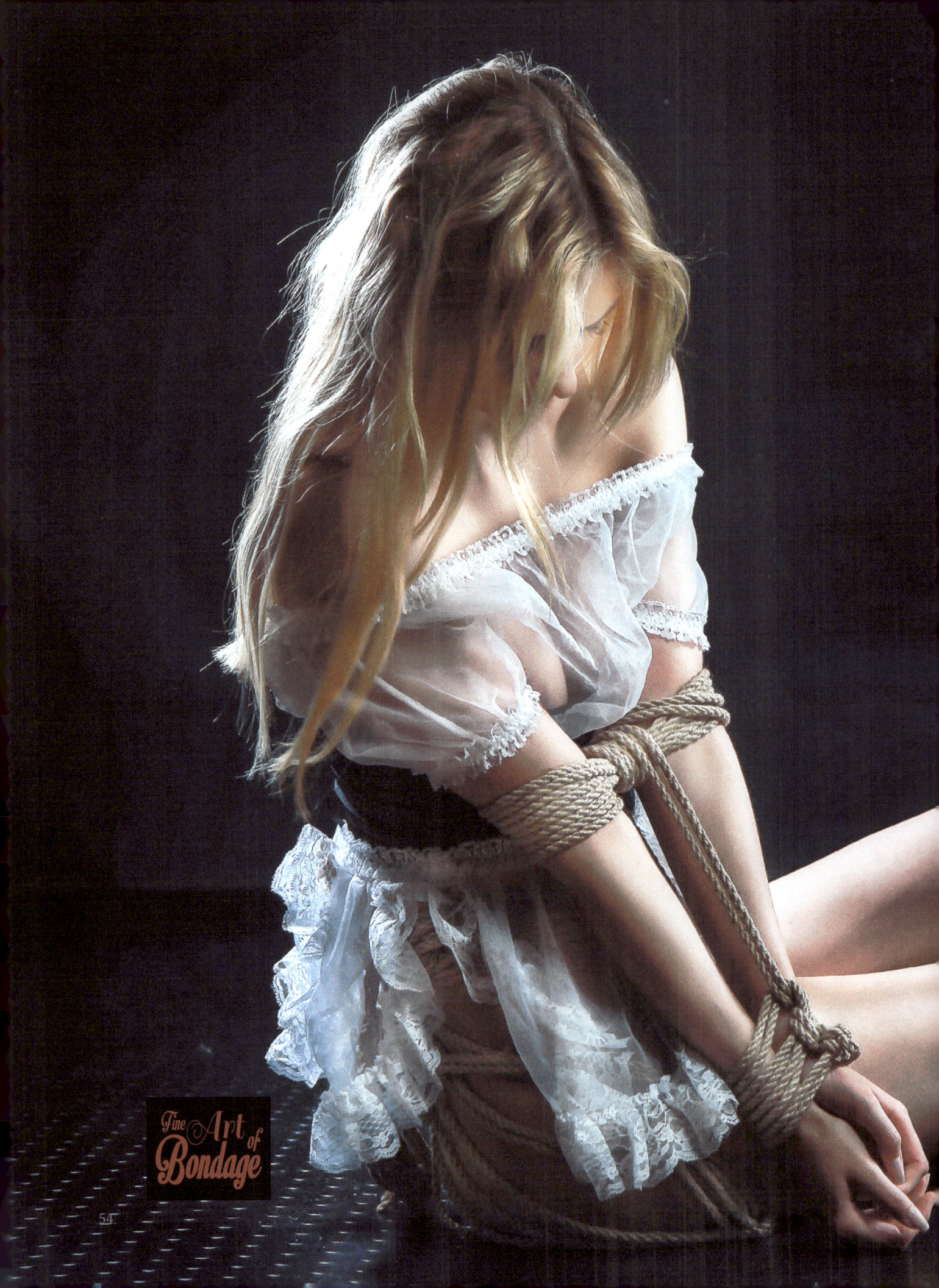

Housemaids Schoolgirls Nuns...

Girls tied in costumes

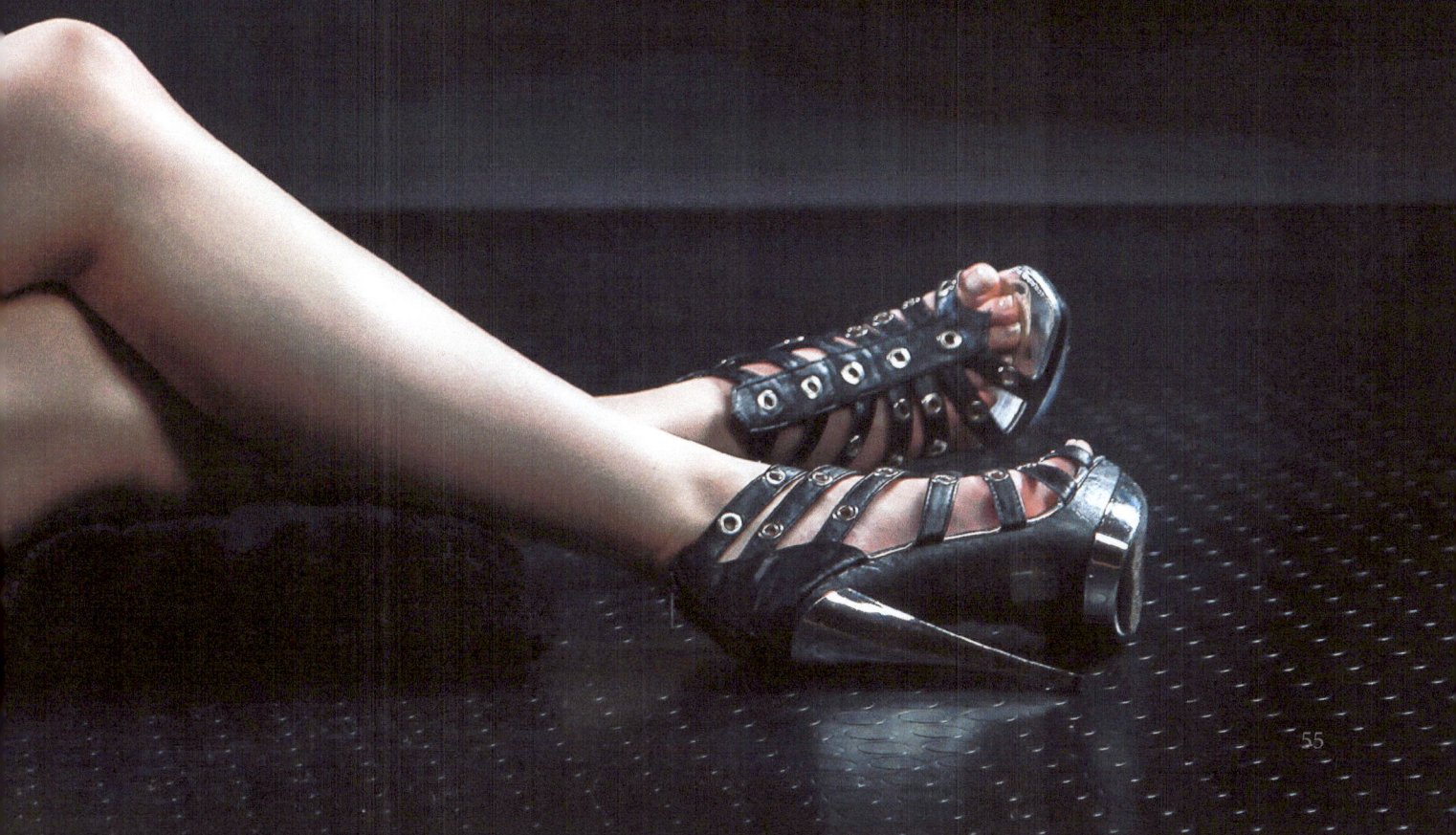

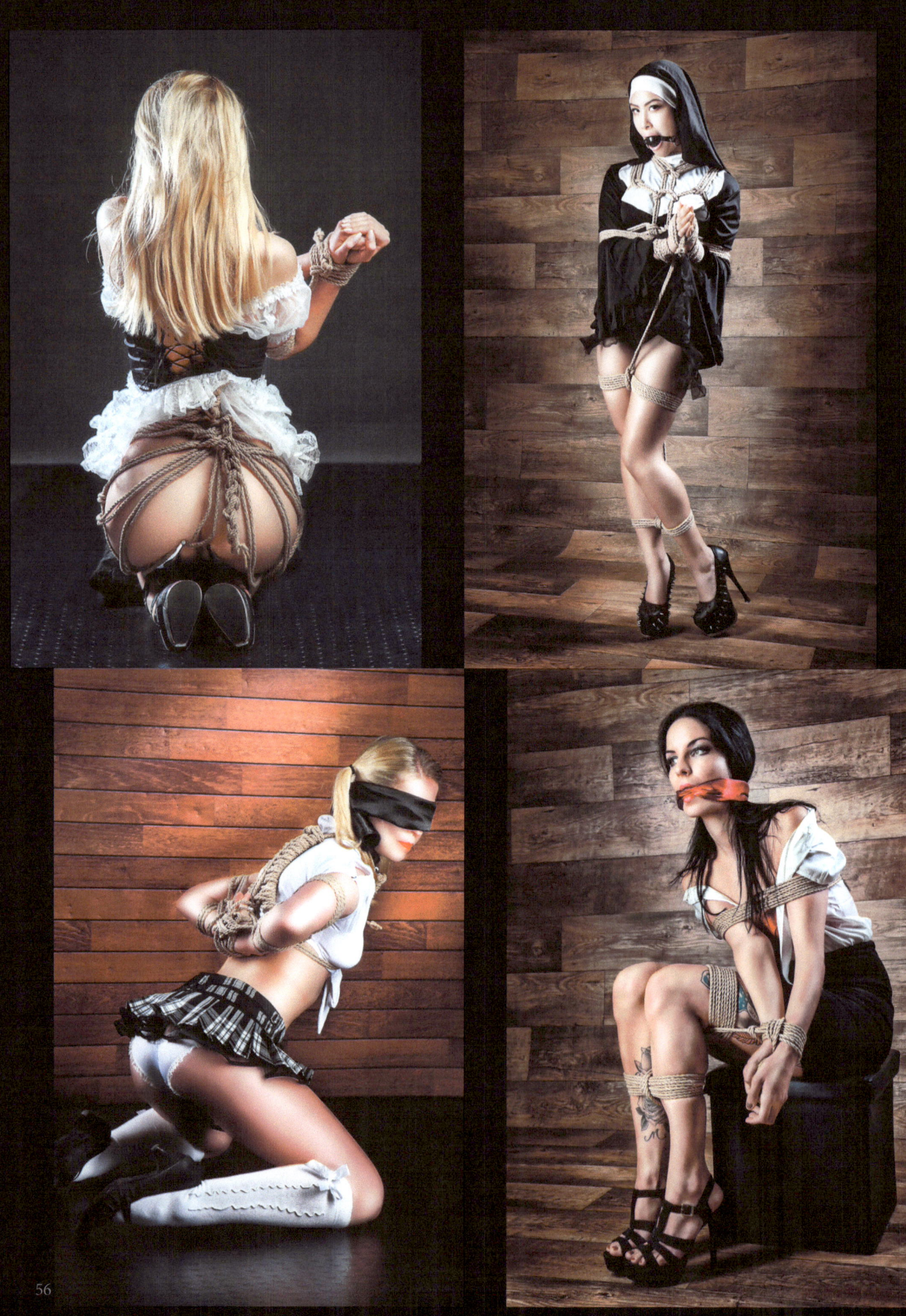

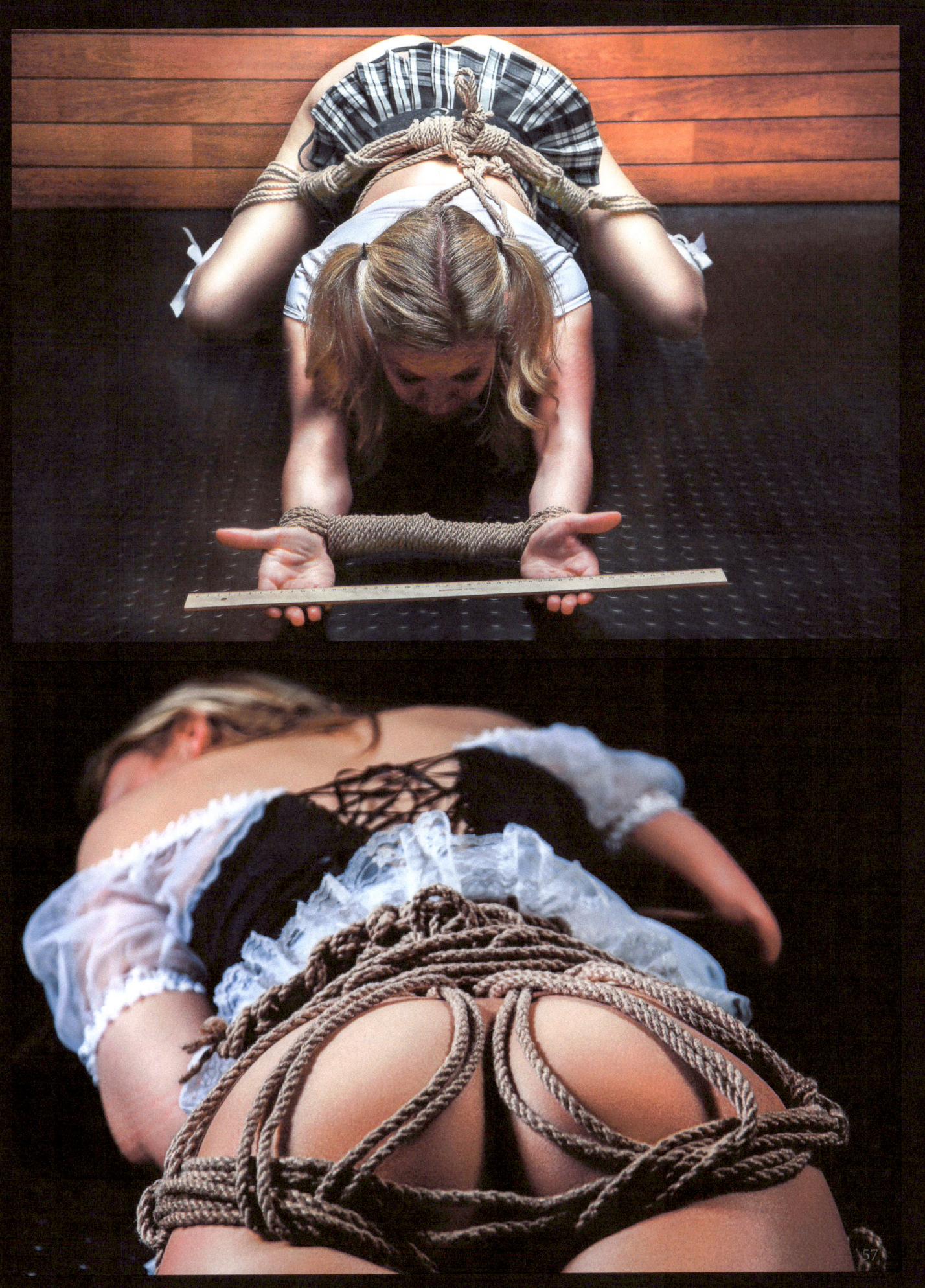

Prints and Wall Art

A lot of these images are available as posters, canvas prints, metal- or acryl prints. Even framed art prints with almost worldwide shipping is possible.

I ordered some of the images for myself as big sized canvas prints - really incredible how people react when they saw them on my wall. They are really impressed about this kind of art.

I work with international art and print on demand galleries - you´ll find all links here:
http://Fine-Art-of-Bondage.com

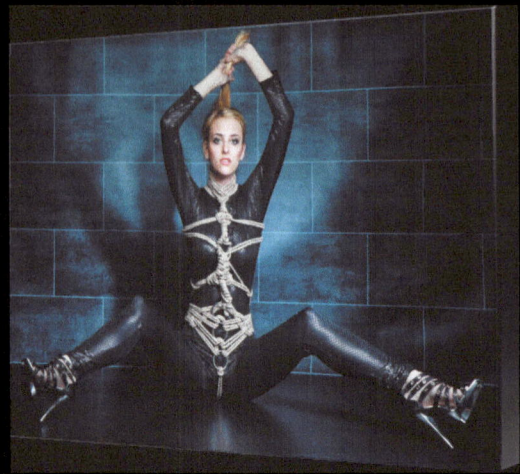

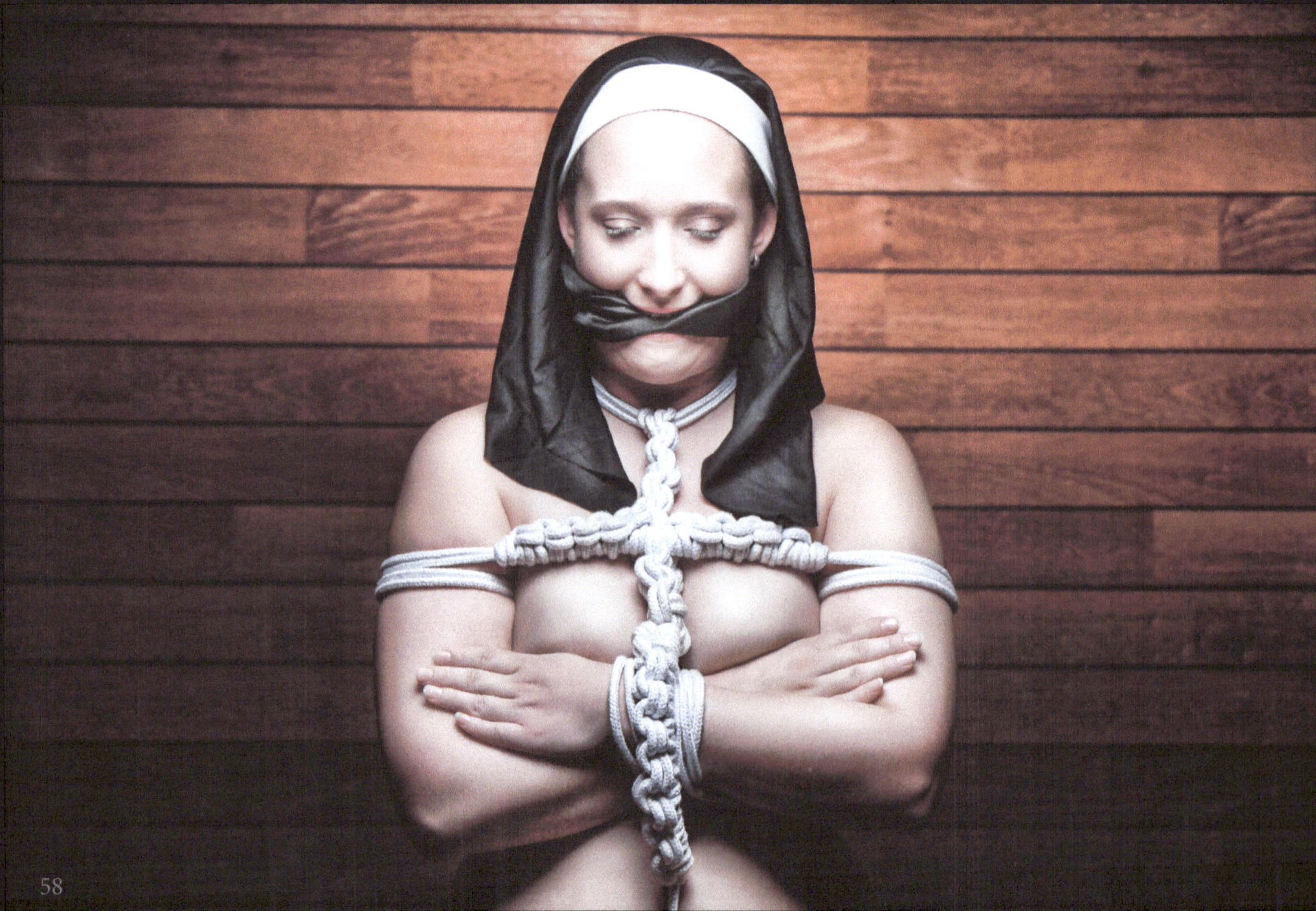

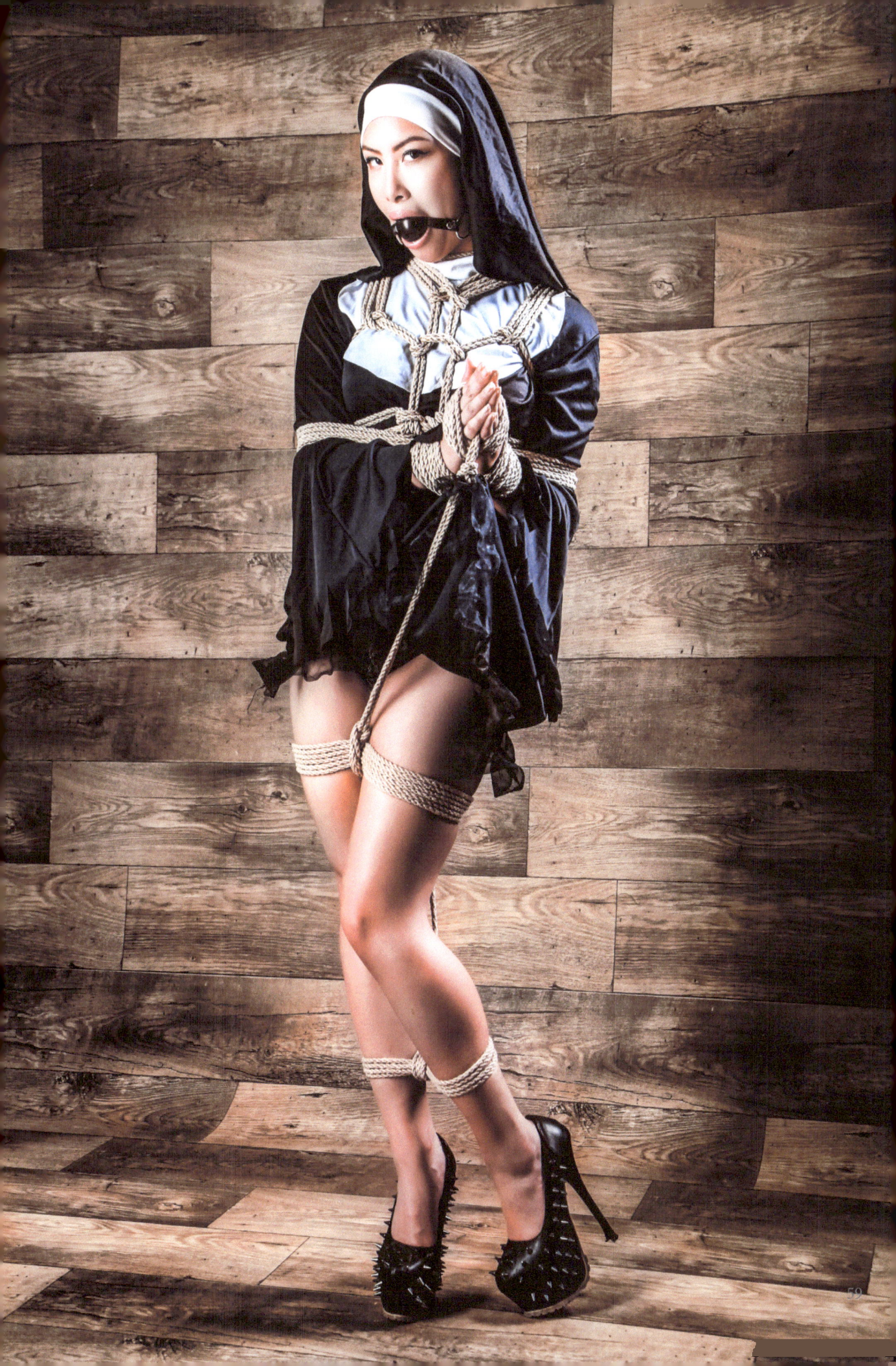

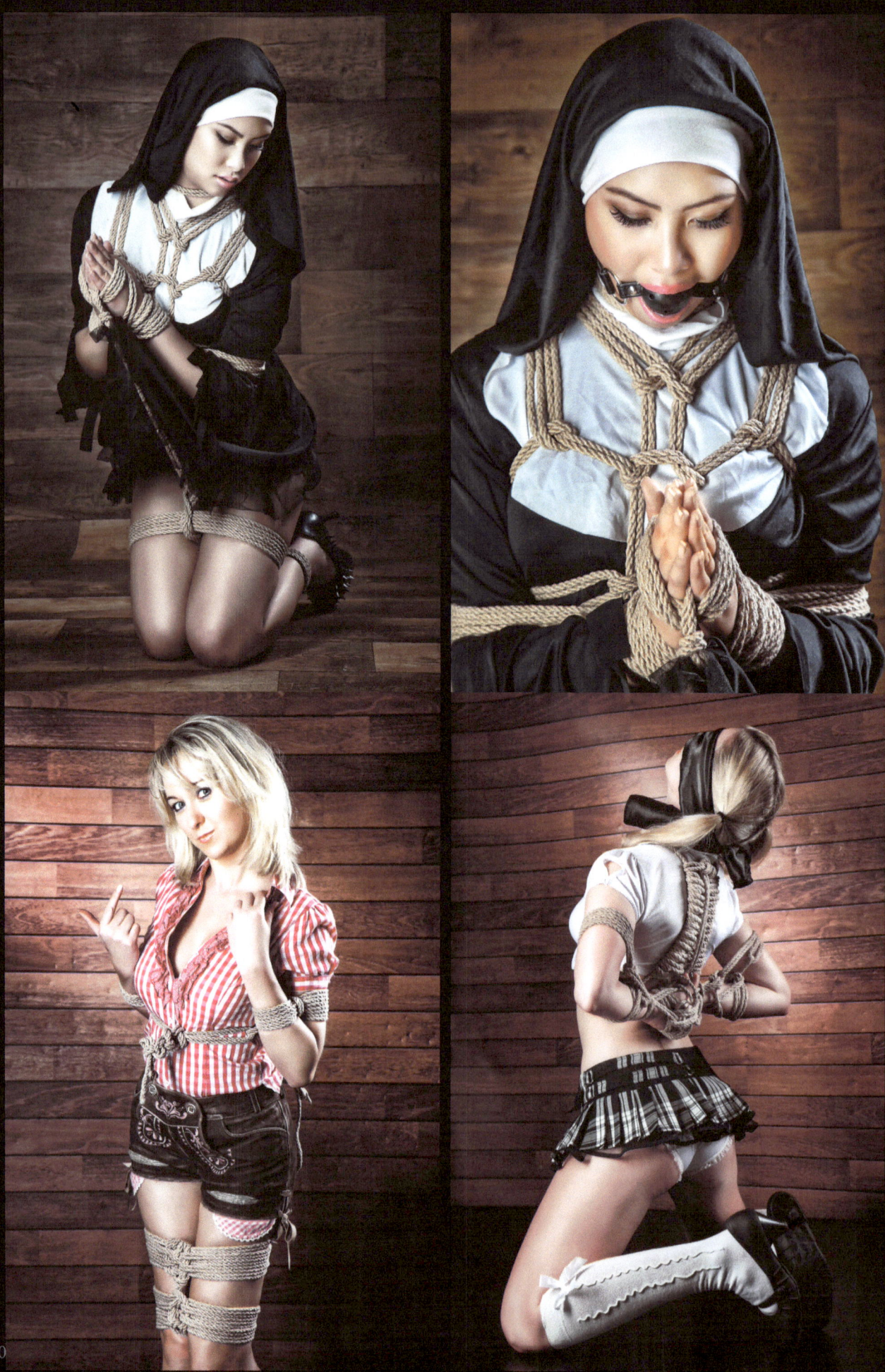

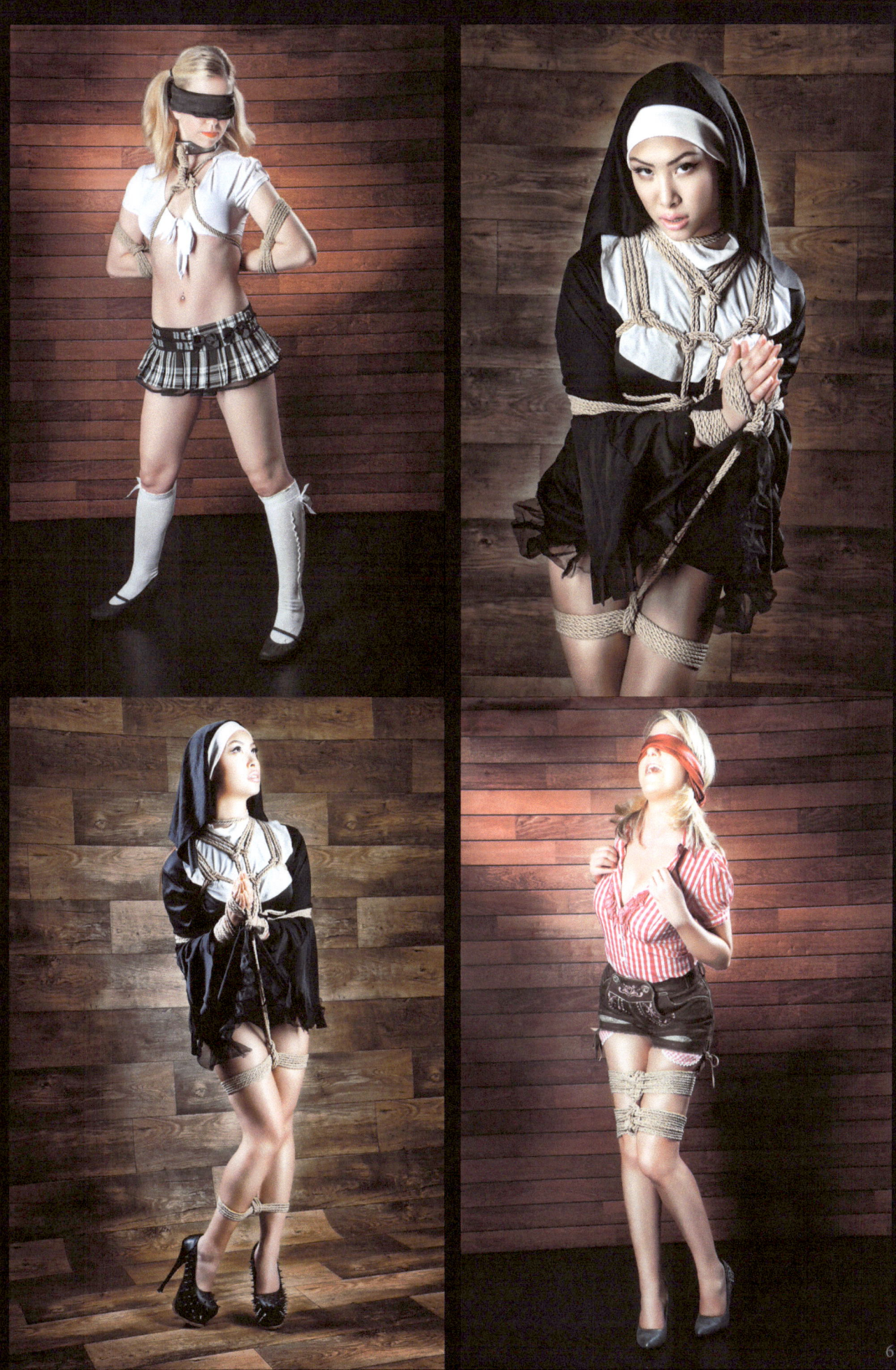

Hard tied

Hogtied, helpless and painful great tied women

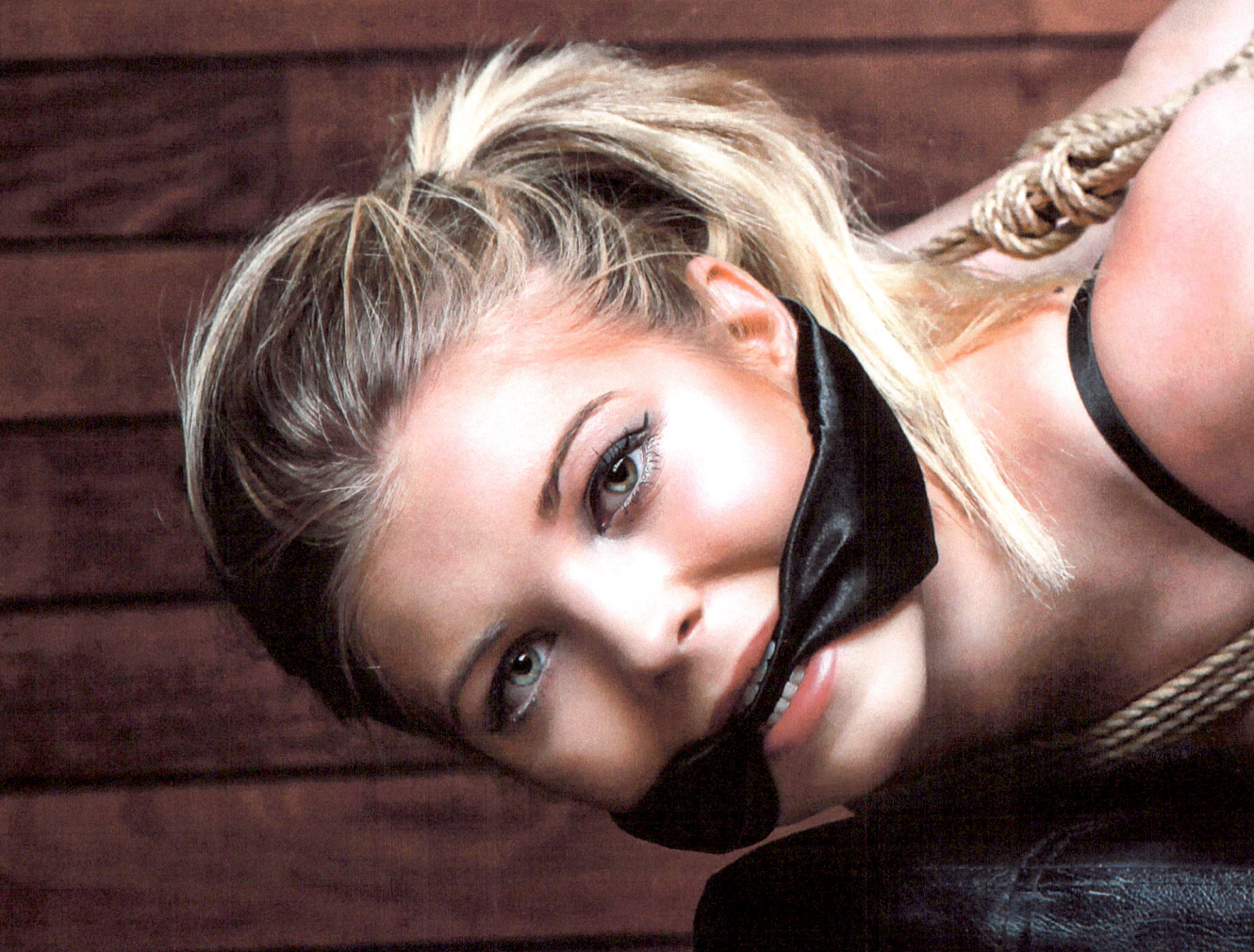

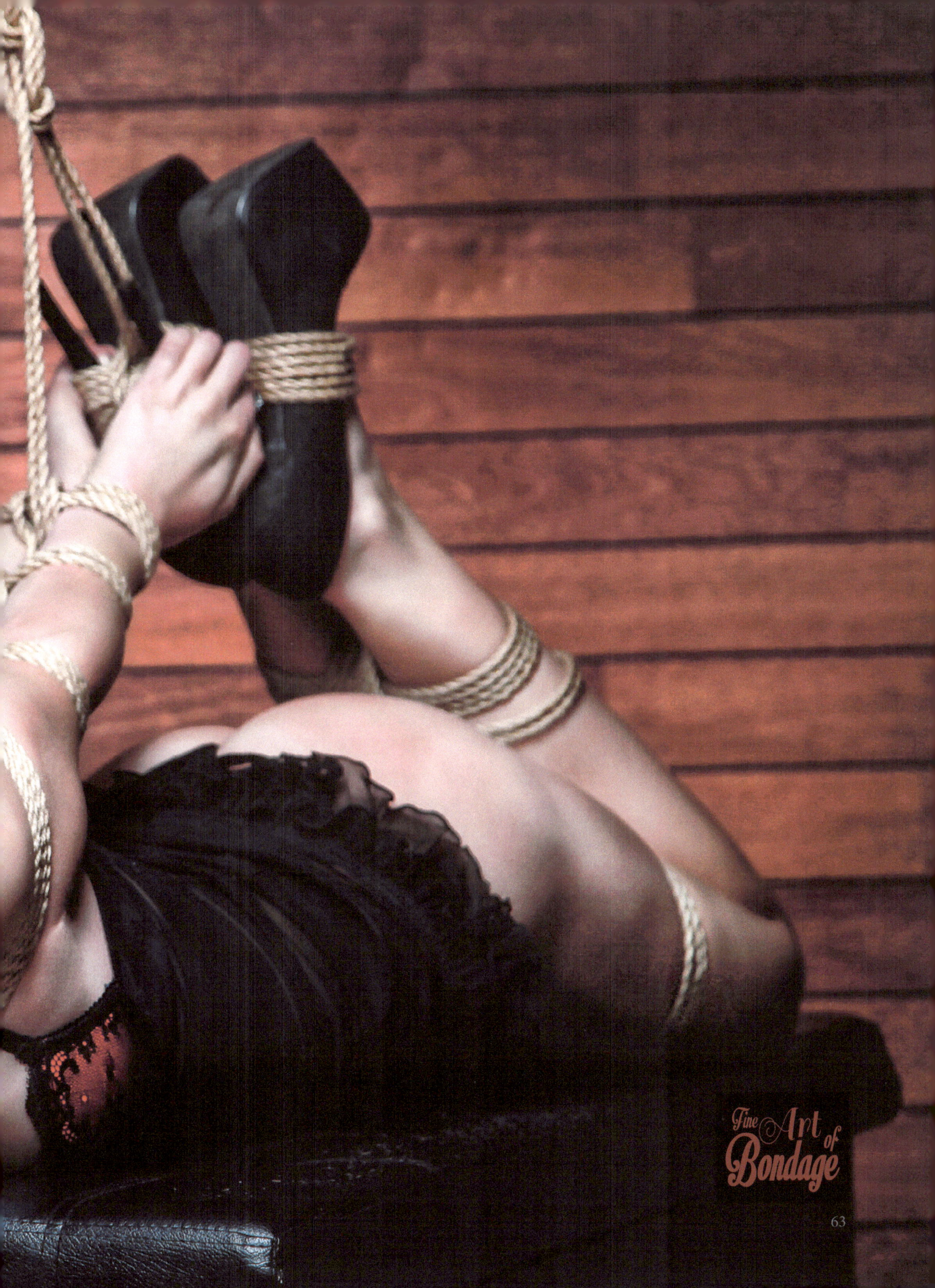

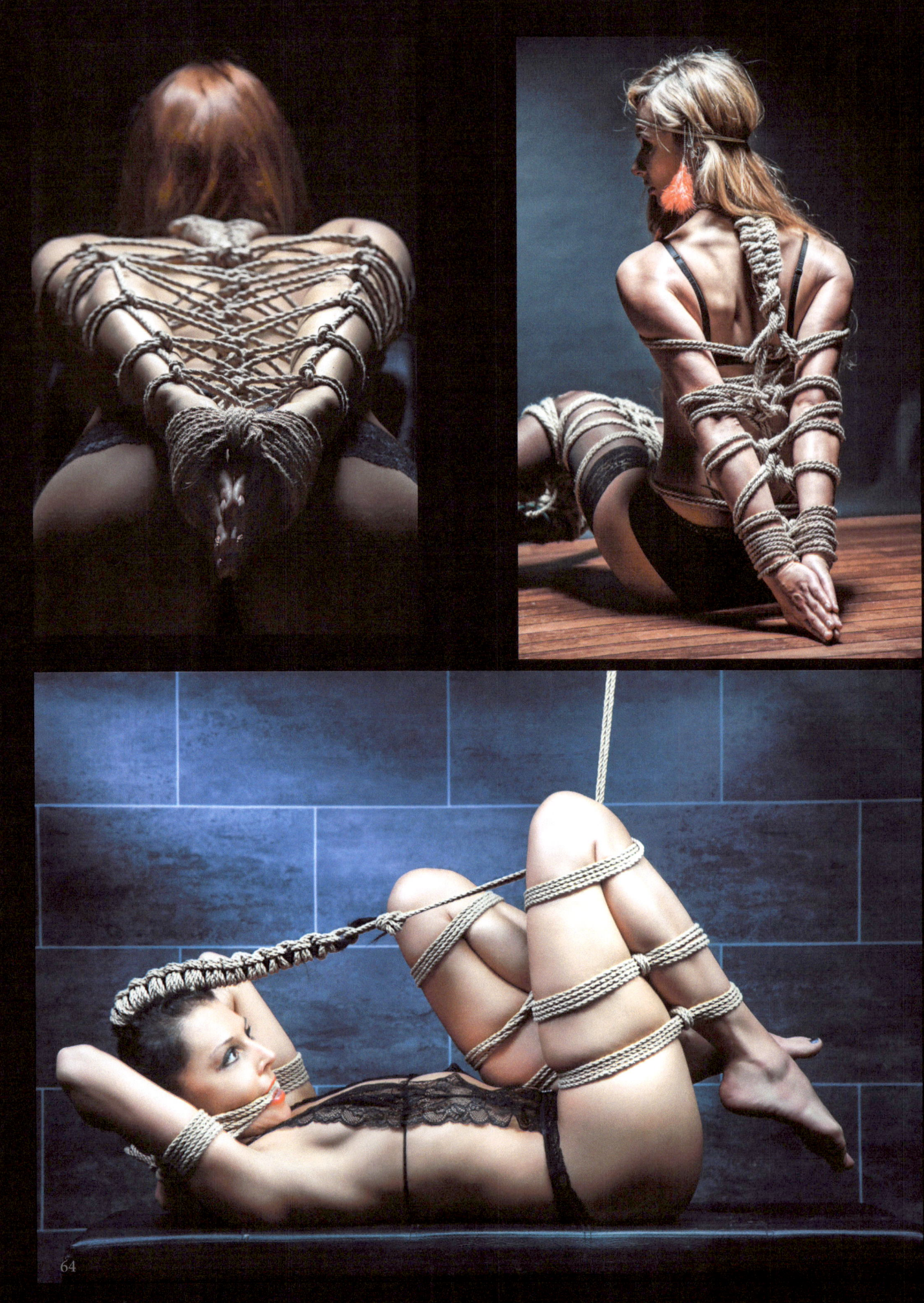

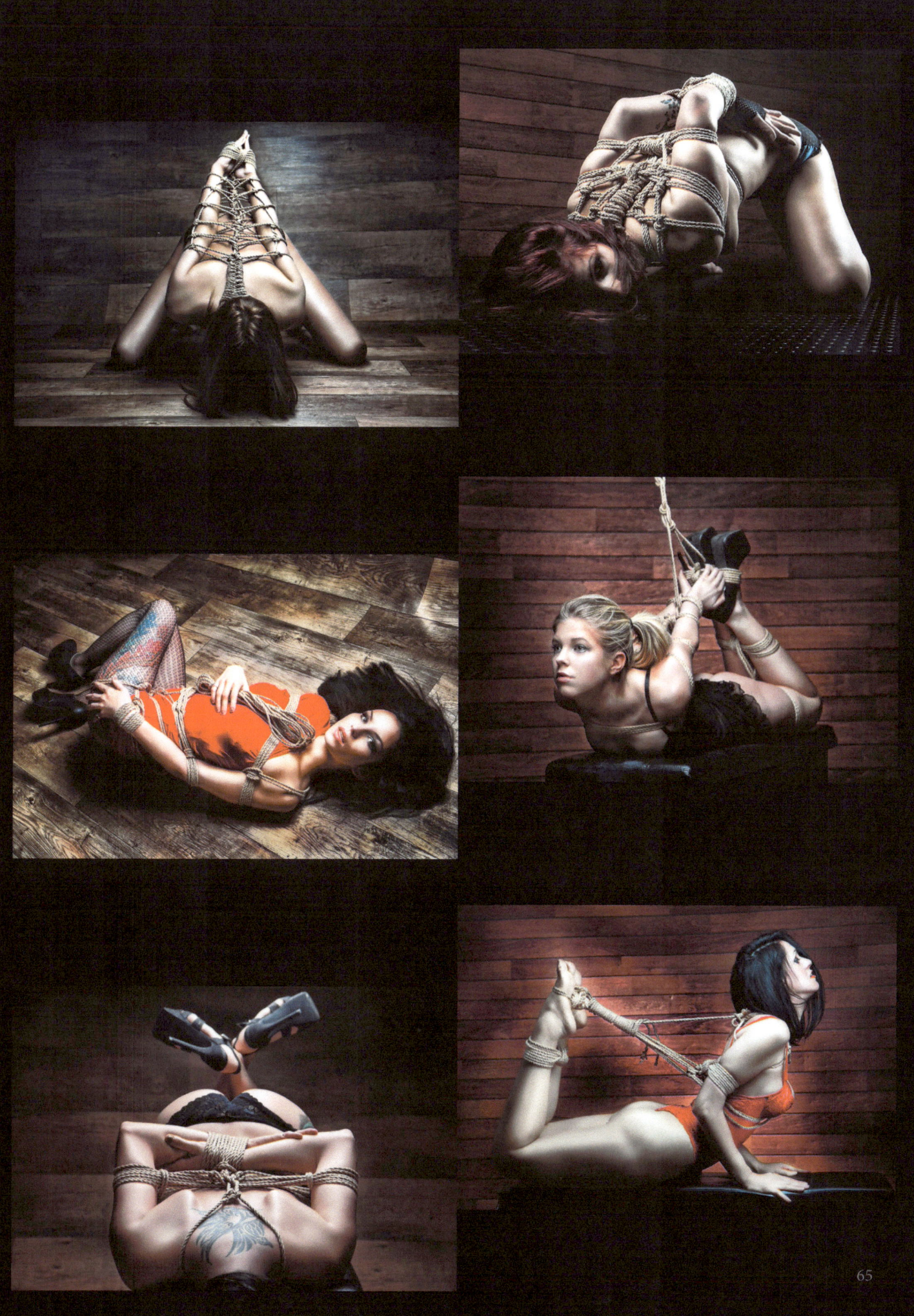

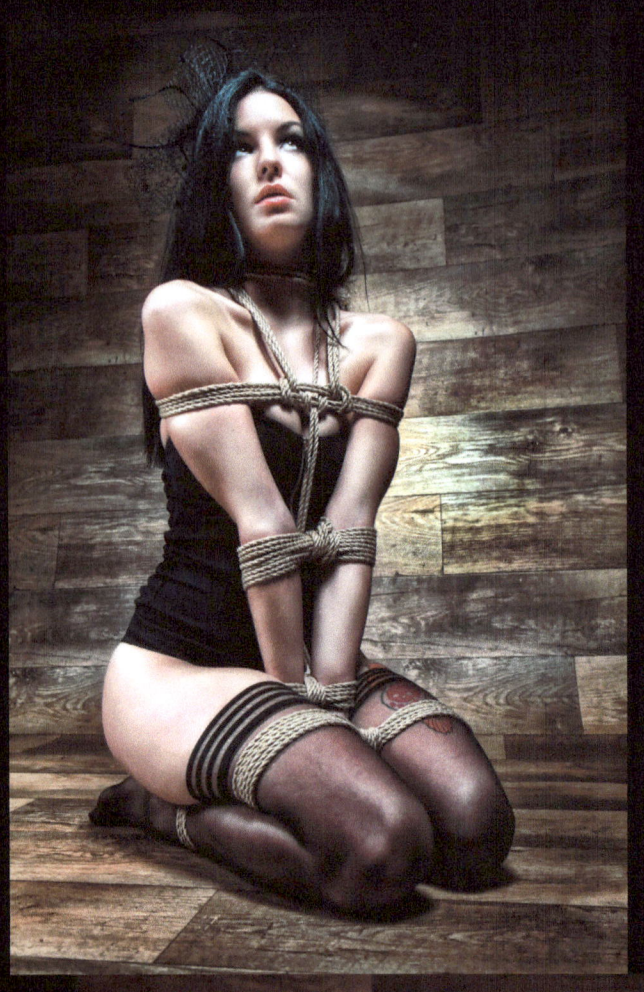
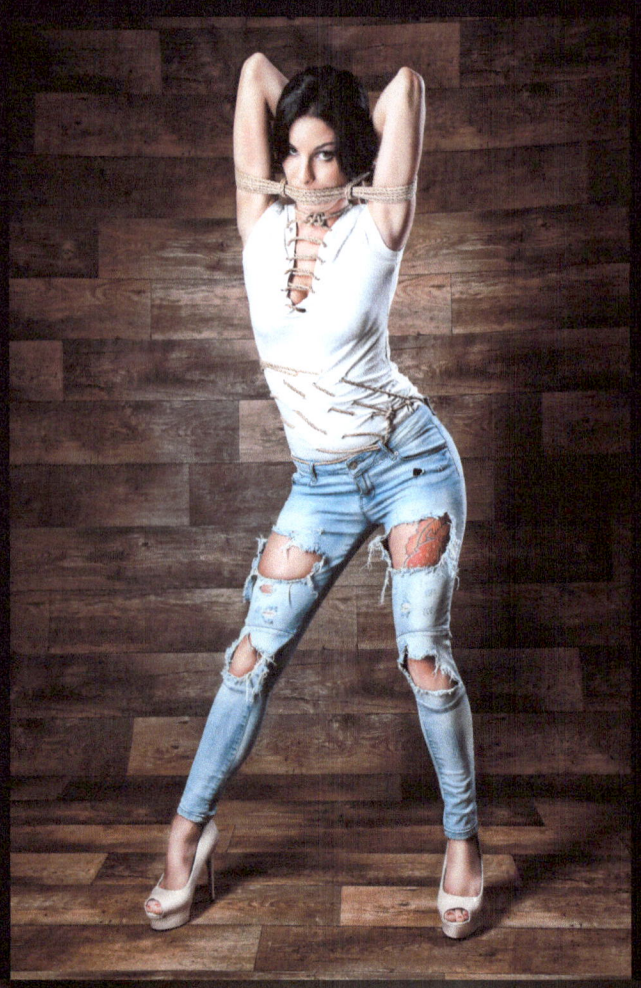
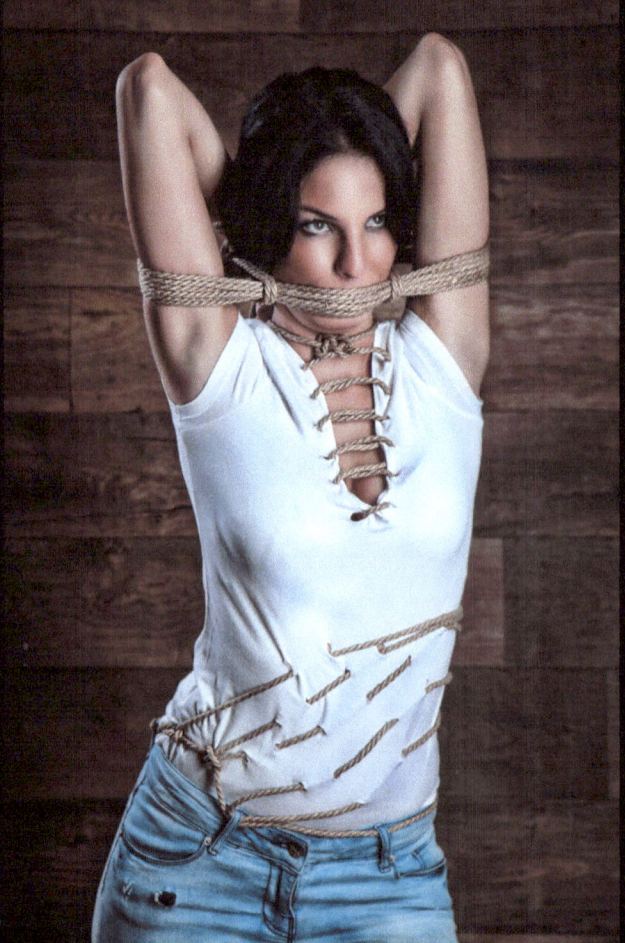
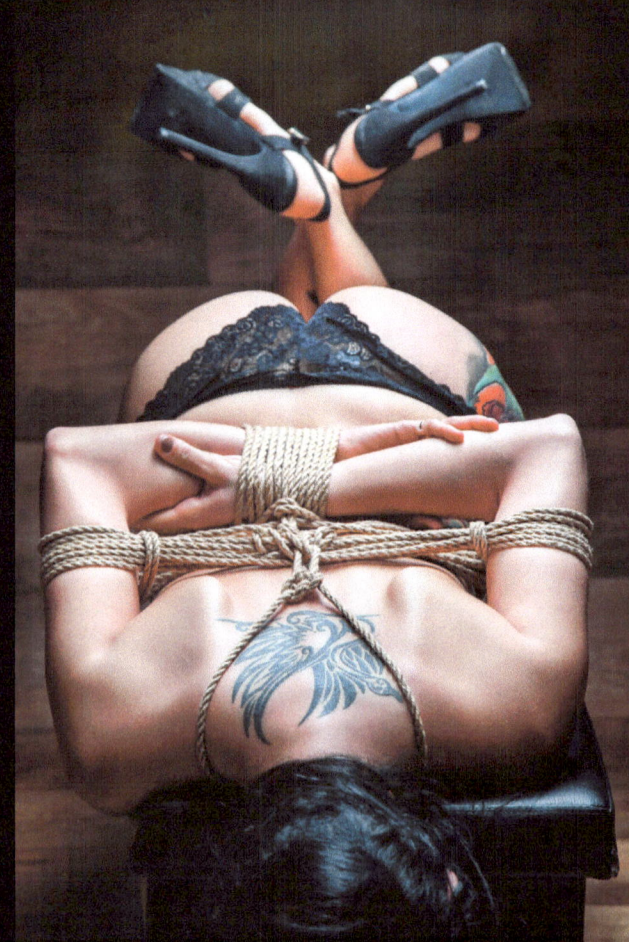

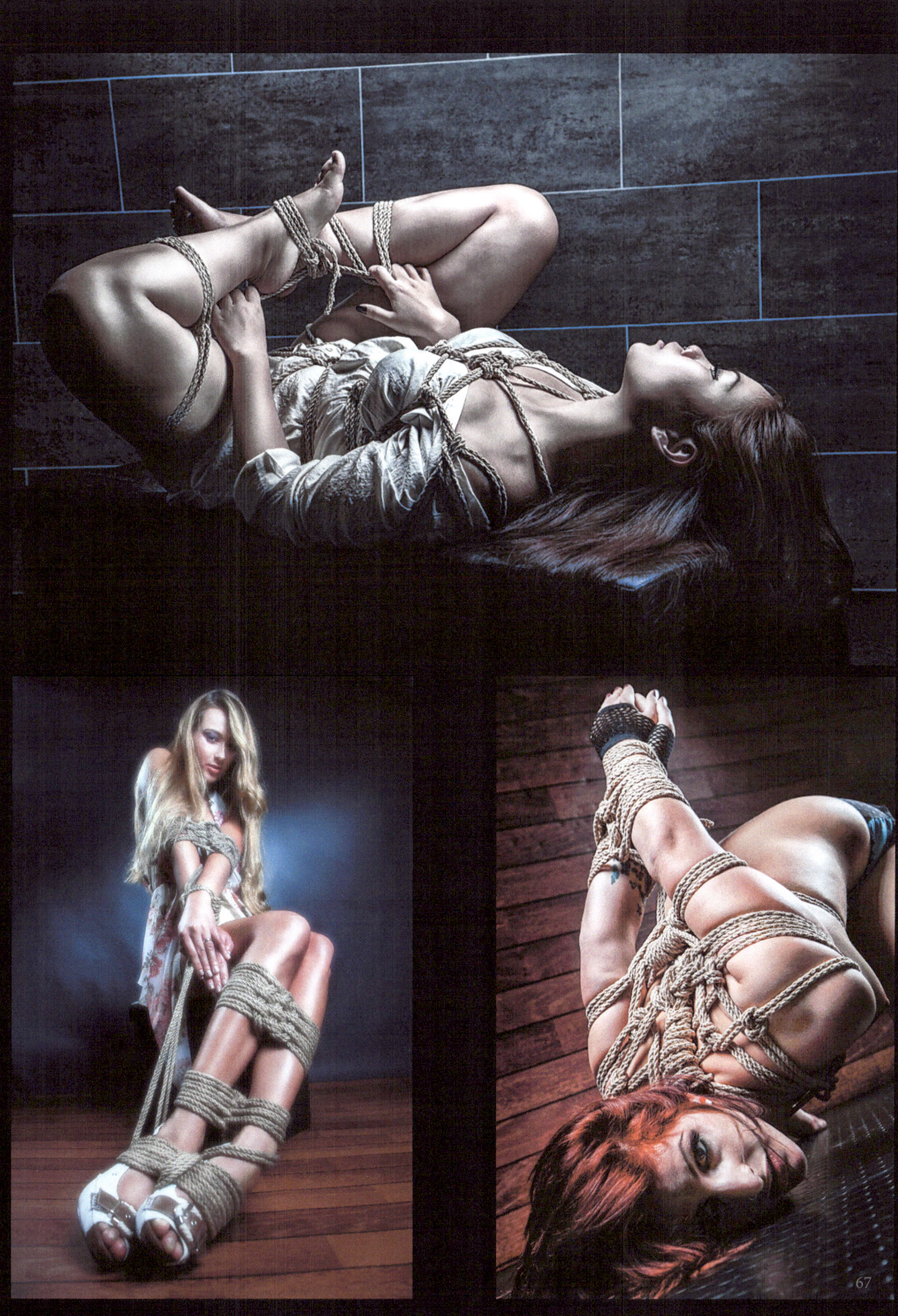

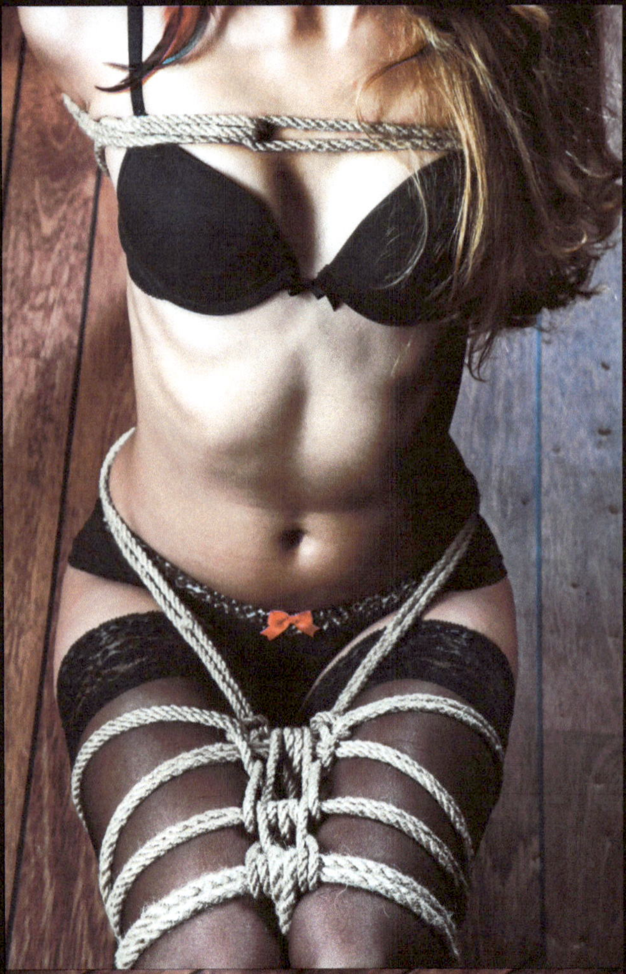

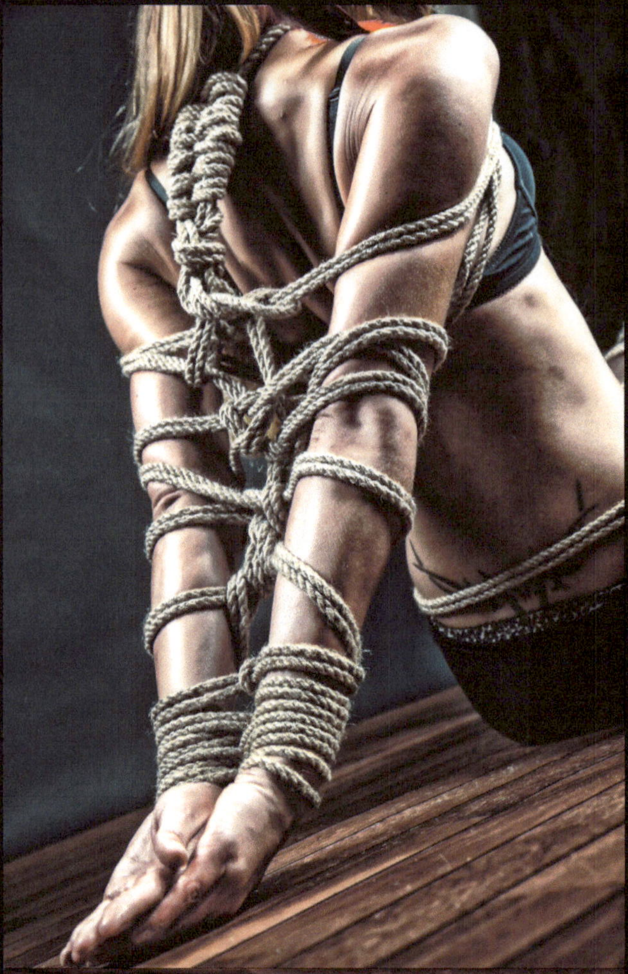

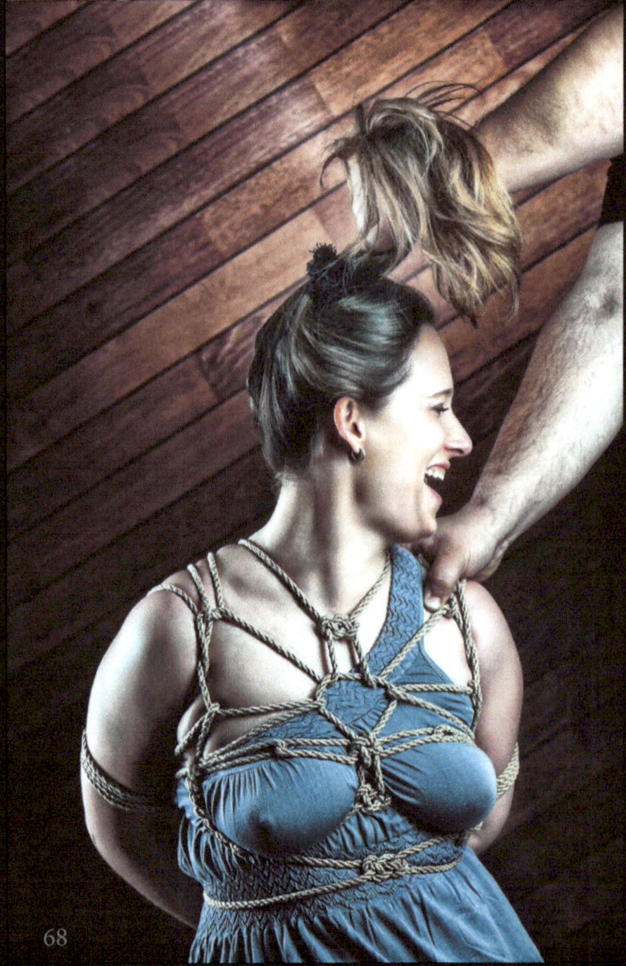

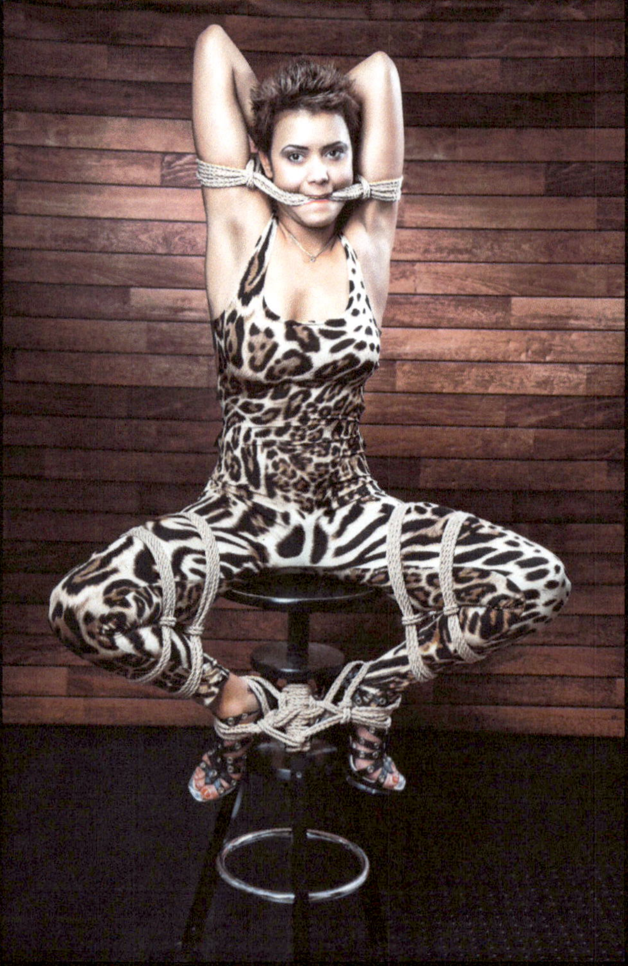

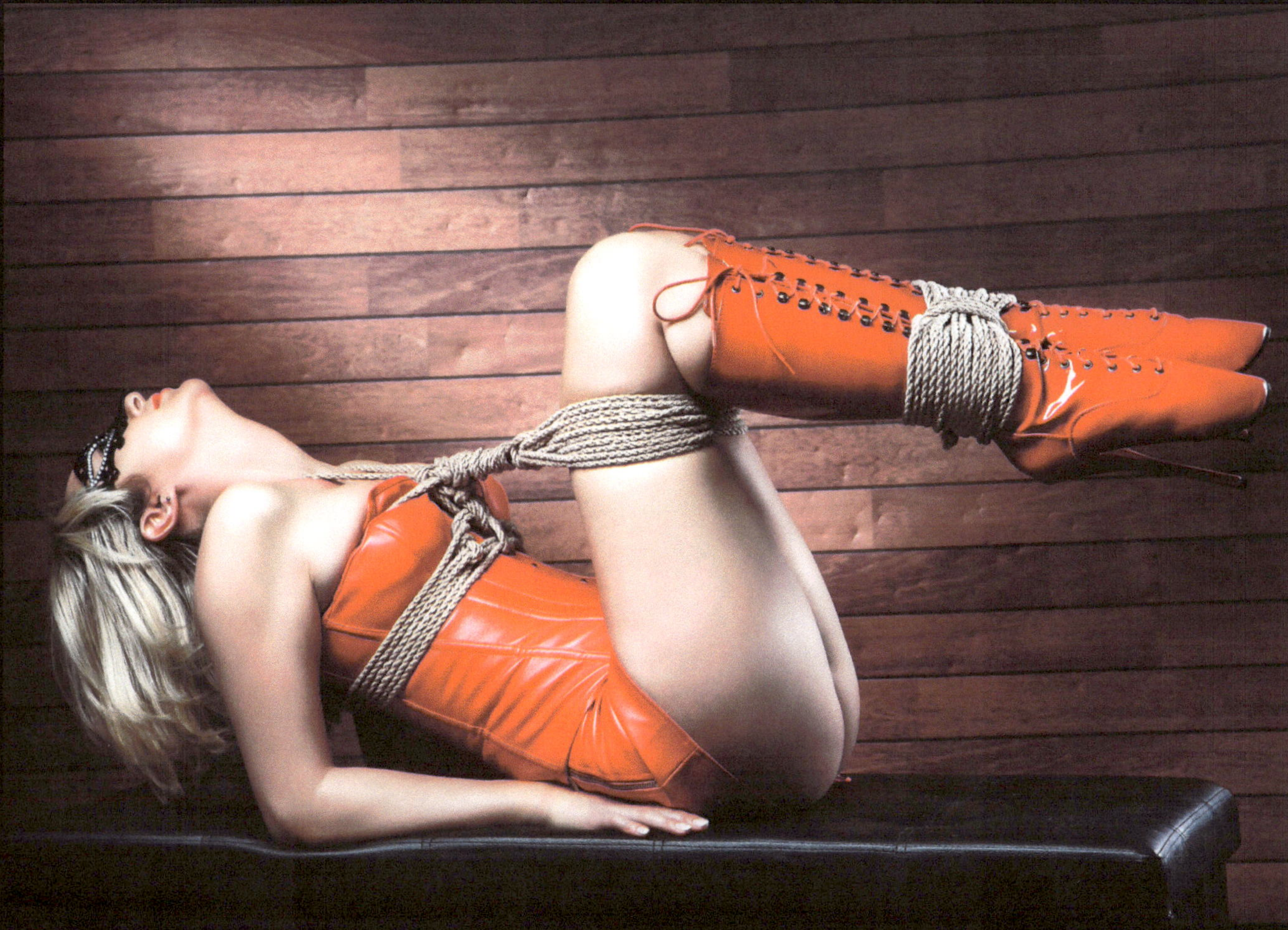

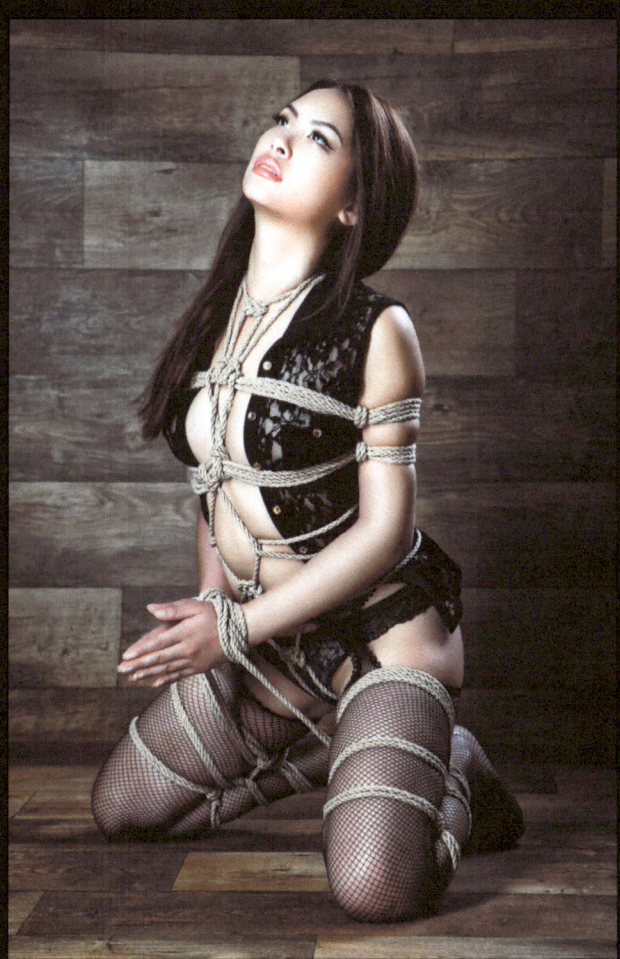
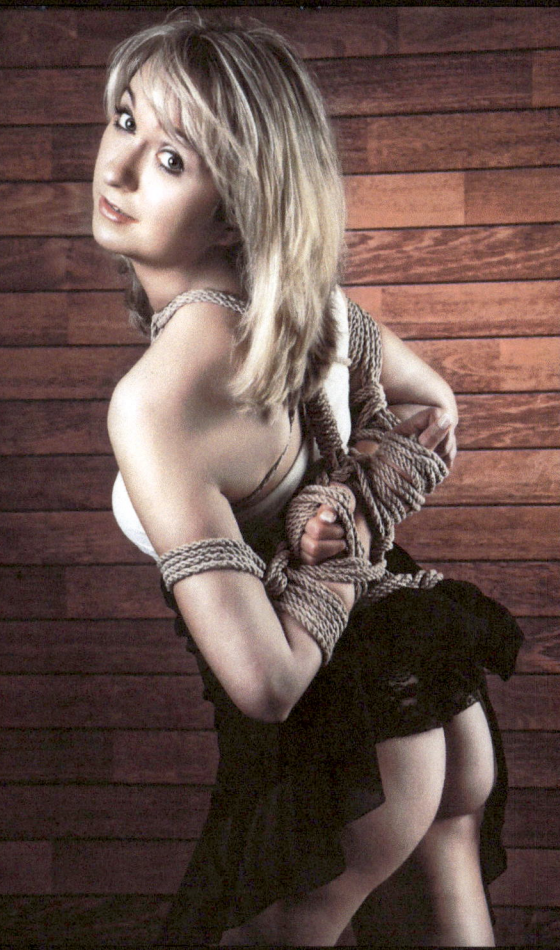

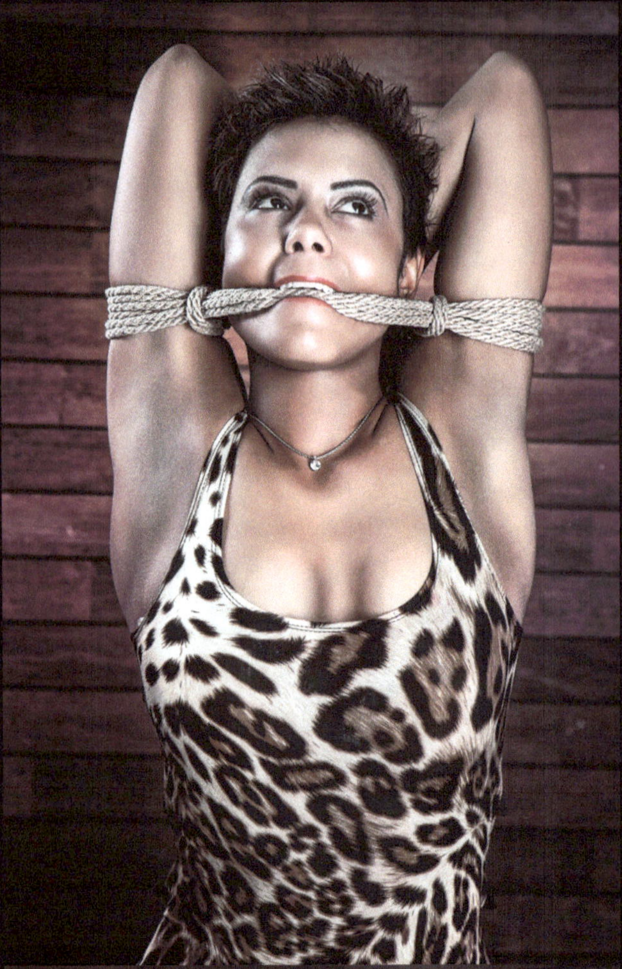

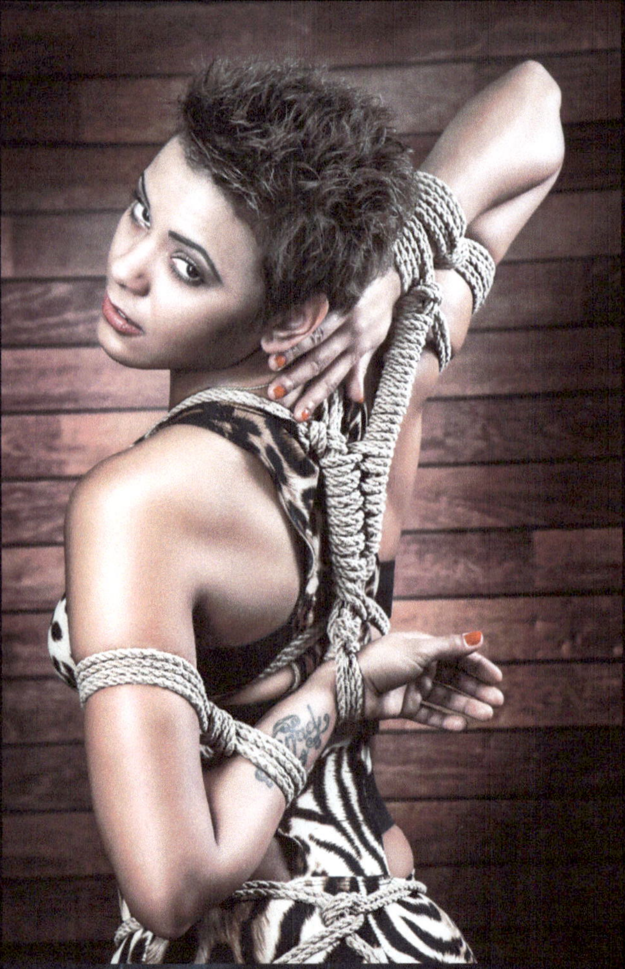

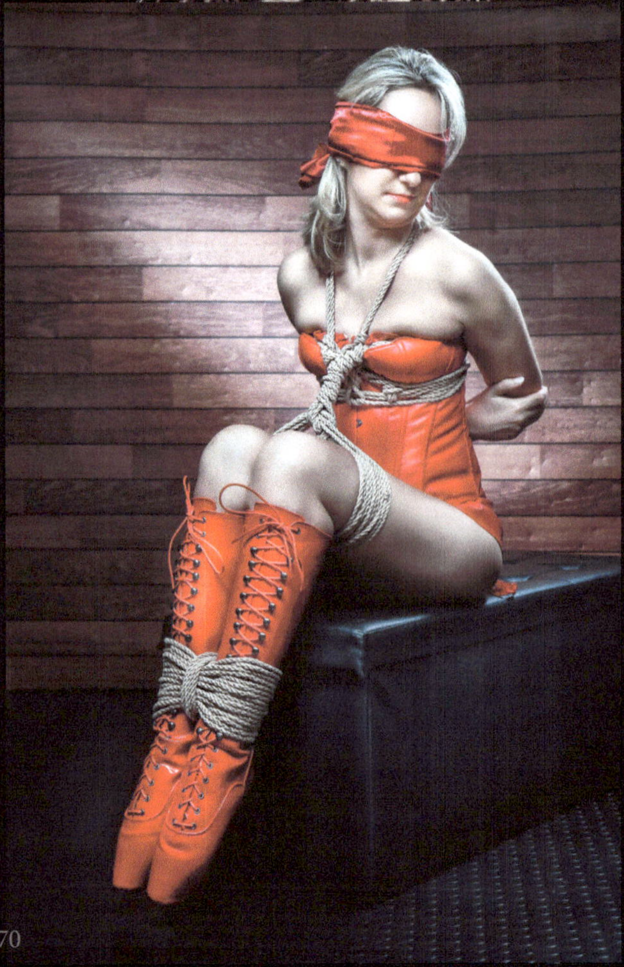

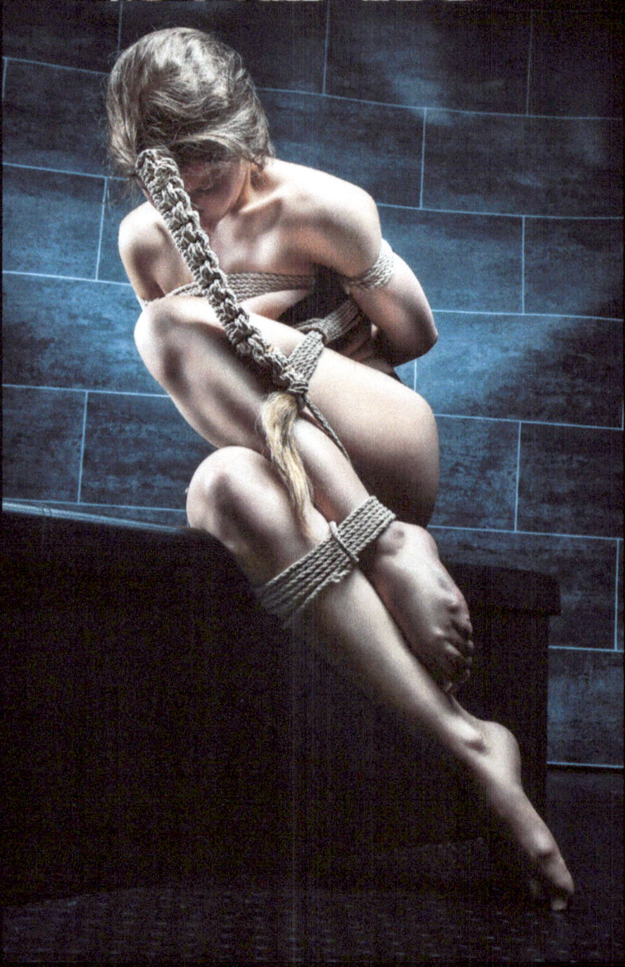

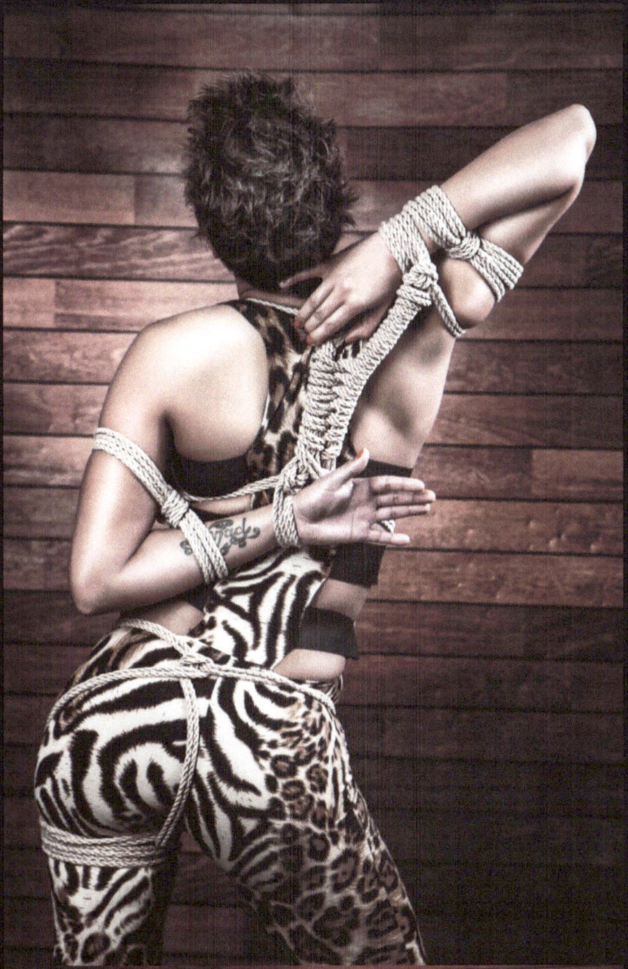

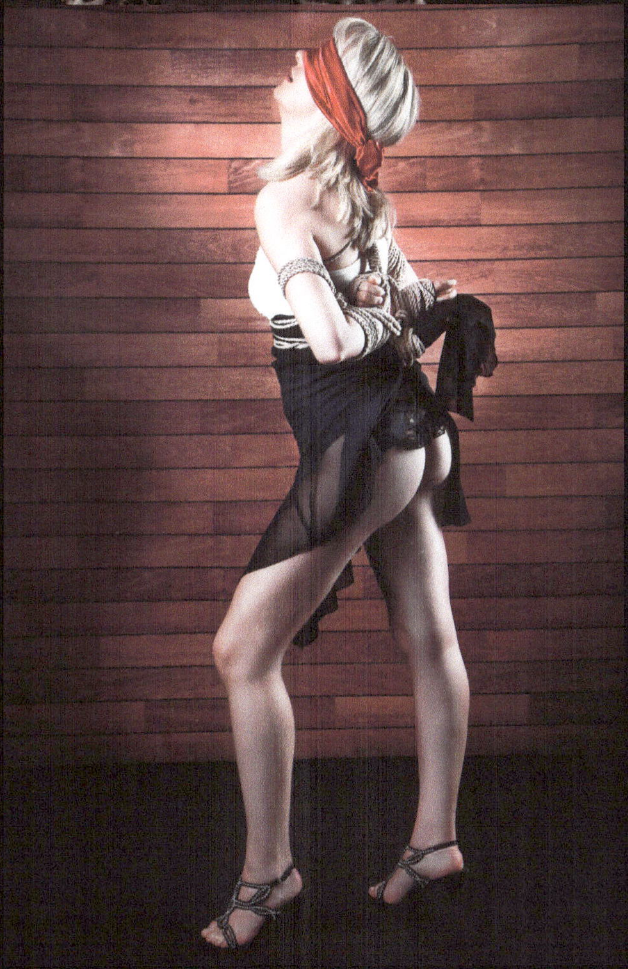

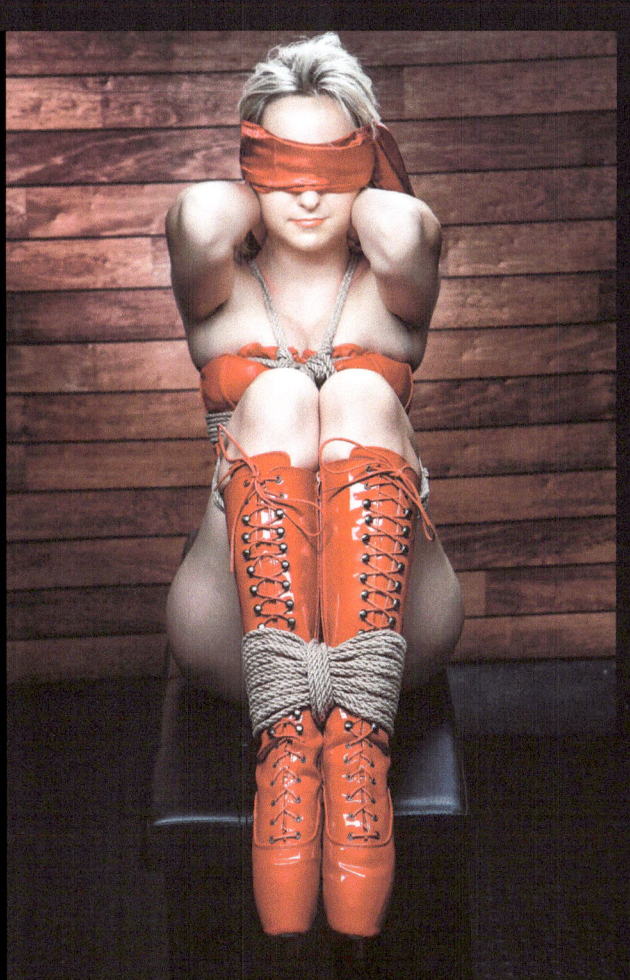
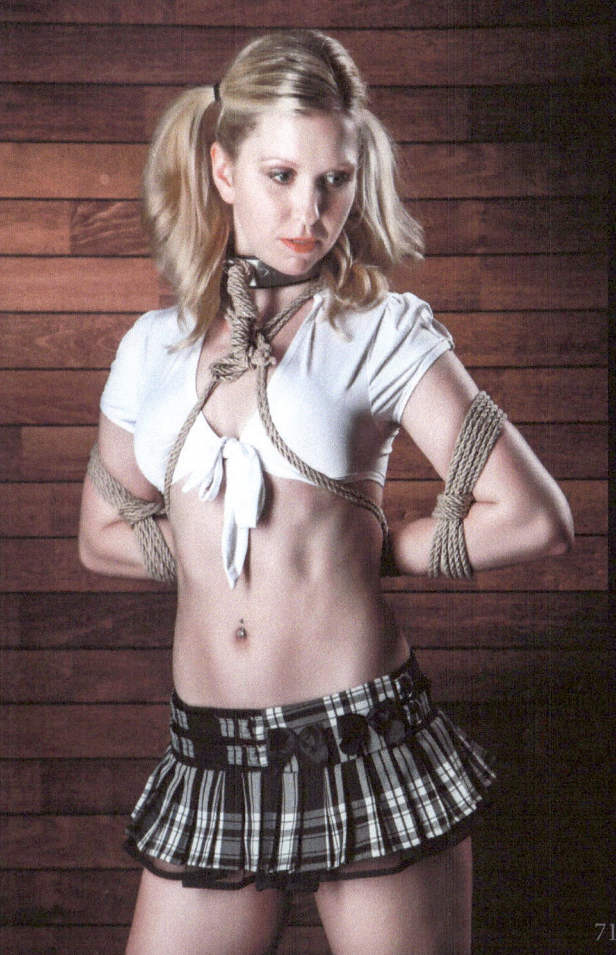

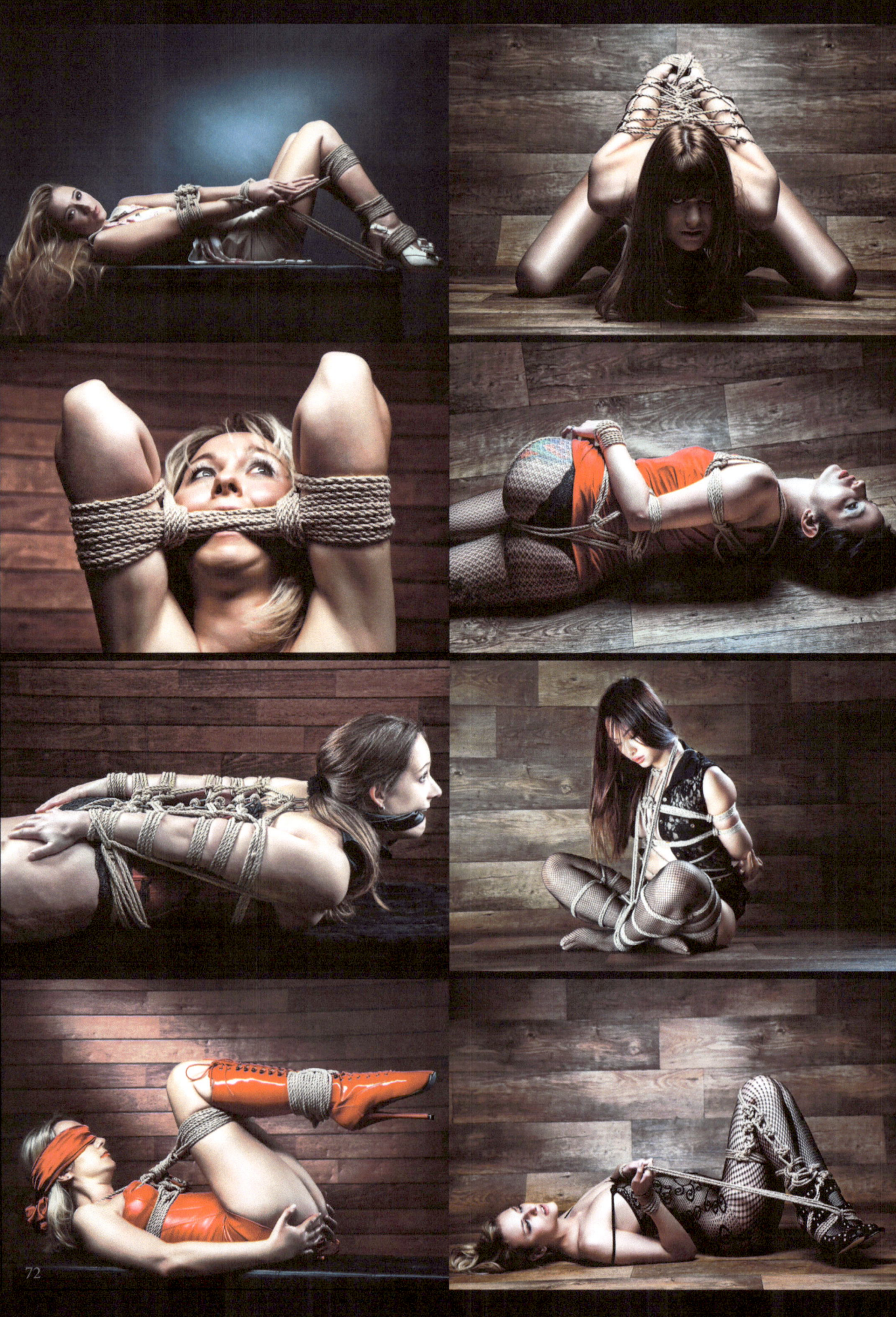

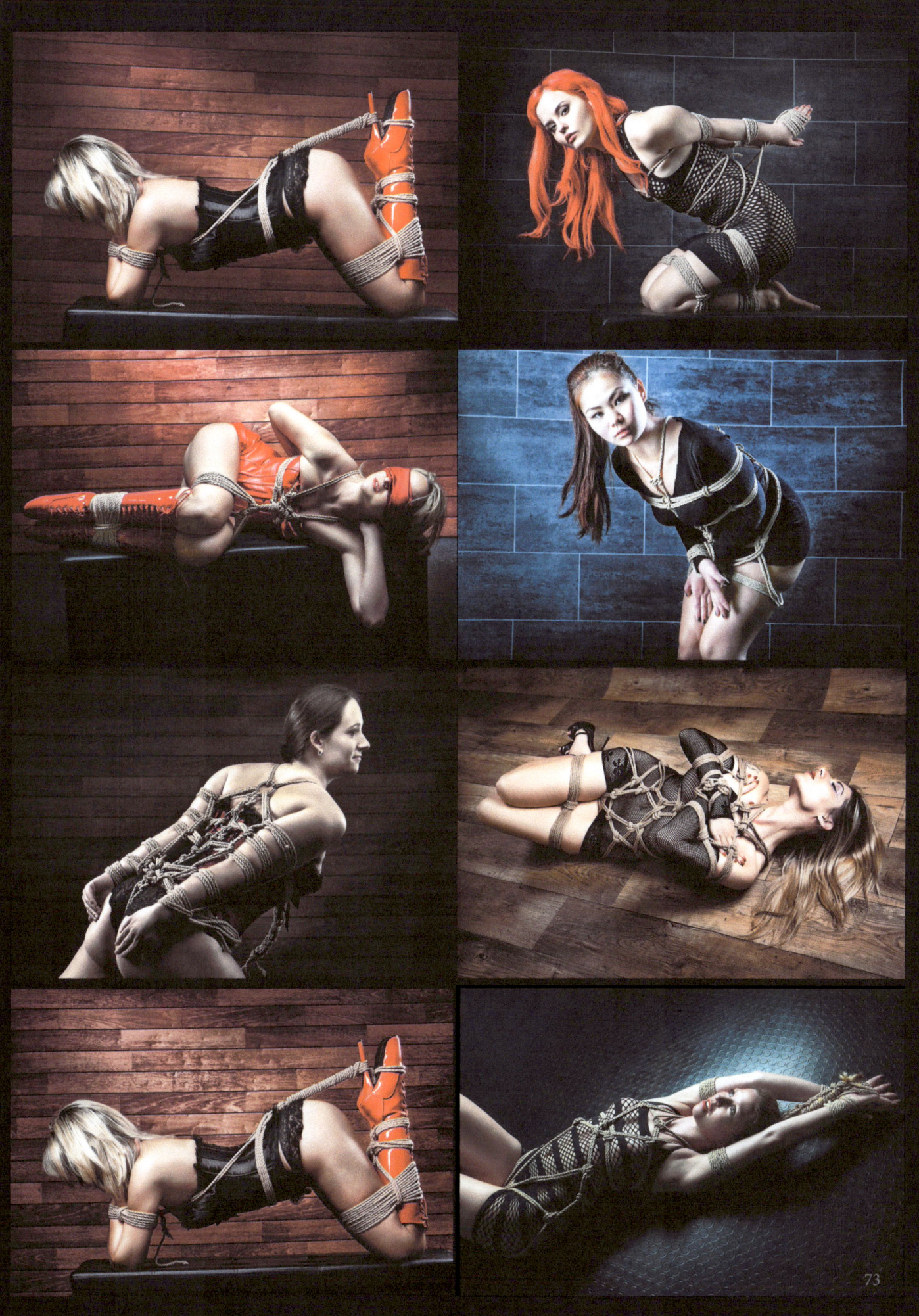

Close up

focused on rope...

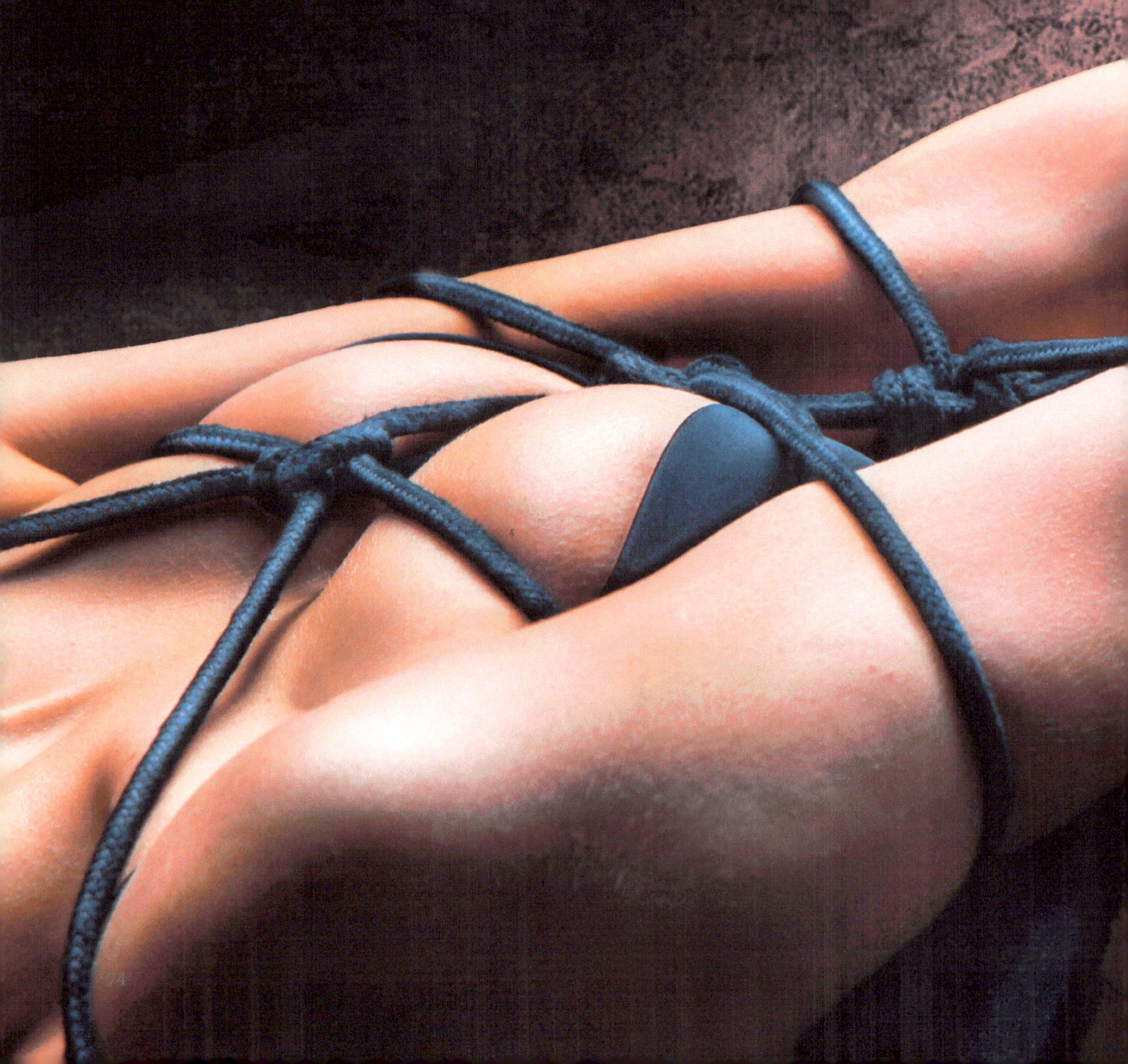

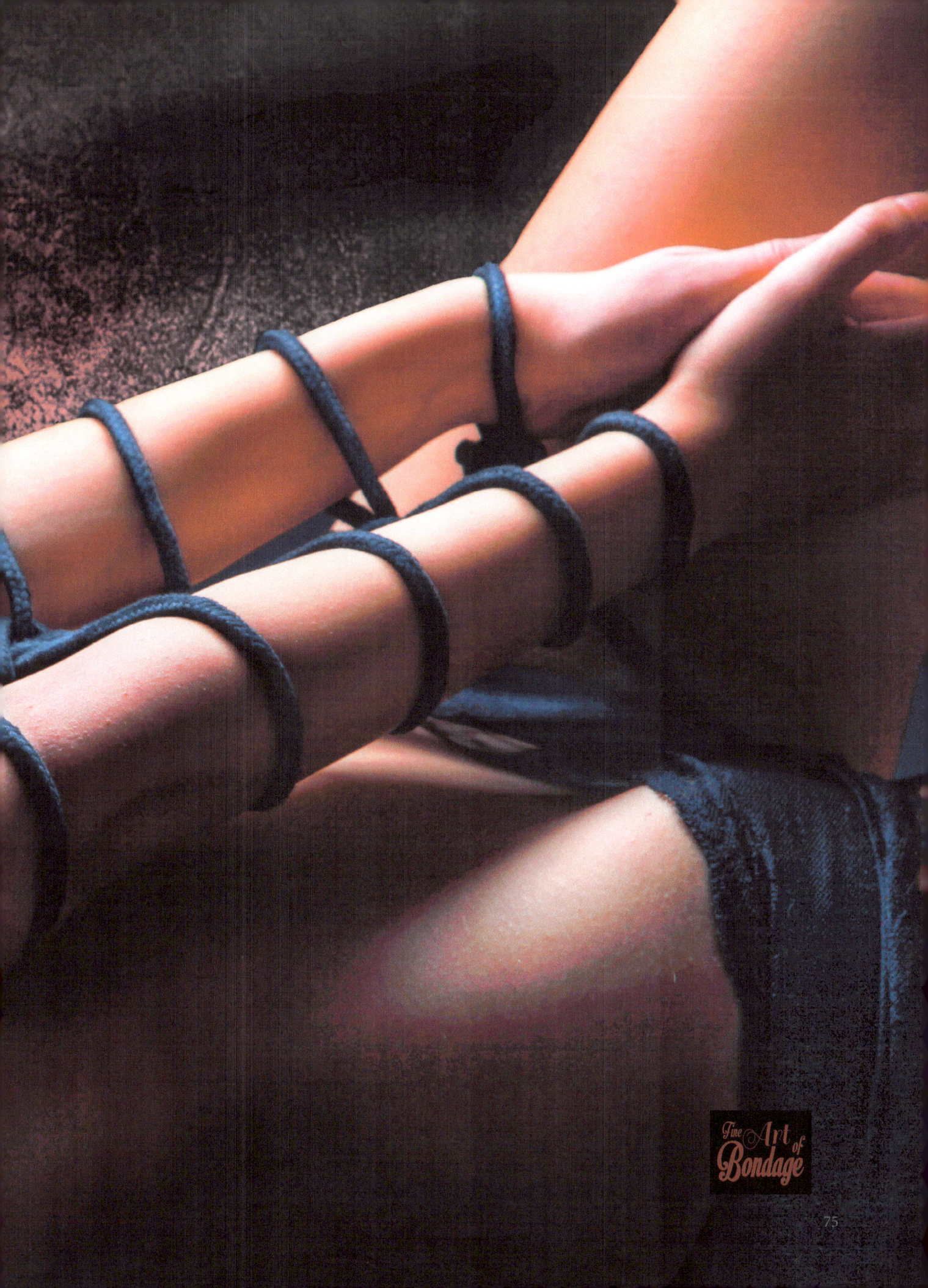

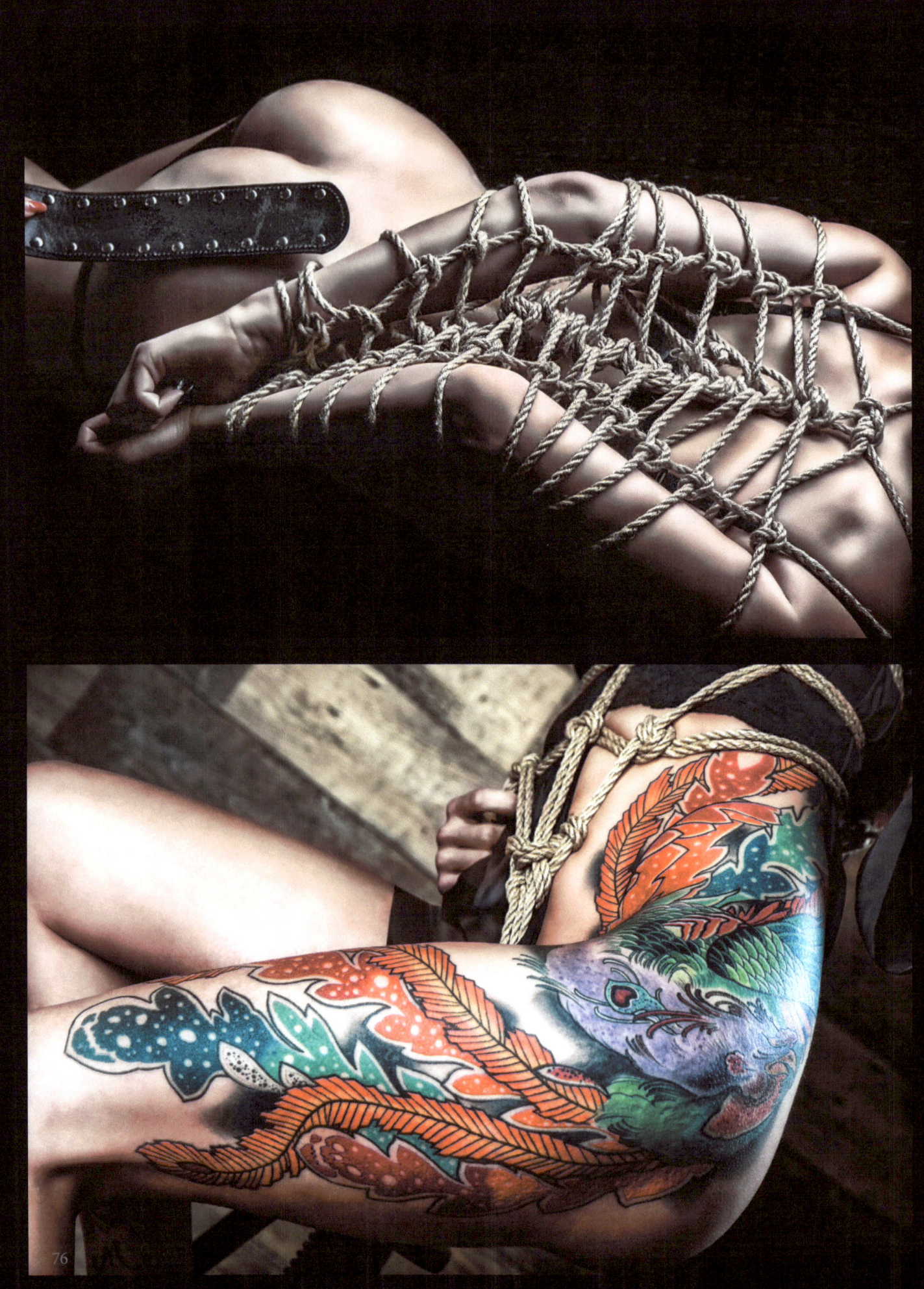

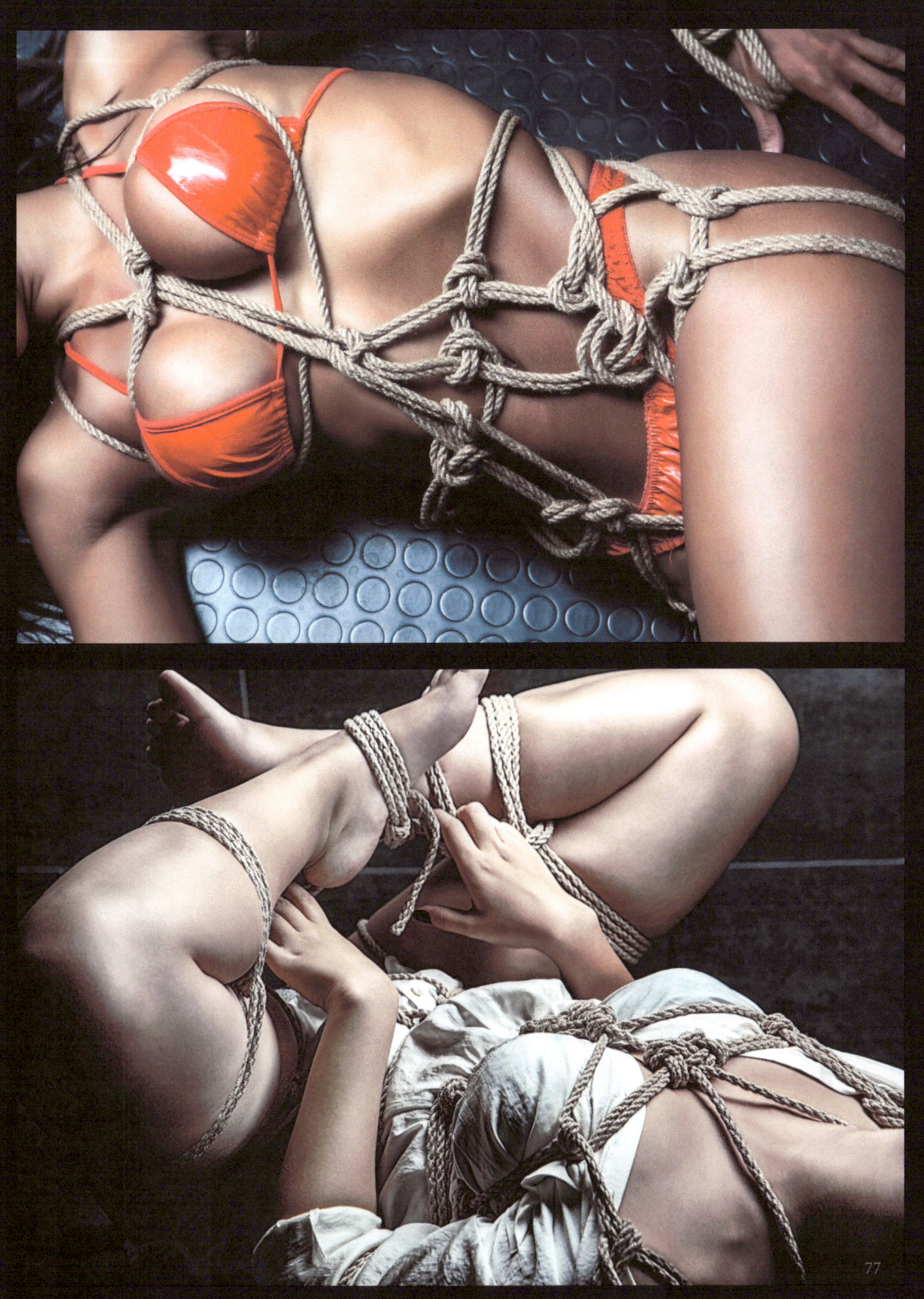

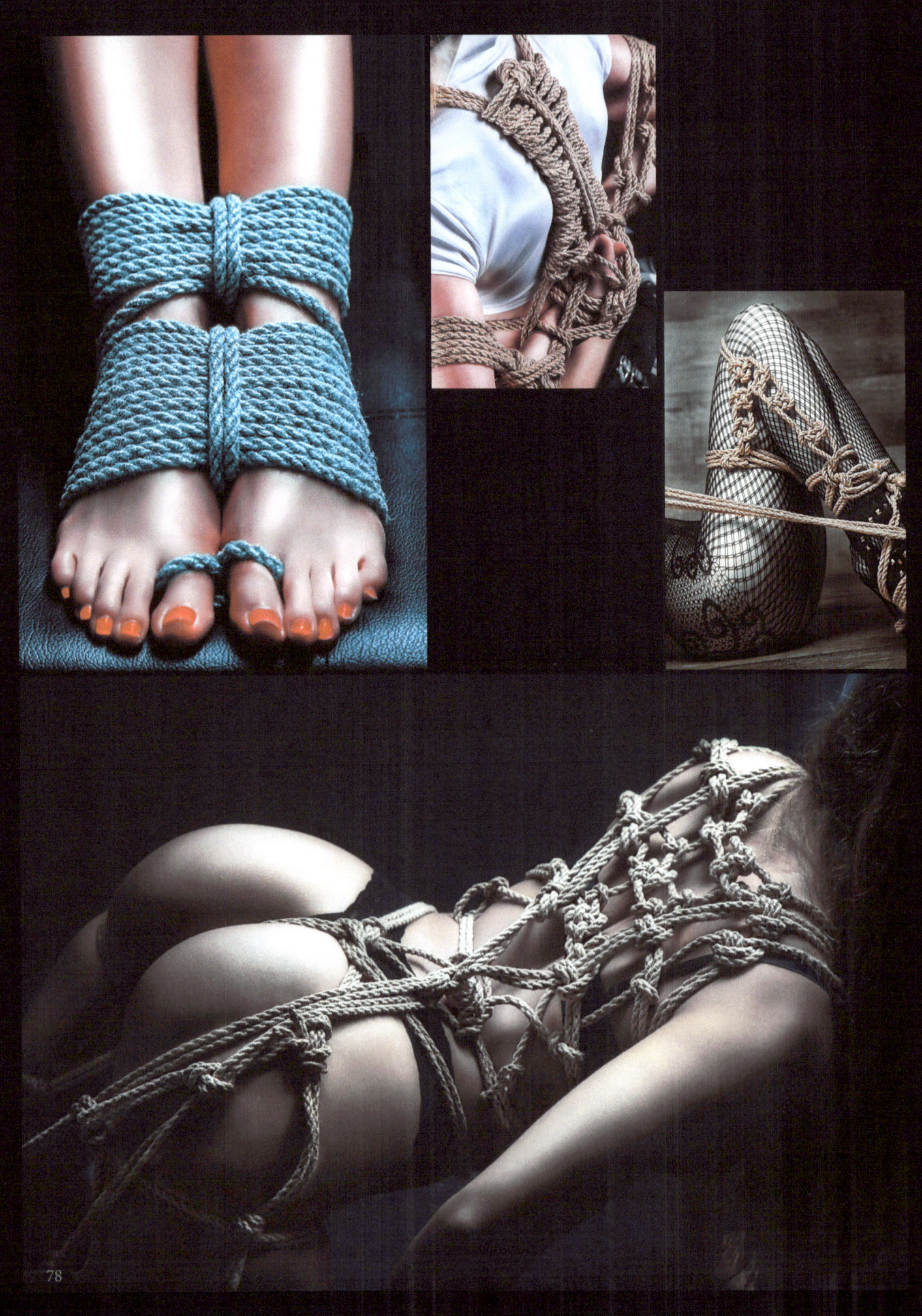

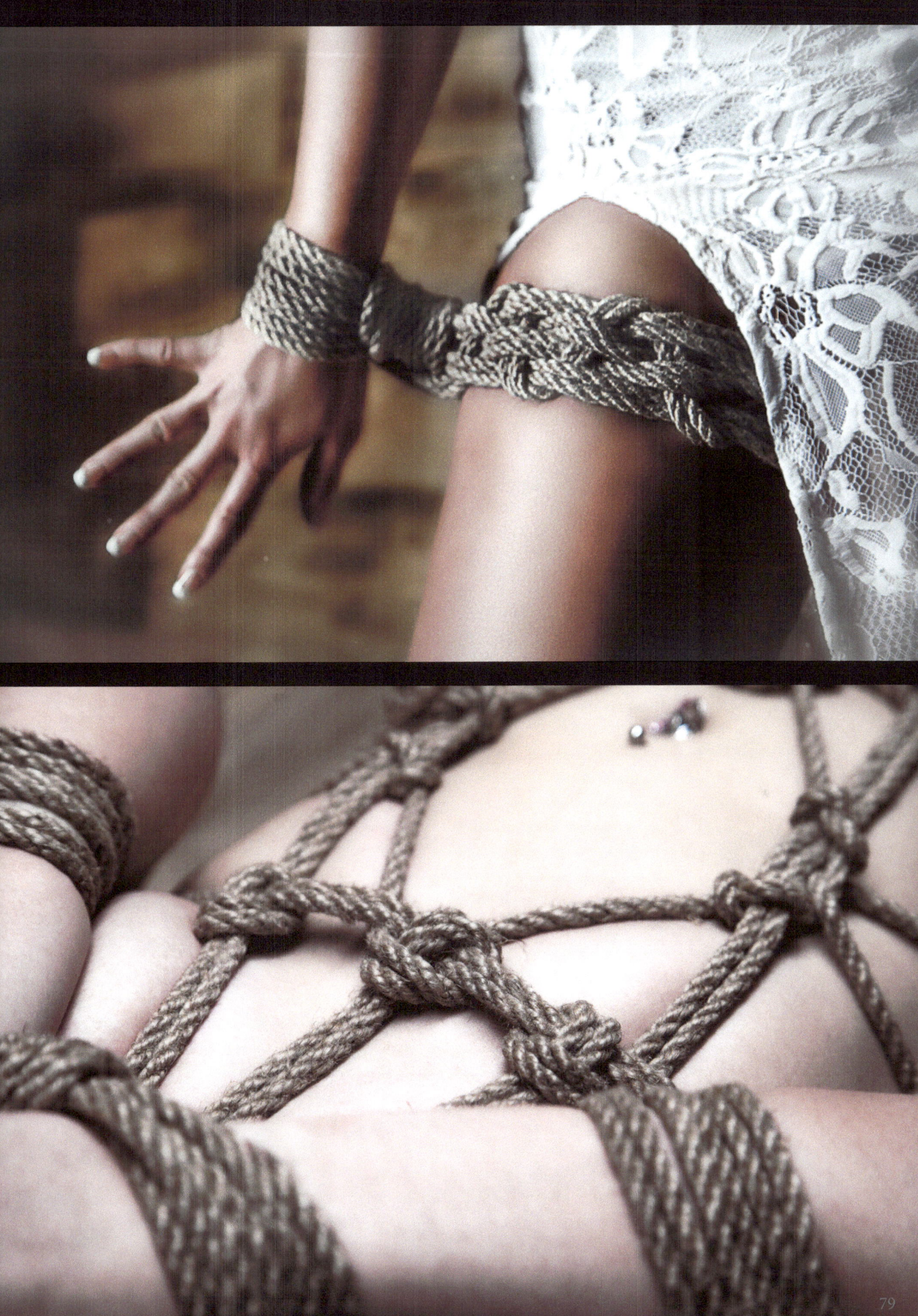

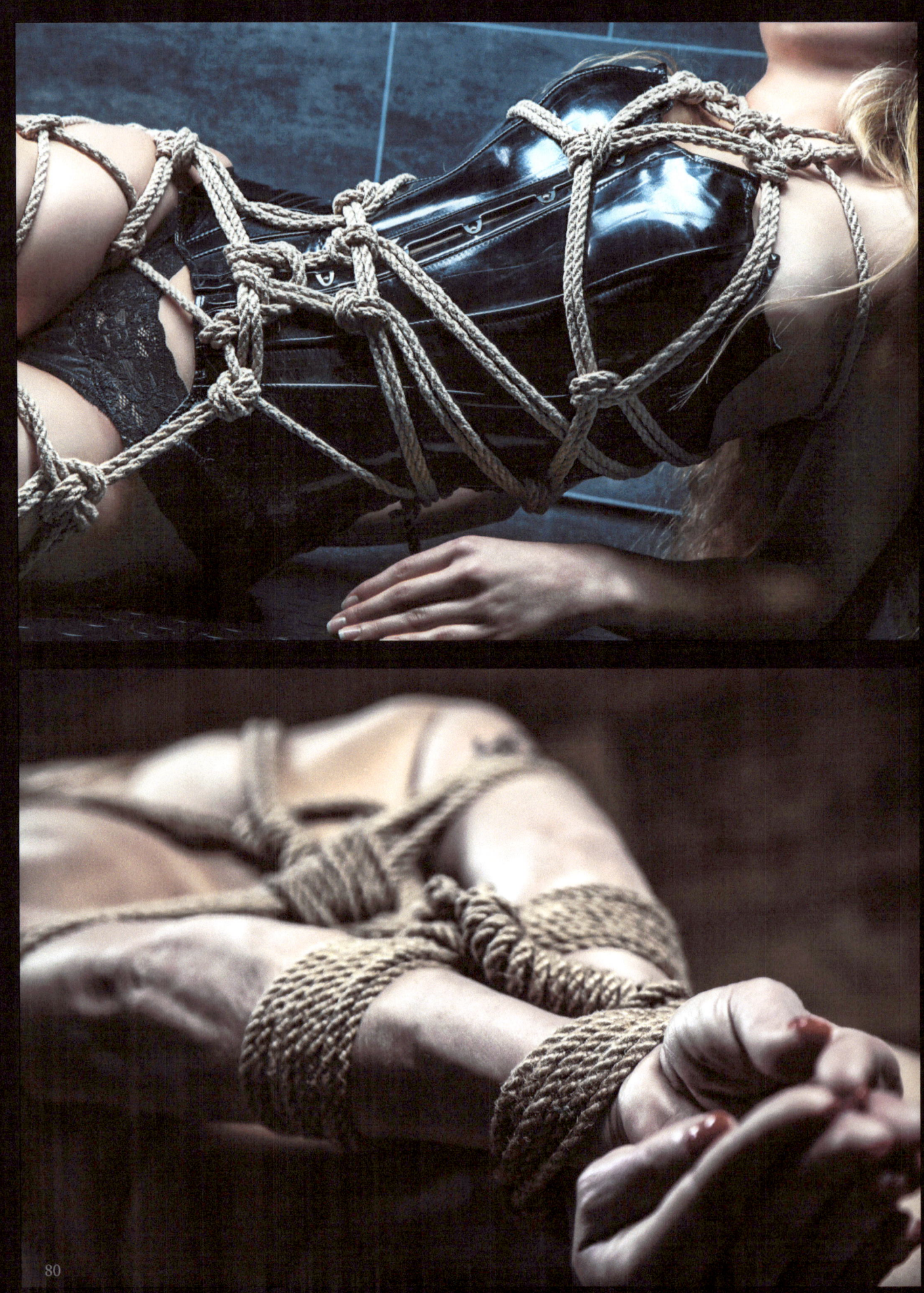

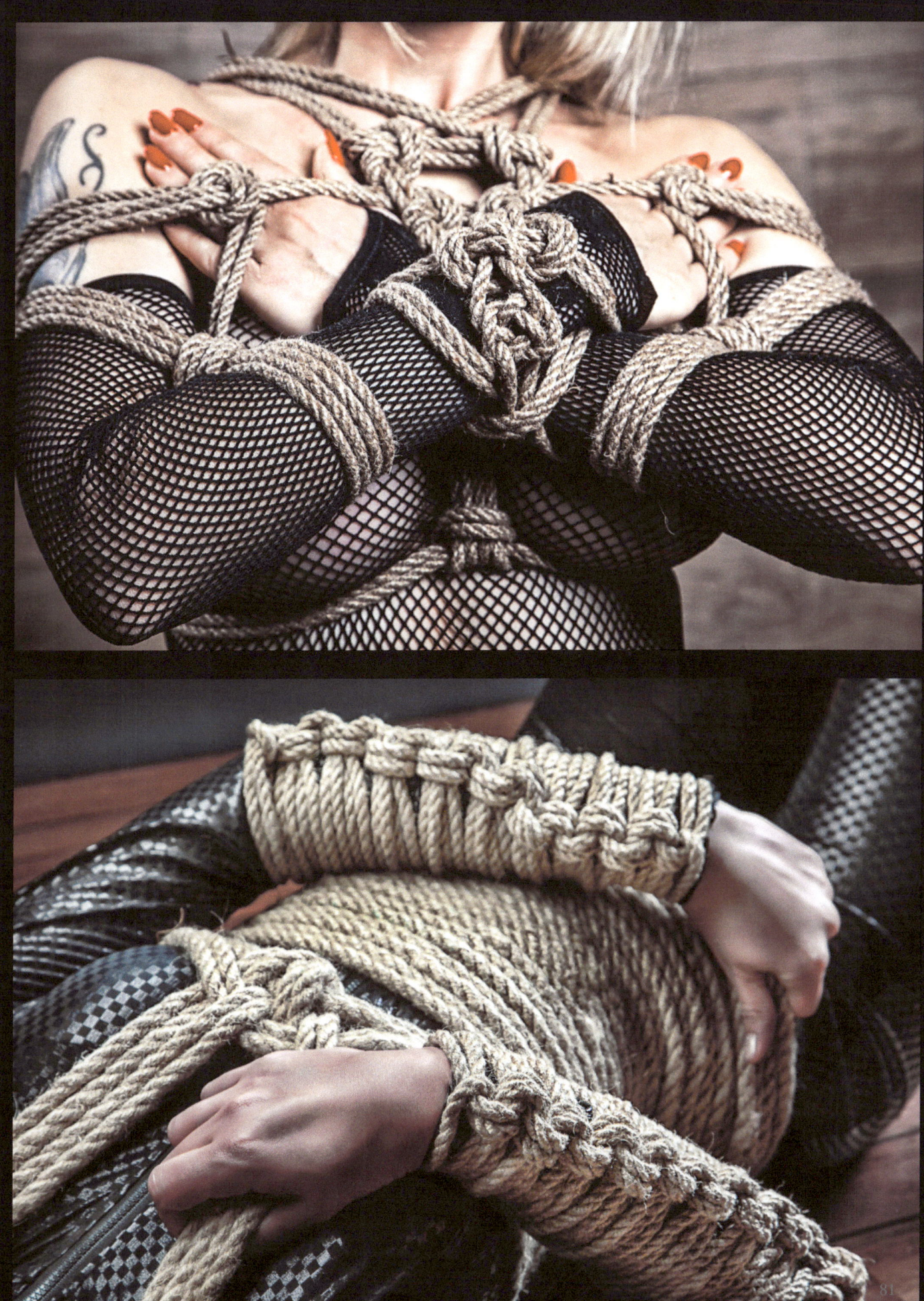

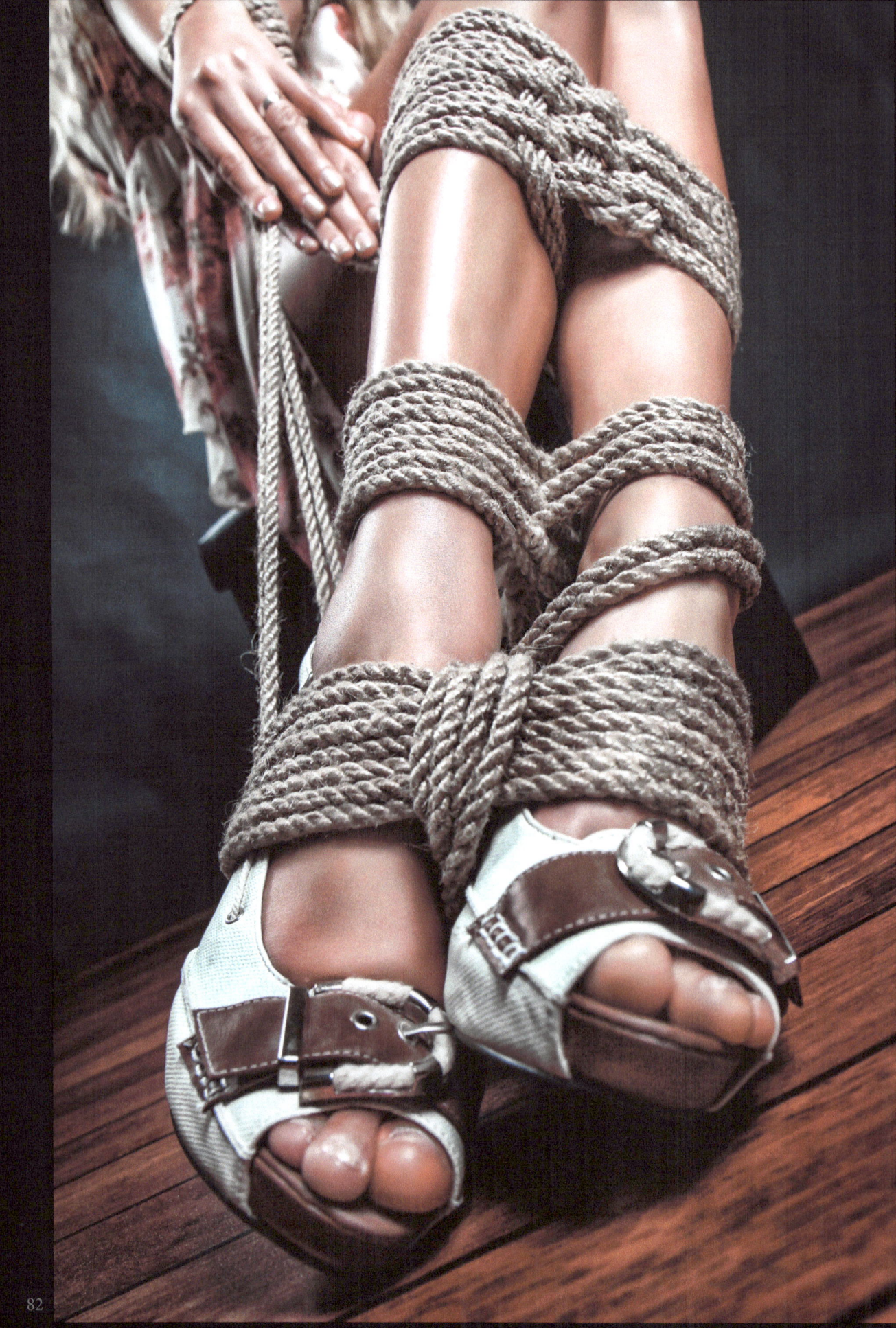

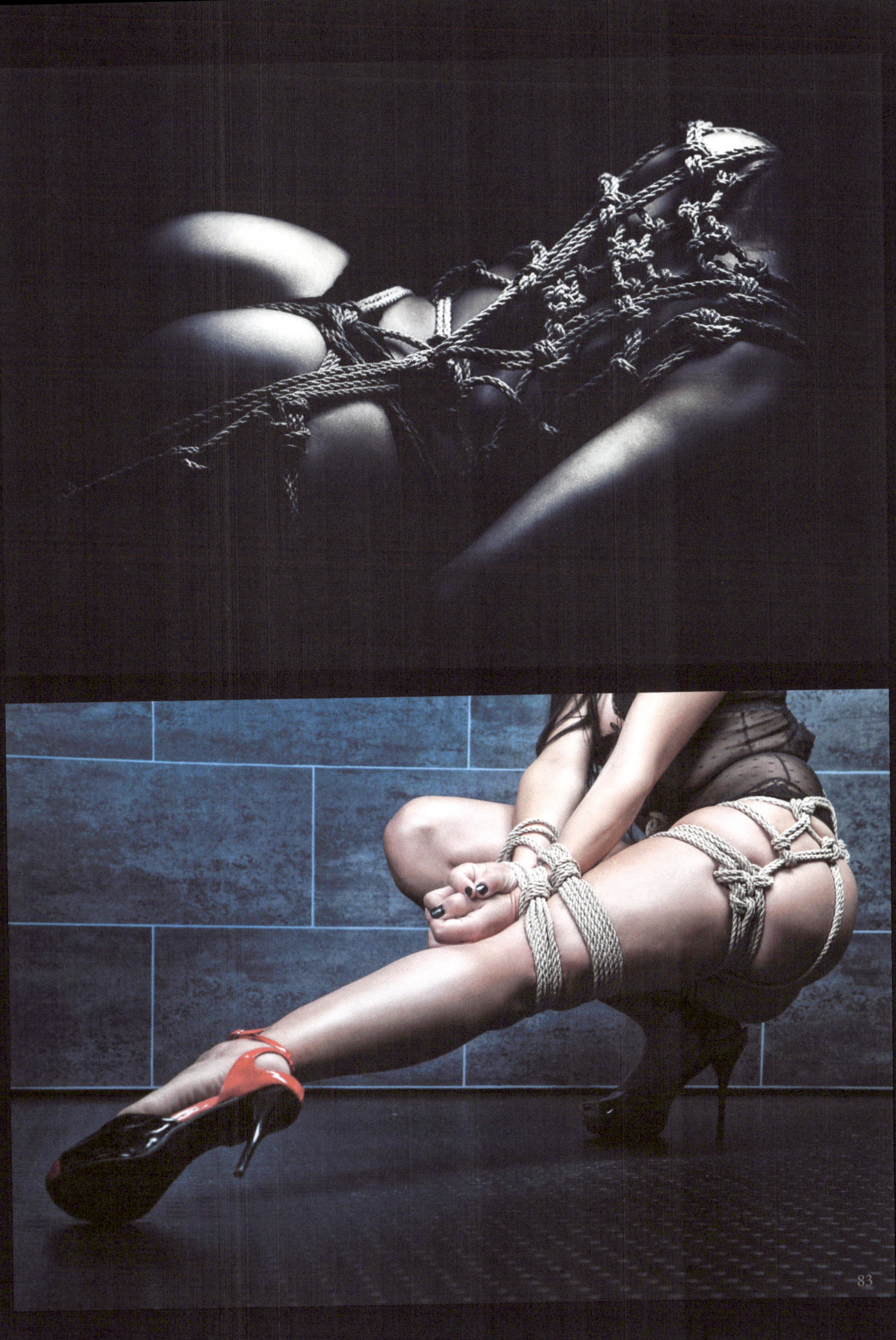

Ropemarks

symbols after the pleasure of rope bondage...

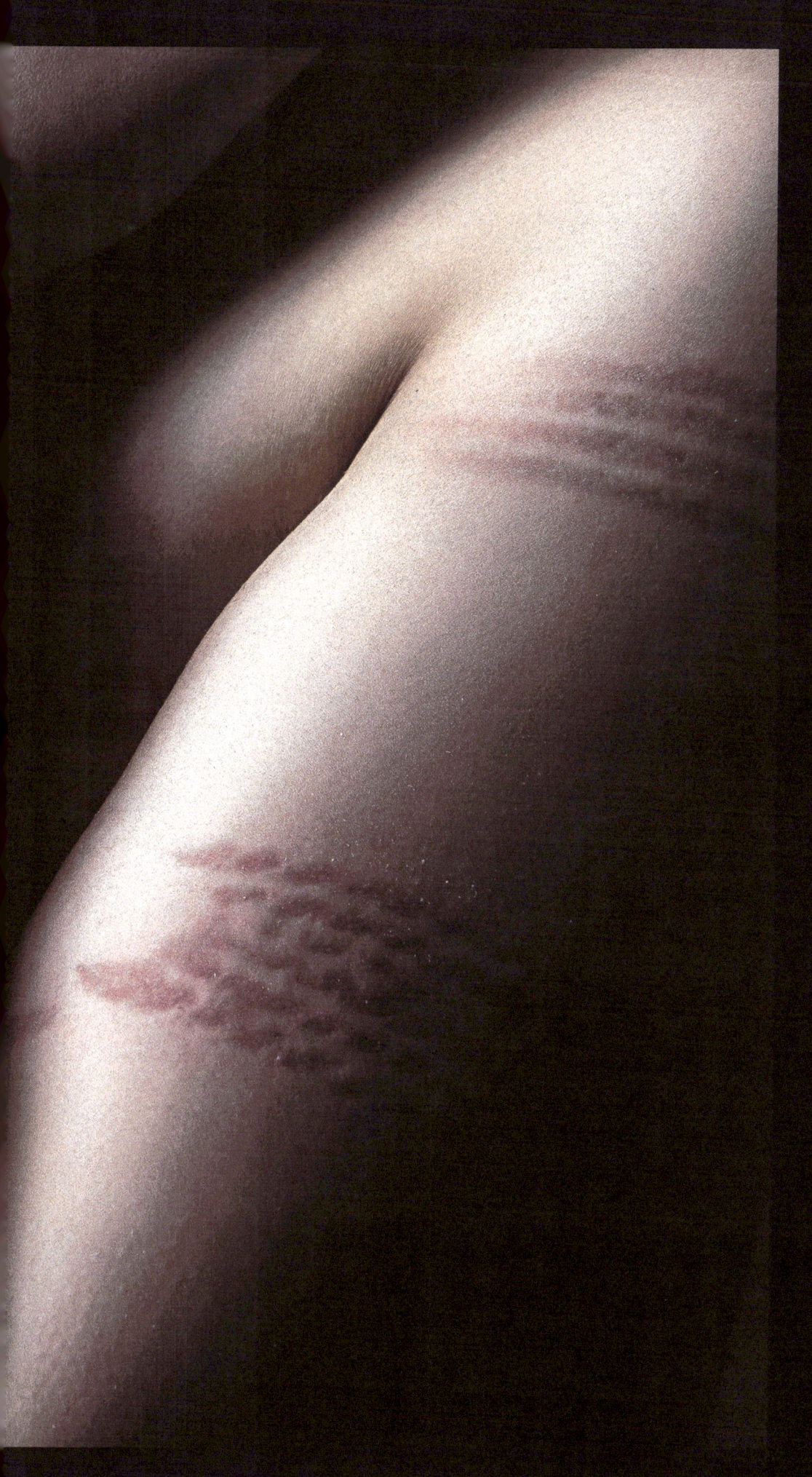

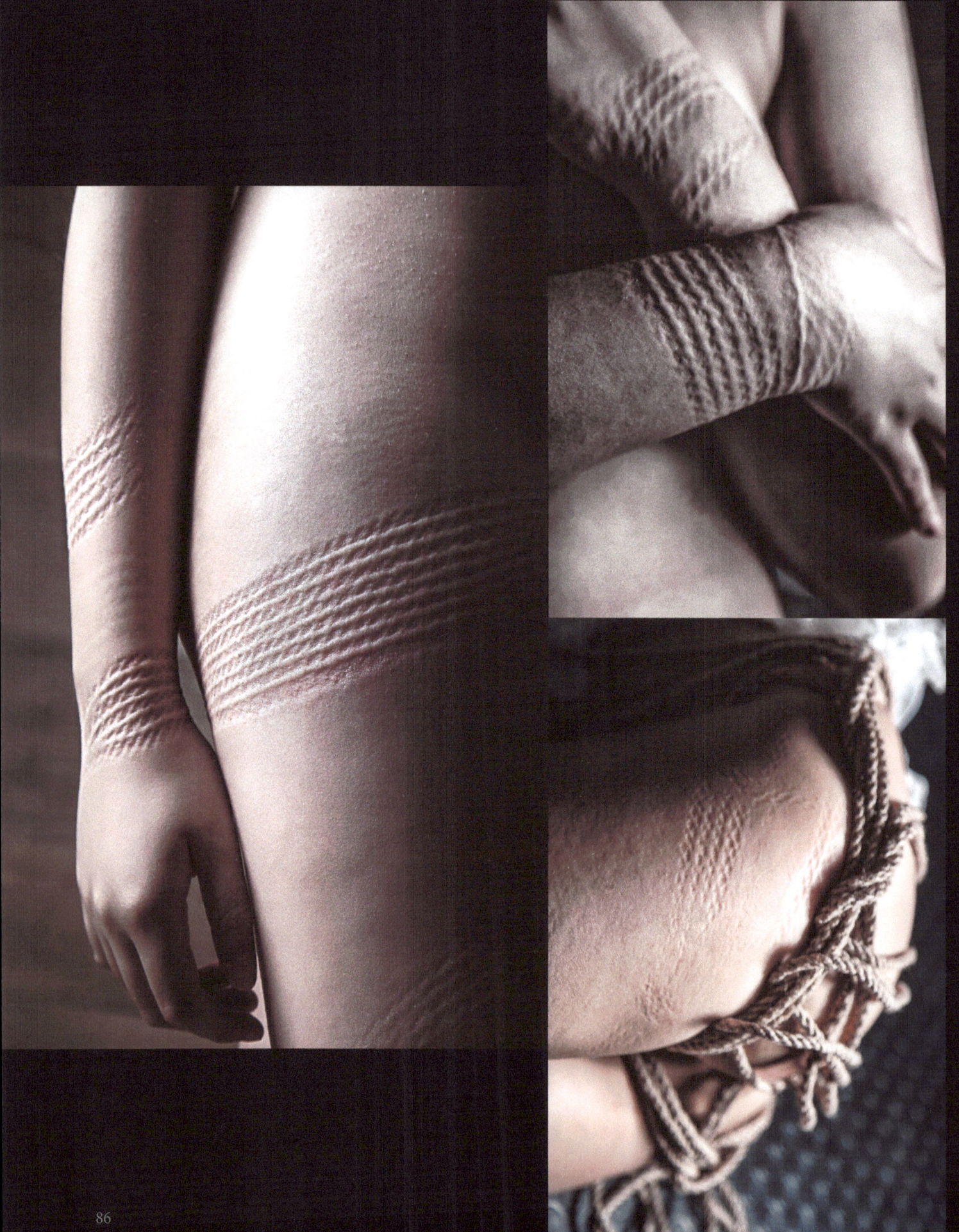

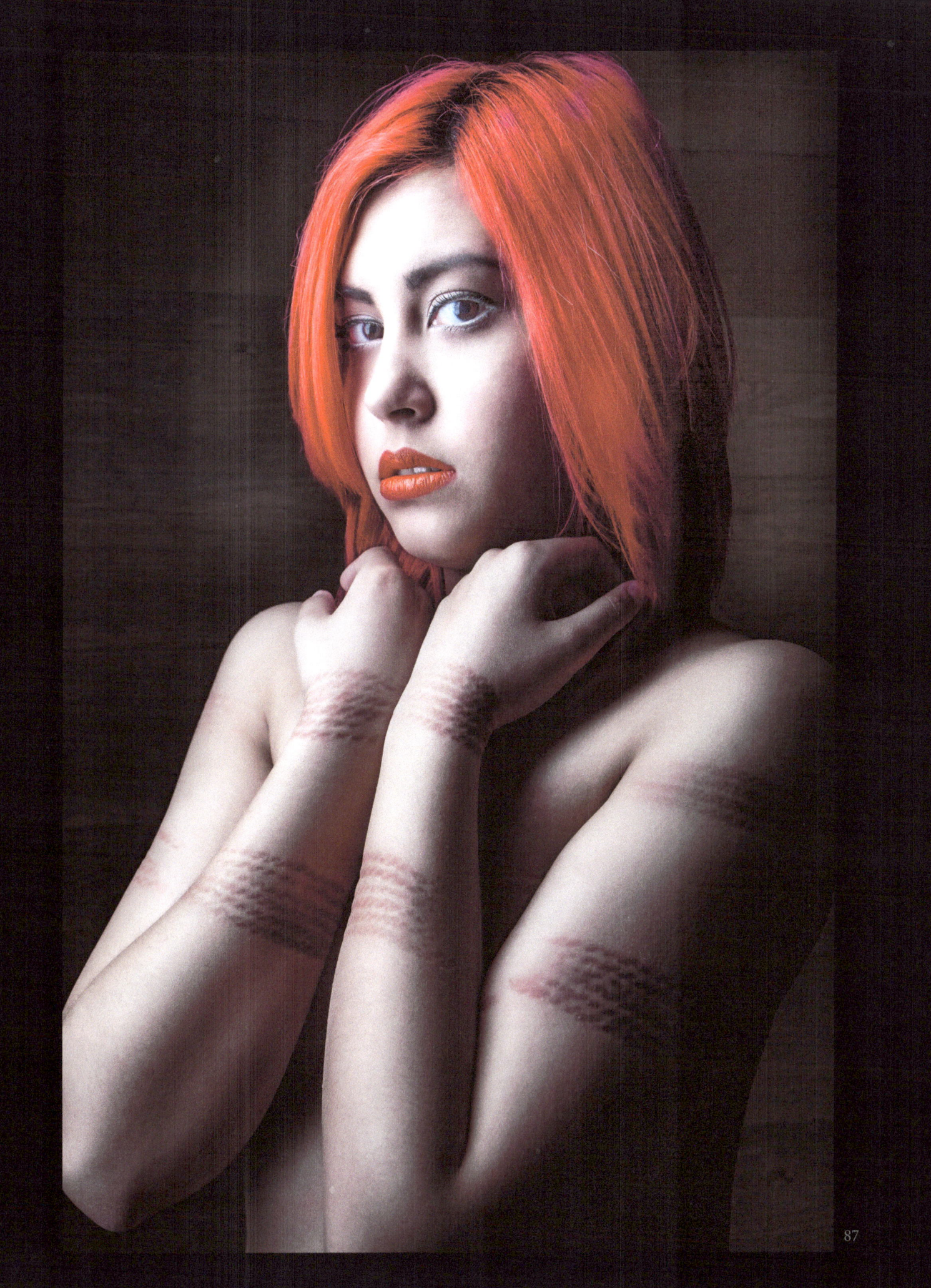

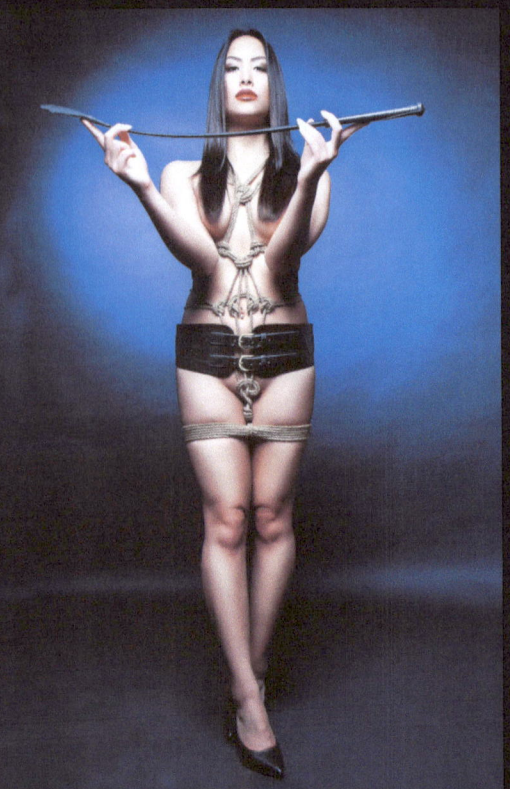

Thank you

for watching my artwork, the awesome response on my social media channels, to the people who bought prints and posters in several art galleries or one of the Fine Art of Bondage calendars.

I will go on doing this kind of artwork. Take a look at the "Fine Art of Bondage" project on facebook, twitter, instagram, tumblr. Follow and don´t miss any new work.

This was collection 1 "beauty of rope". At least two more books are almost finished: One with only nude art bondage and another with couples. Stay tuned, have fun and be careful when you play with ropes..

Rod Meier
www.Fine-Art-of-Bondage.com

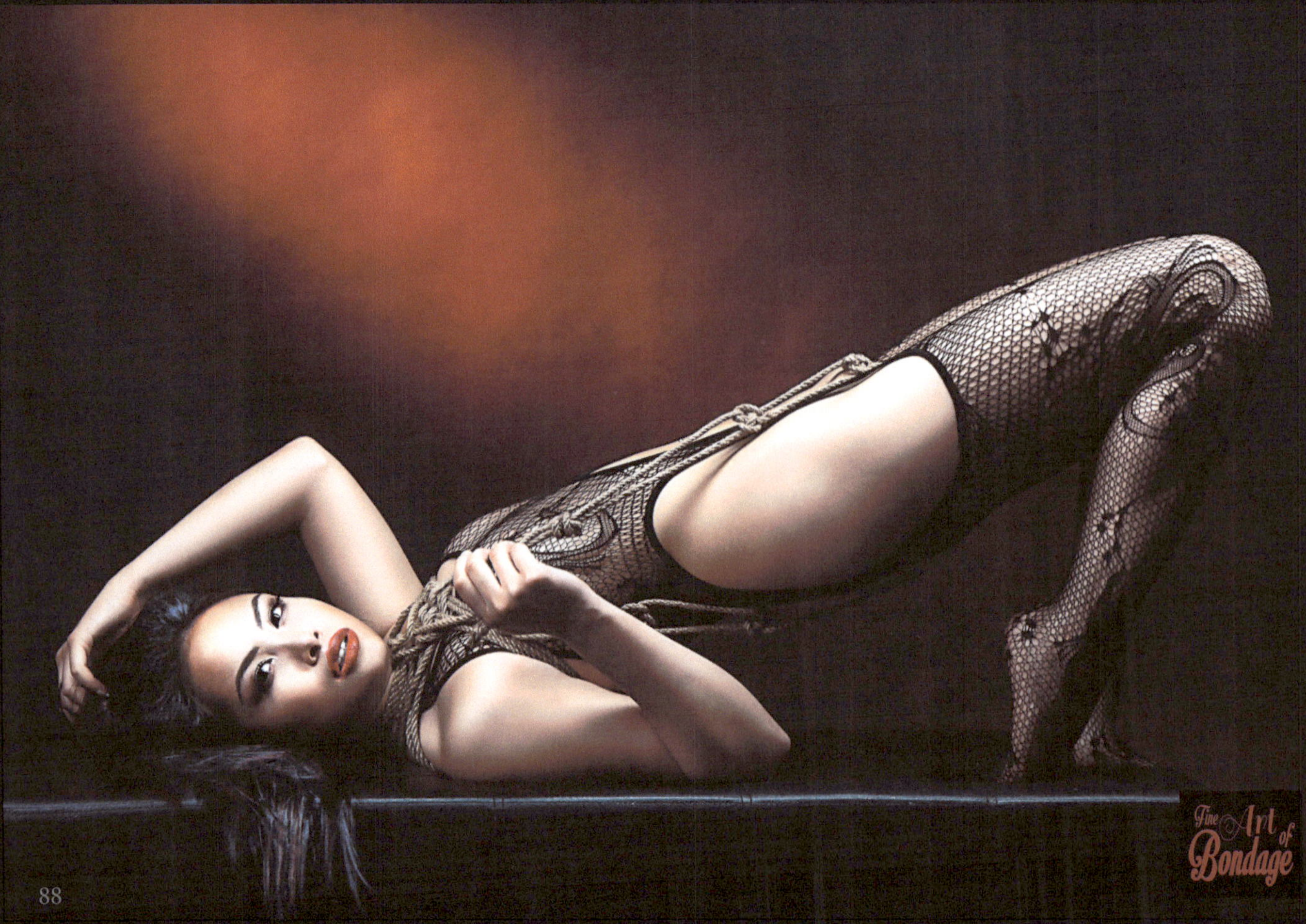

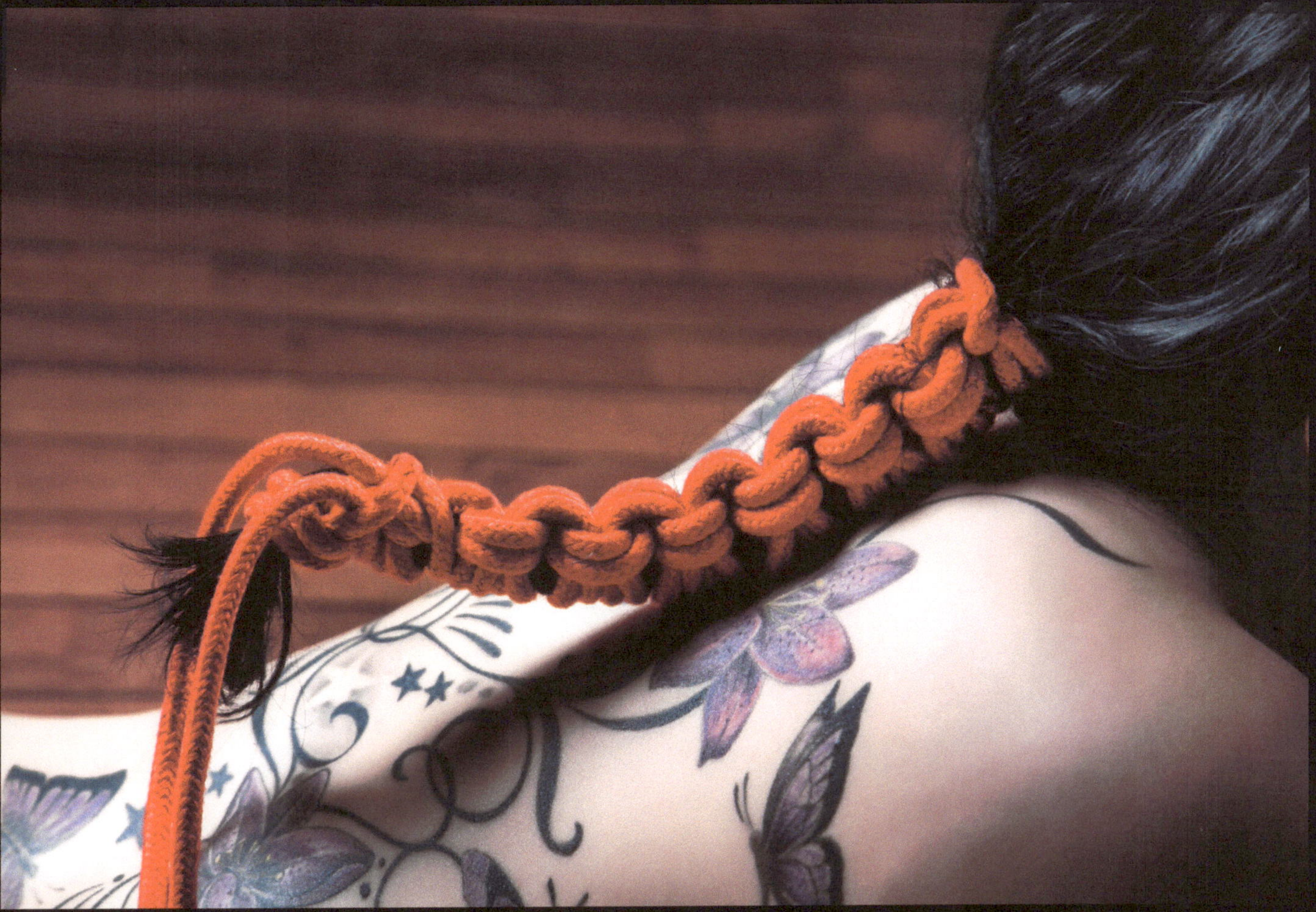

more books to come...

In this book you only see non-nude images. But I already work on the next Fine Art of Bondage books. At the end it will be a large collection.

Collection 2 is about **nudes and rope** followed by collection 3 with **couples and rope** in it.

On the following pages you´ll find some preview images of these books.

Rod Meier
www.Fine-Art-of-Bondage.com

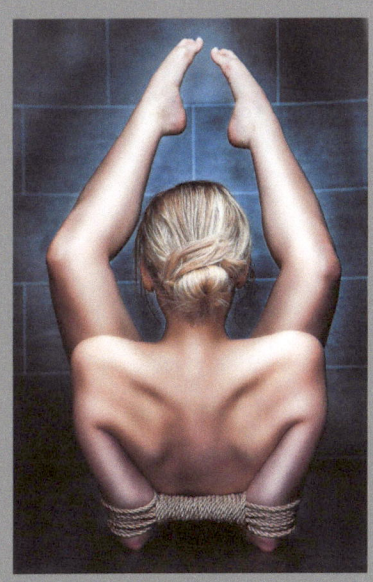

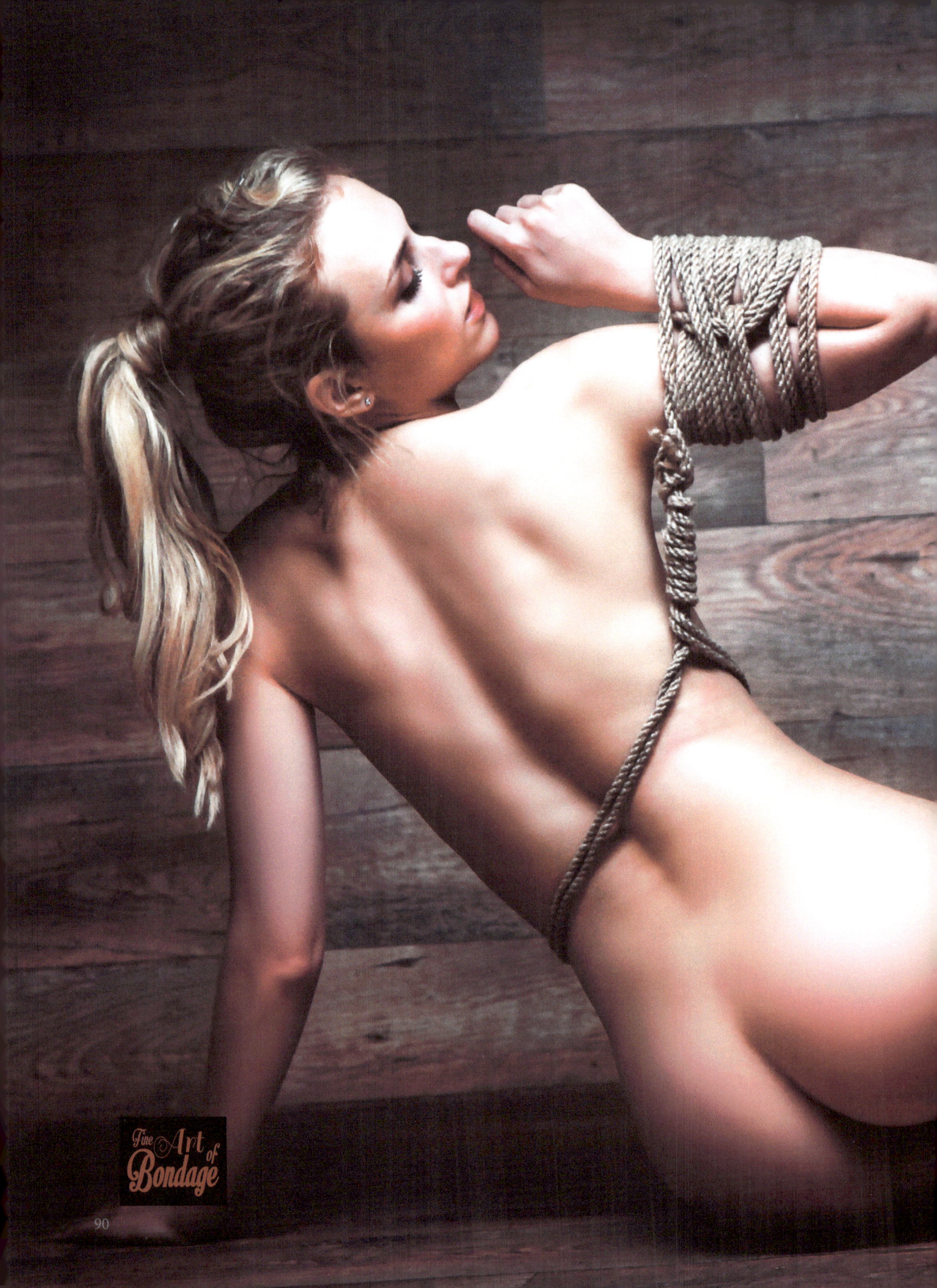

Nudes and Rope

"just skin and rope"
the second book

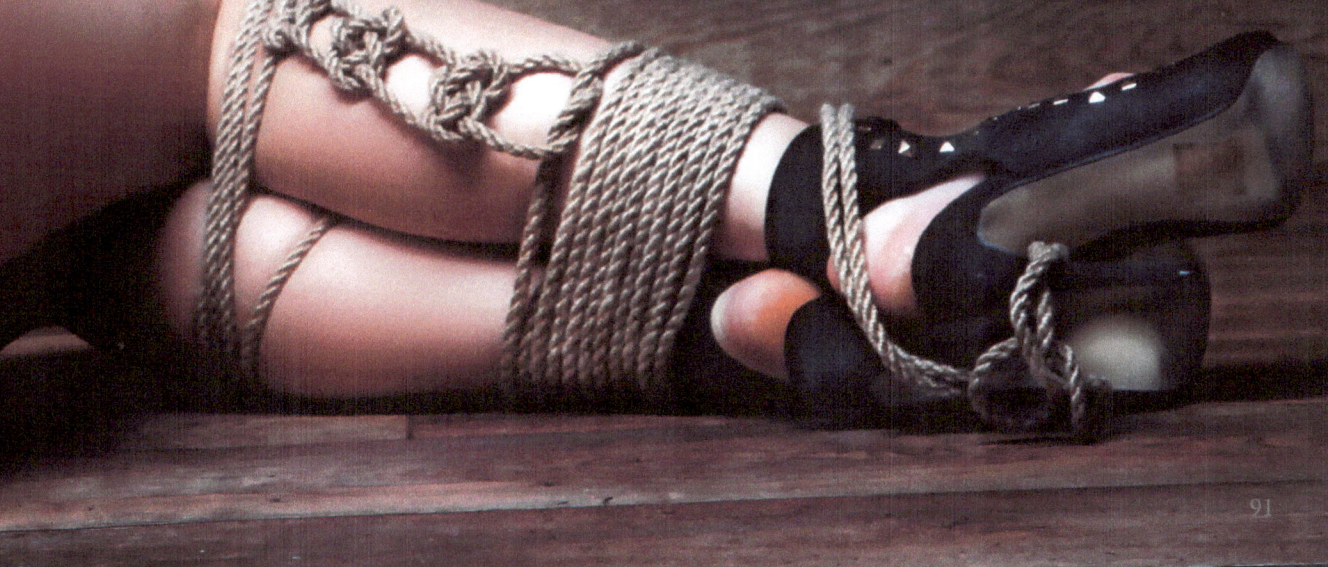

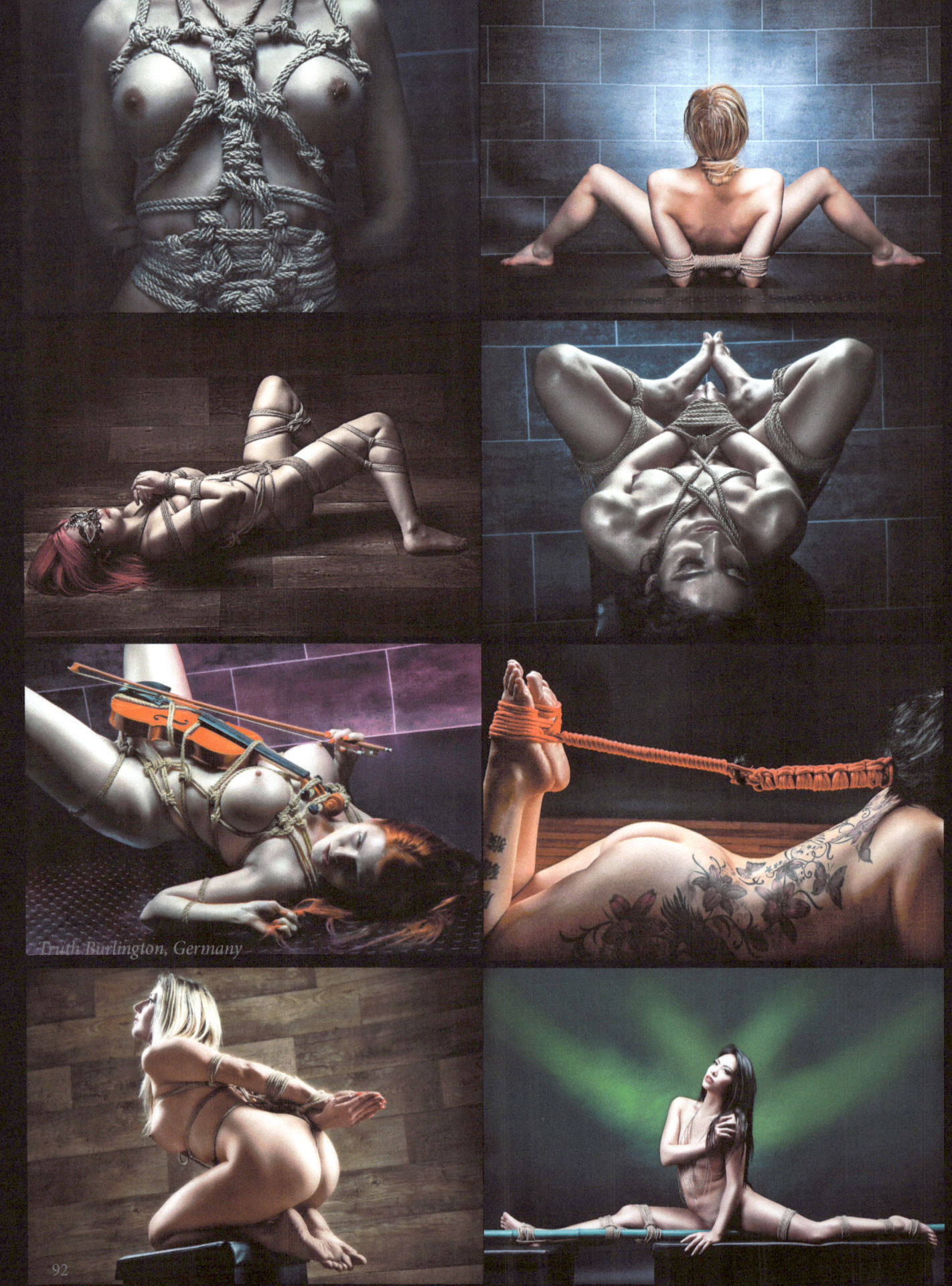

Truth Burlington, Germany

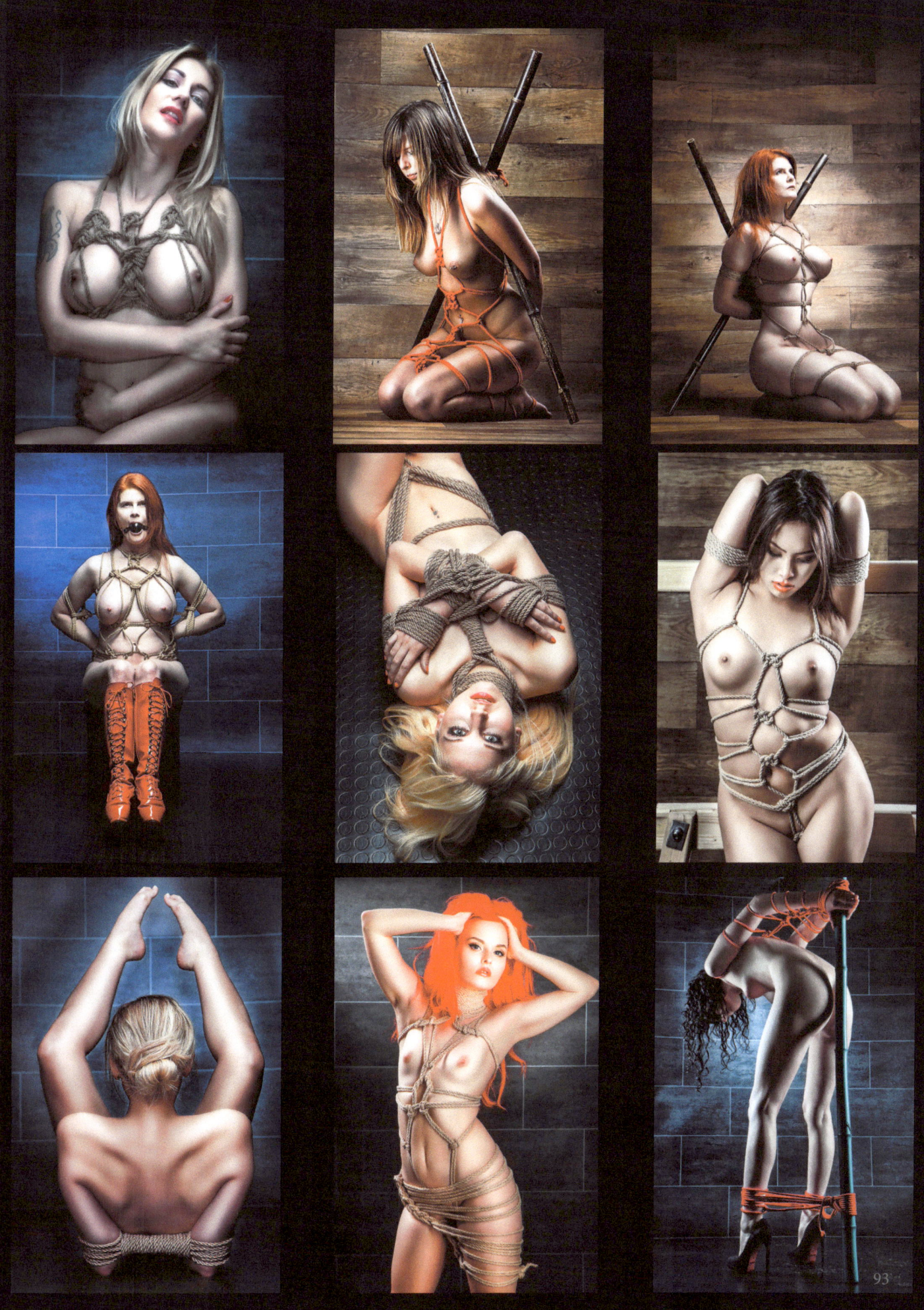

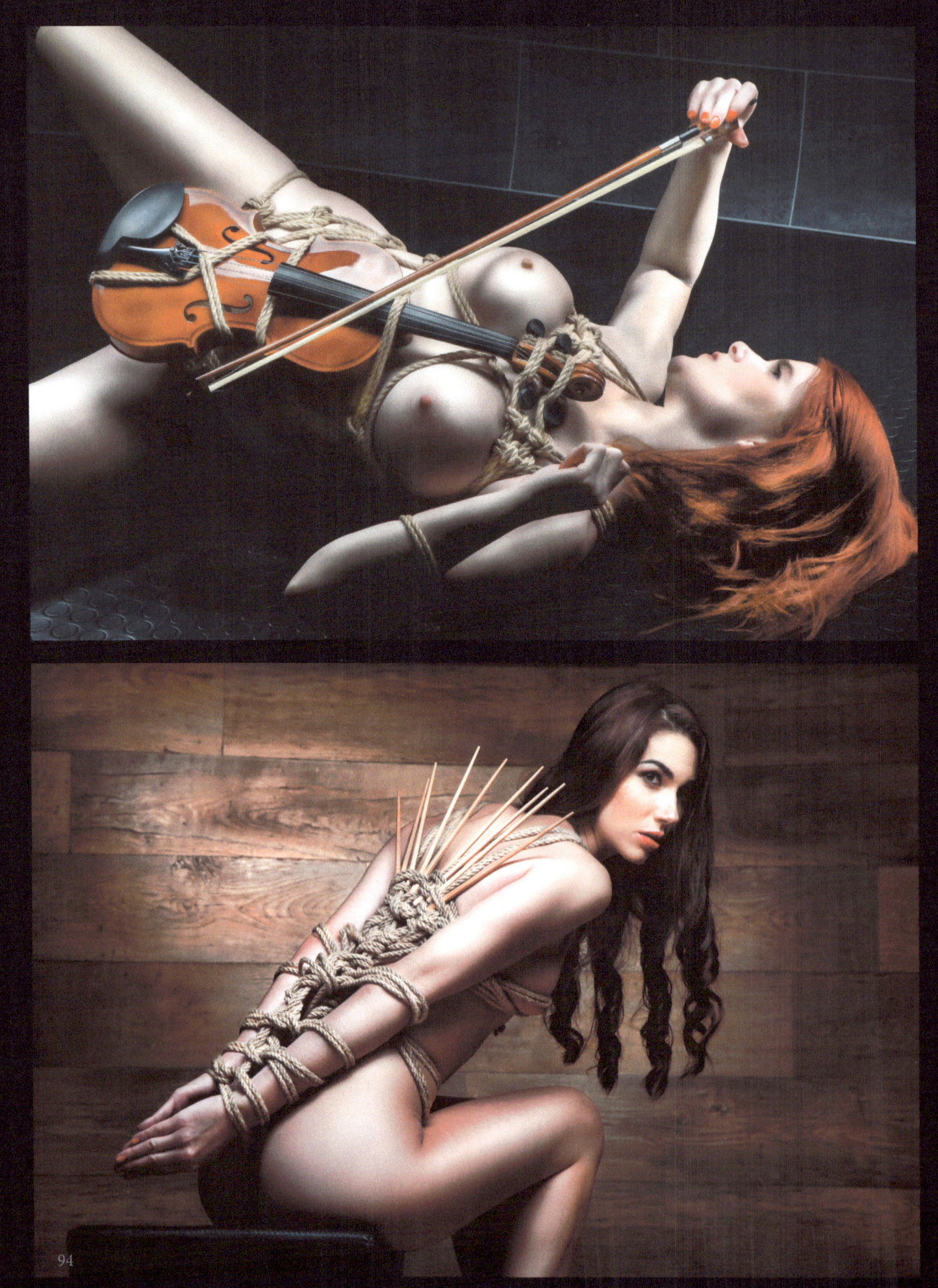

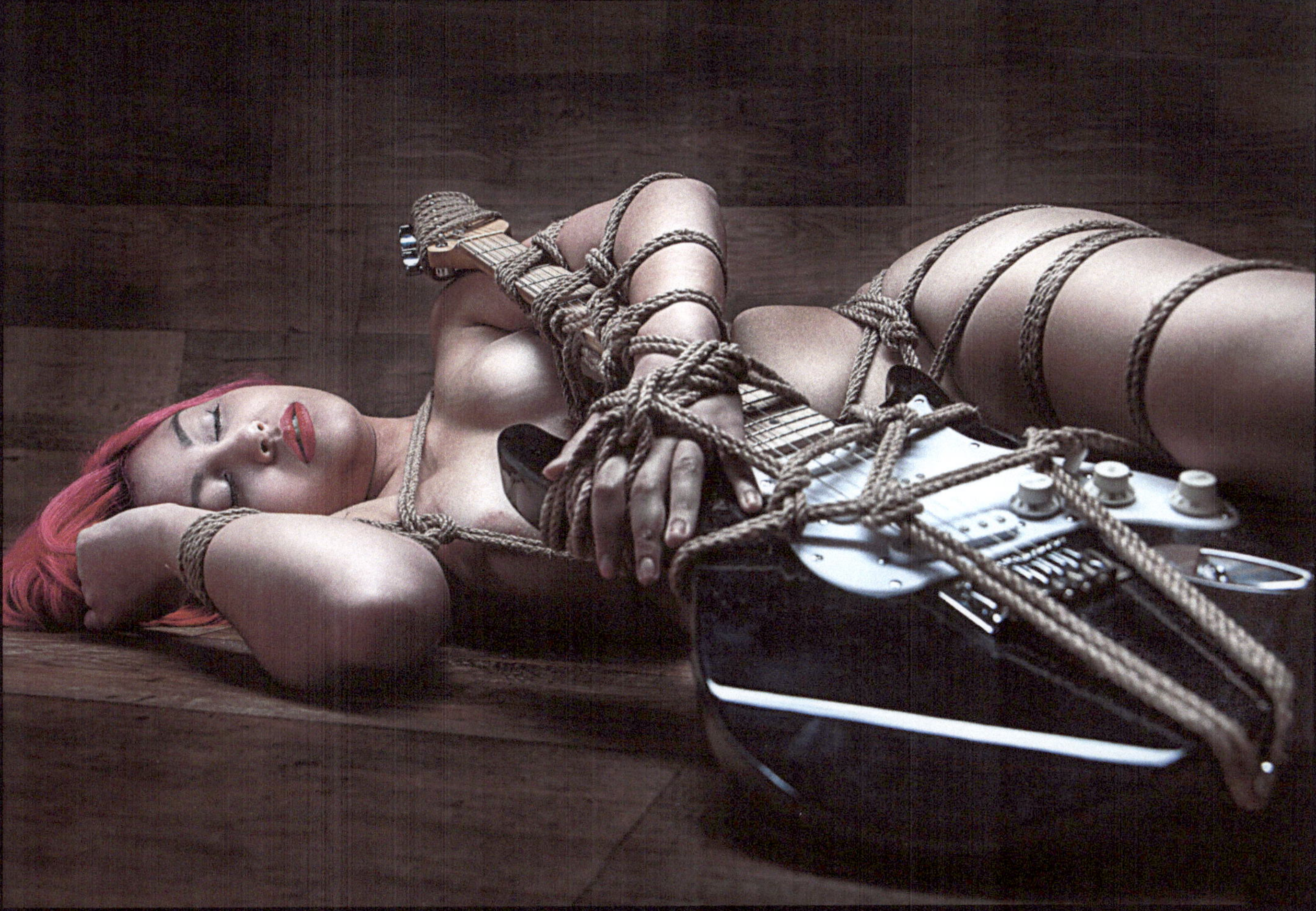

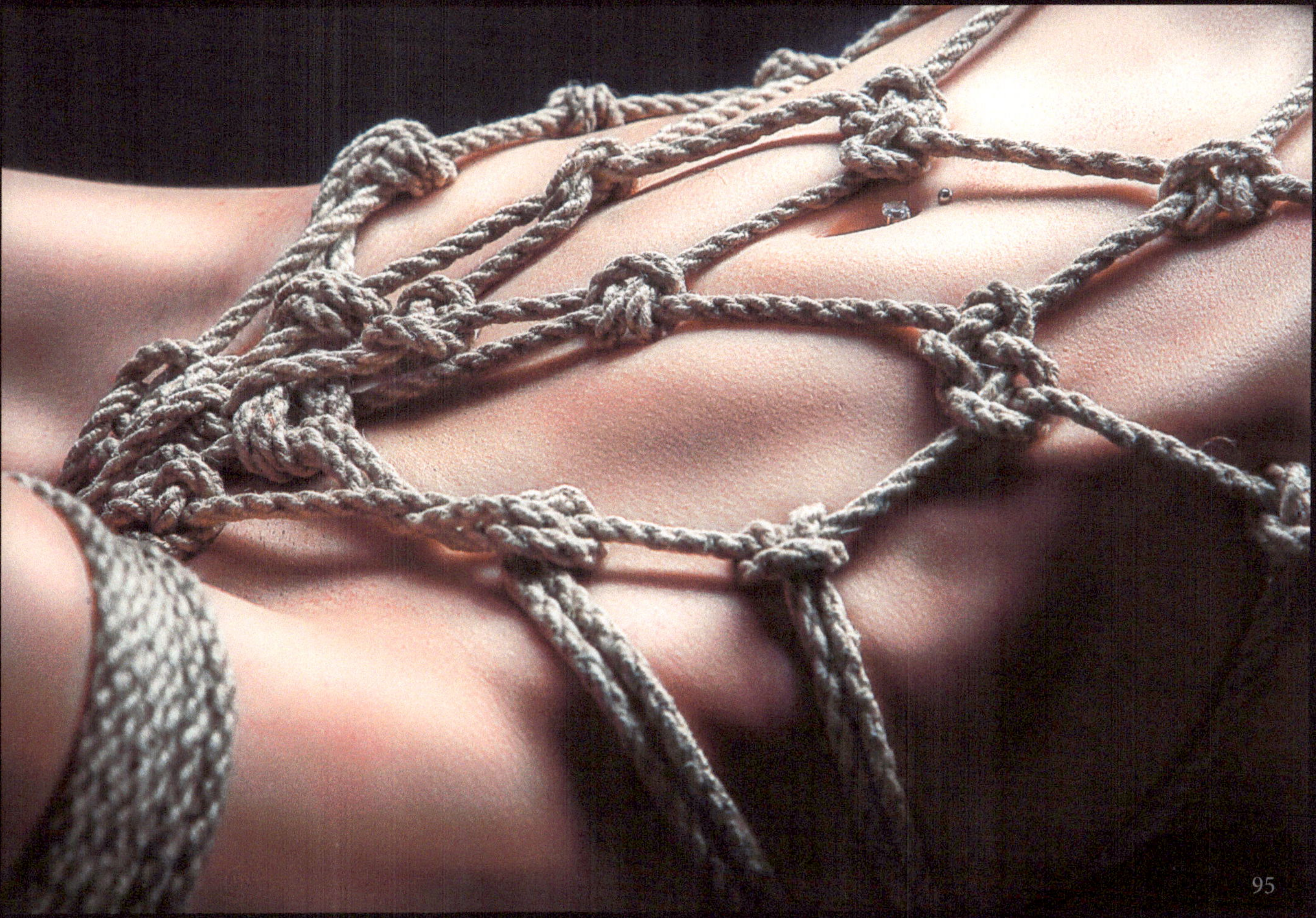

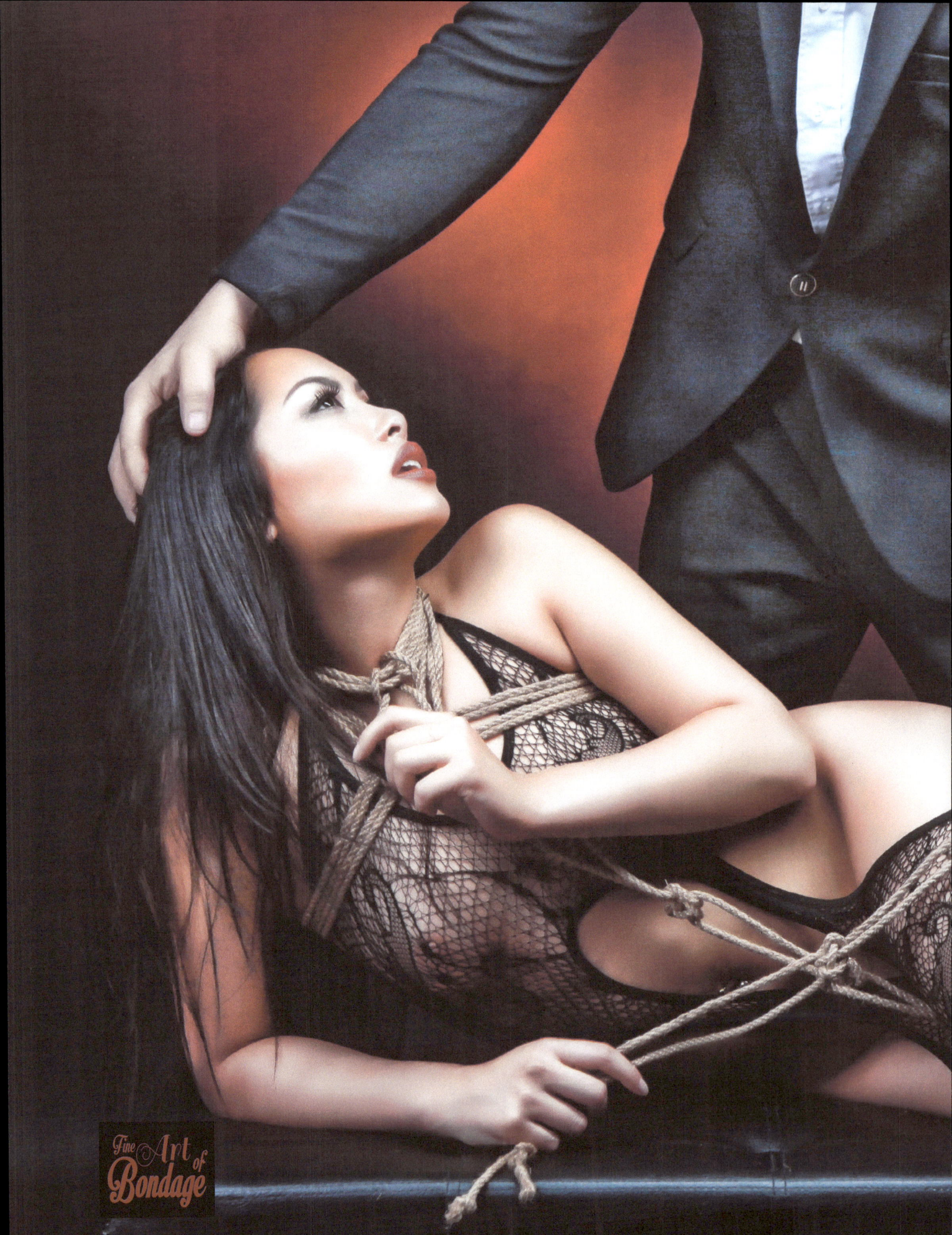

Couples and Rope

"couples and rope, playing"
the third book

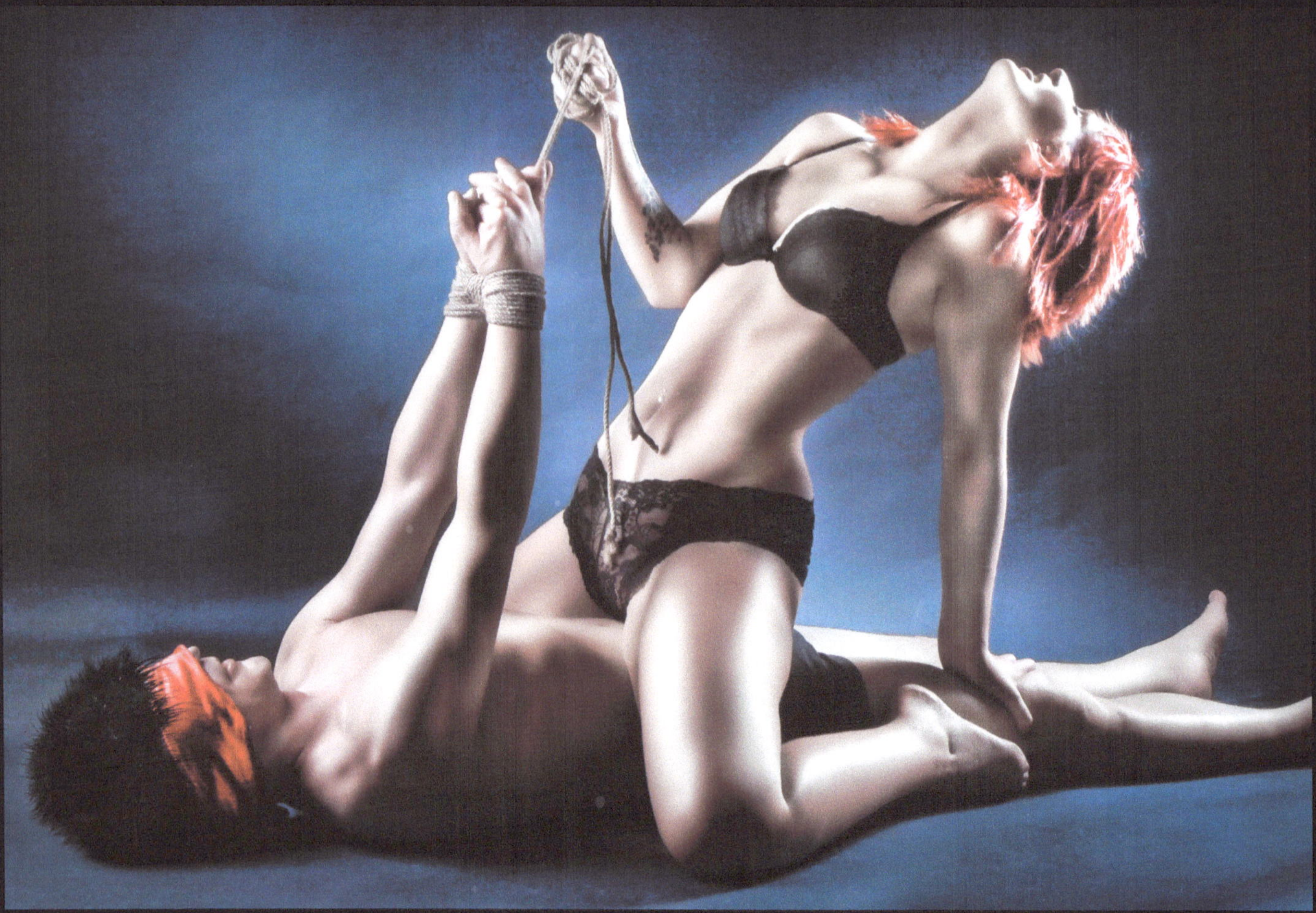

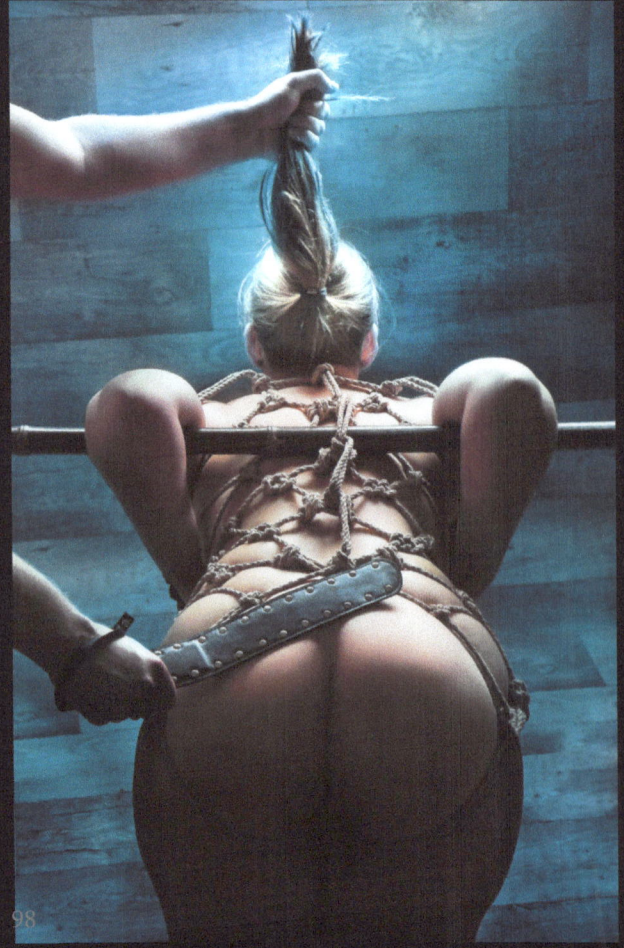
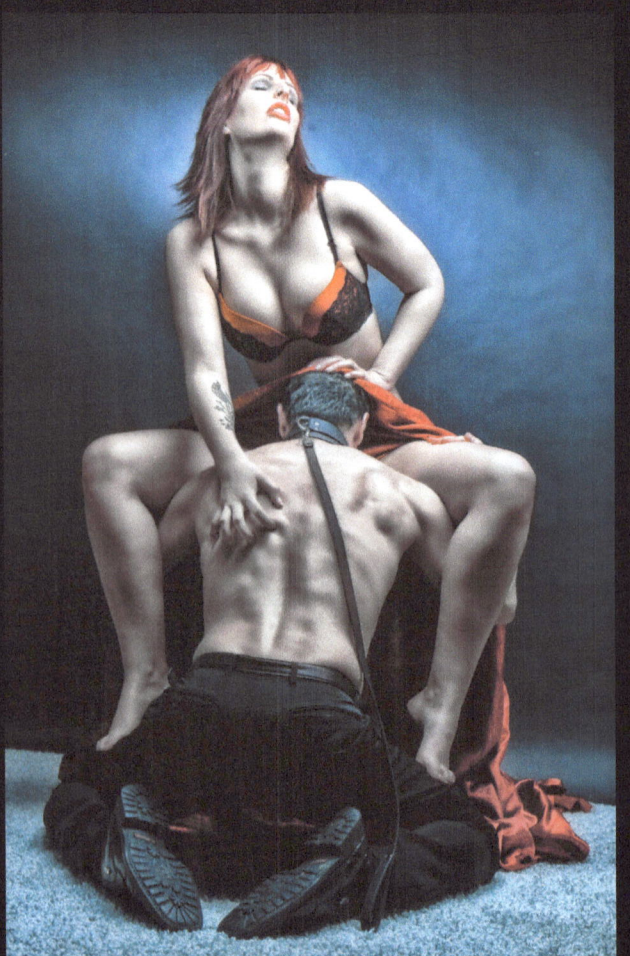

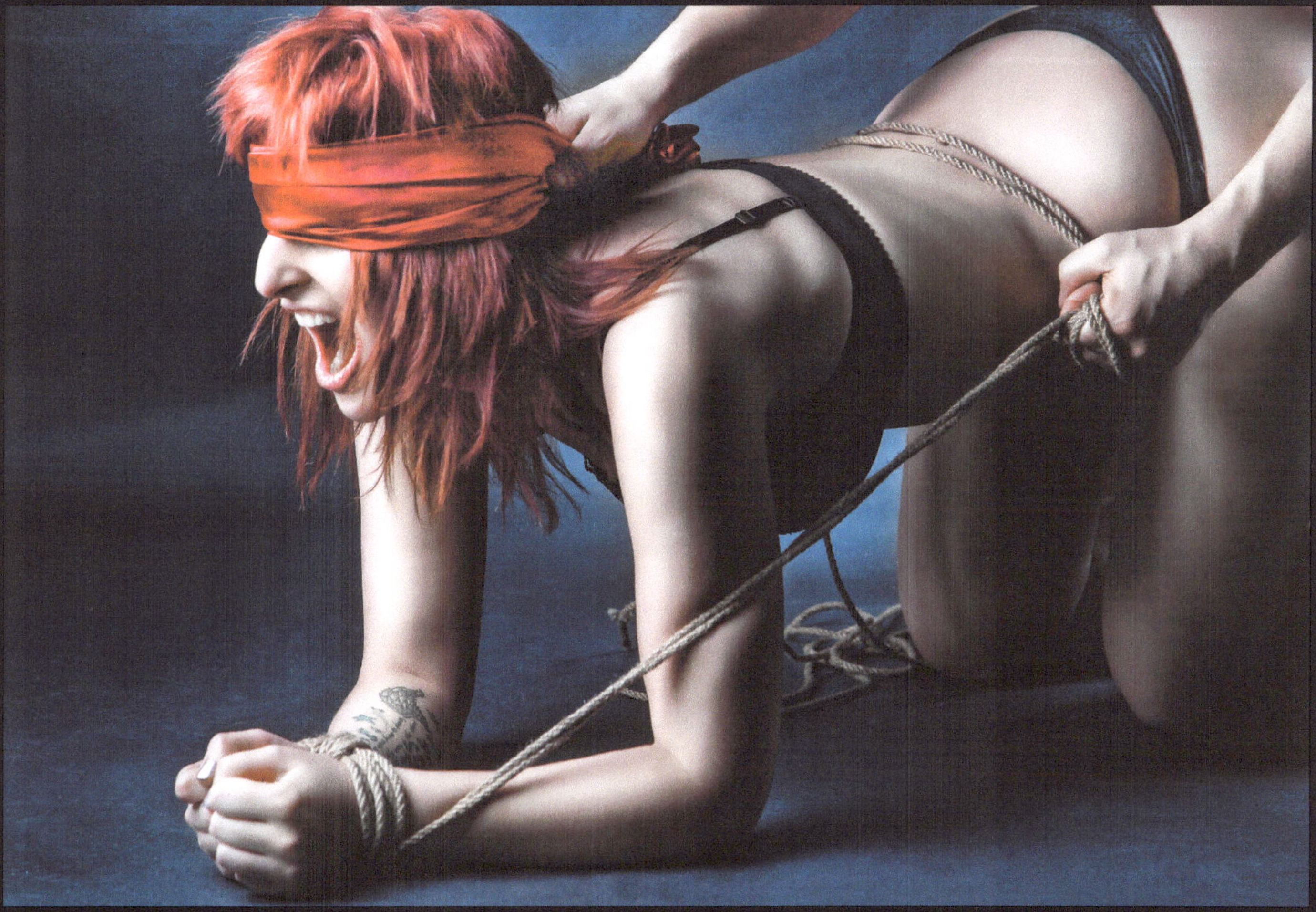

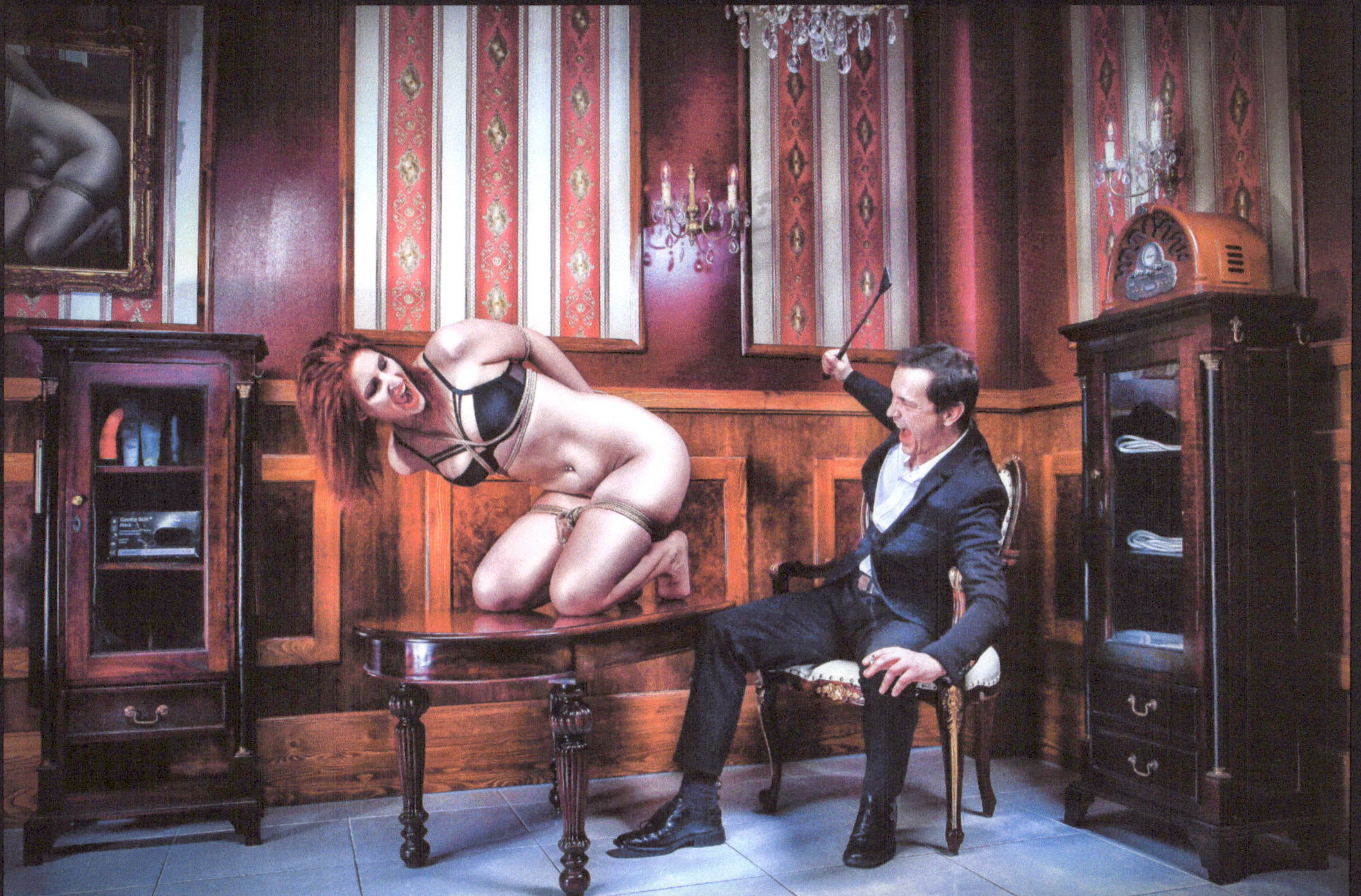

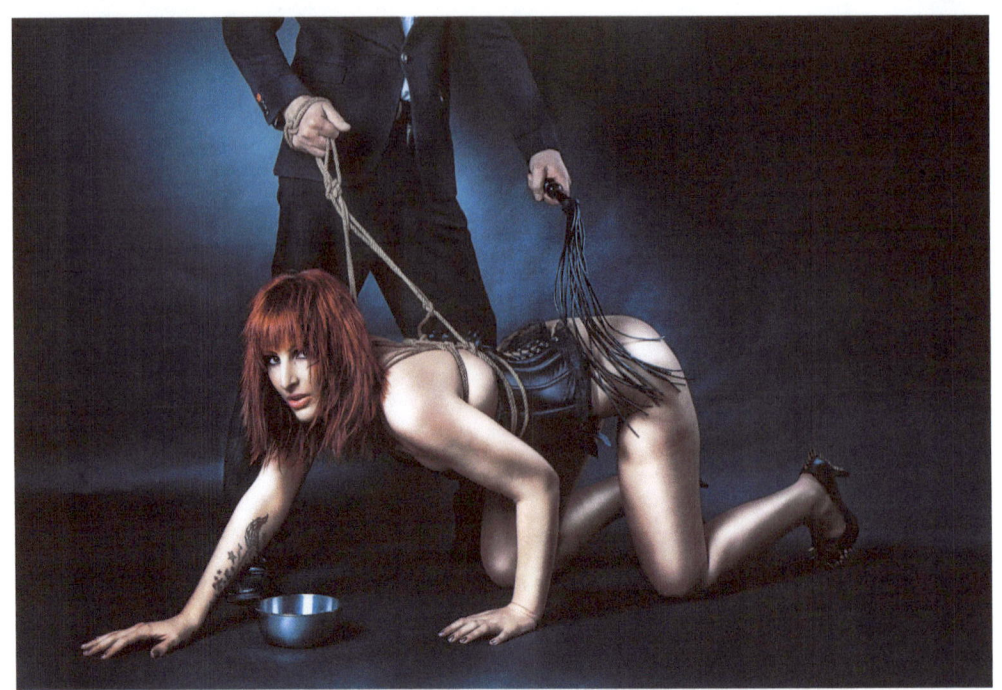

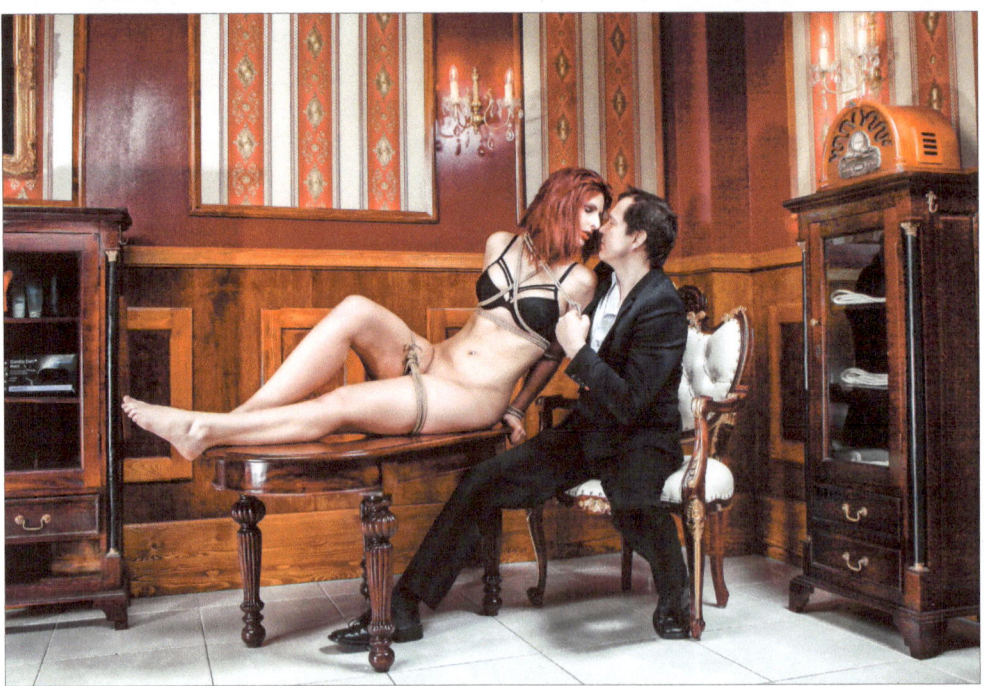

(c) 2016 by Rod Meier Media - all rights reserved

Photos, concept, rigging and most of the retouching by Rod Meier
www.Fine-Art-of-Bondage.com
Mail: Info@Fine-Art-of-Bondage.com
Photography Homepage - www.Model-Space.de

published by Rod Meier Media, Brueckenstr. 1, 89231 Ulm/Germany
http://Rod-Meier-Media.com

ISBN: 978-3-946768-00-5
First Edition